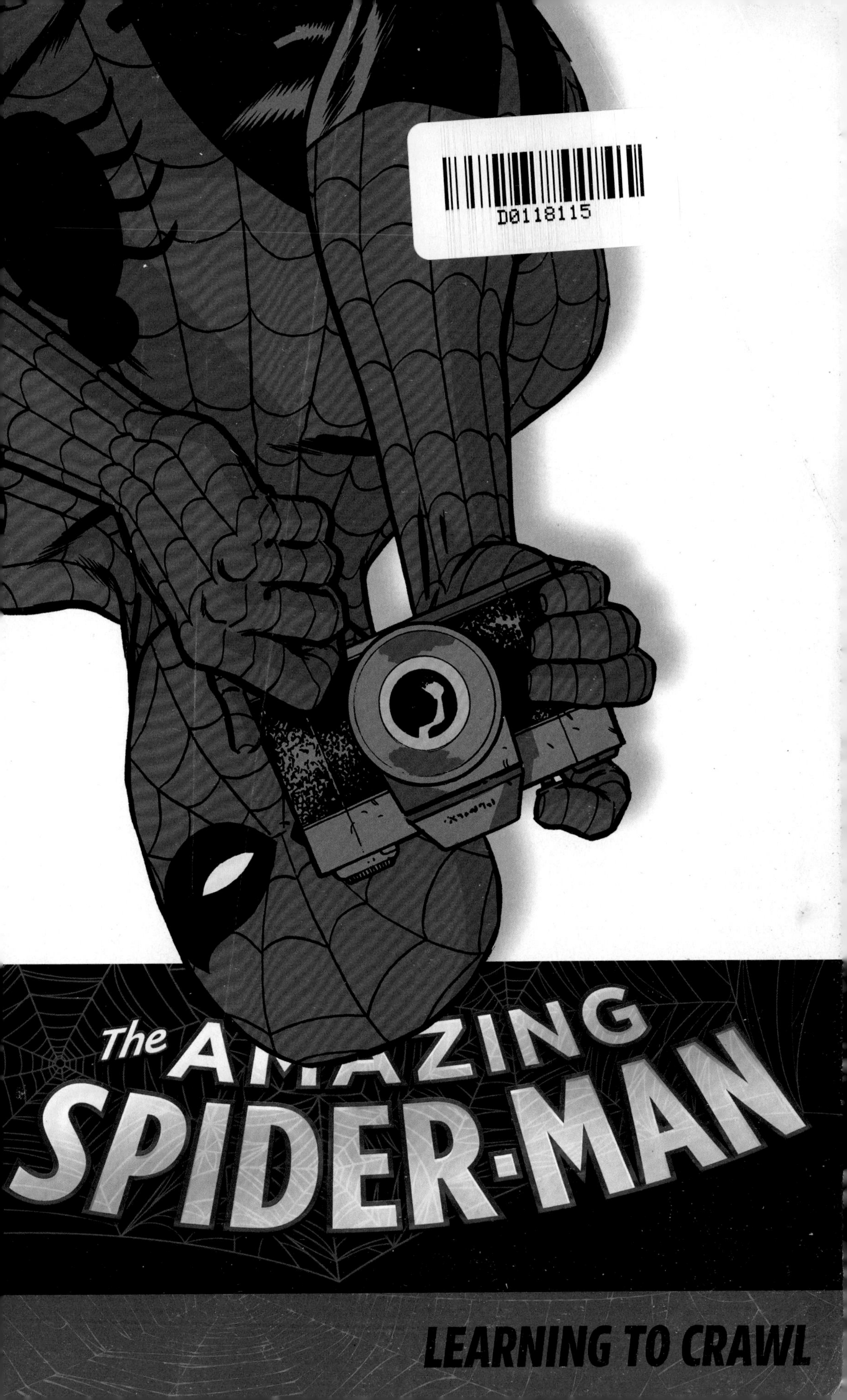

The AMAZING SPIDER-MAN

LEARNING TO CRAWL

Collection Editor: **Jennifer Grünwald**
Assistant Editor: **Sarah Brunstad**
Associate Managing Editor: **Alex Starbuck**
Editor, Special Projects: **Mark D. Beazley**
Senior Editor, Special Projects: **Jeff Youngquist**
SVP Print, Sales & Marketing: **David Gabriel**
Book Designer: **Nelson Ribeiro**

Editor in Chief: **Axel Alonso**
Chief Creative Officer: **Joe Quesada**
Publisher: **Dan Buckley**
Executive Producer: **Alan Fine**

AMAZING SPIDER-MAN VOL. 1.1: LEARNING TO CRAWL. Contains material originally published in magazine form as AMAZING SPIDER-MAN #1 and #1.1-1.5. First printing 2014. ISBN# 978-0-7851-6677-1. Published by MARVEL WORLDWIDE, INC., a subsidiary of MARVEL ENTERTAINMENT, LLC. OFFICE OF PUBLICATION: 135 West 50th Street, New York, NY 10020. **Printed in Canada.** ALAN FINE, EVP - Office of the President, Marvel Worldwide, Inc. and EVP & CMO Marvel Characters B.V.; DAN BUCKLEY, Publisher & President - Print, Animation & Digital Divisions; JOE QUESADA, Chief Creative Officer; TOM BREVOORT, SVP of Publishing; DAVID BOGART, SVP of Operations & Procurement, Publishing; C.B. CEBULSKI, SVP of Creator & Content Development; DAVID GABRIEL, SVP Print, Sales & Marketing; JIM O'KEEFE, VP of Operations & Logistics; DAN CARR, Executive Director of Publishing Technology; SUSAN CRESPI, Editorial Operations Manager; ALEX MORALES, Publishing Operations Manager; STAN LEE, Chairman Emeritus. For information regarding advertising in Marvel Comics or on Marvel.com, please contact Niza Disla, Director of Marvel Partnerships, at ndisla@marvel.com. For Marvel subscription inquiries, please call 800-217-9158. **Manufactured between 10/3/2014 and 11/10/2014 by SOLISCO PRINTERS, SCOTT, QC, CANADA.**

10 9 8 7 6 5 4 3 2 1

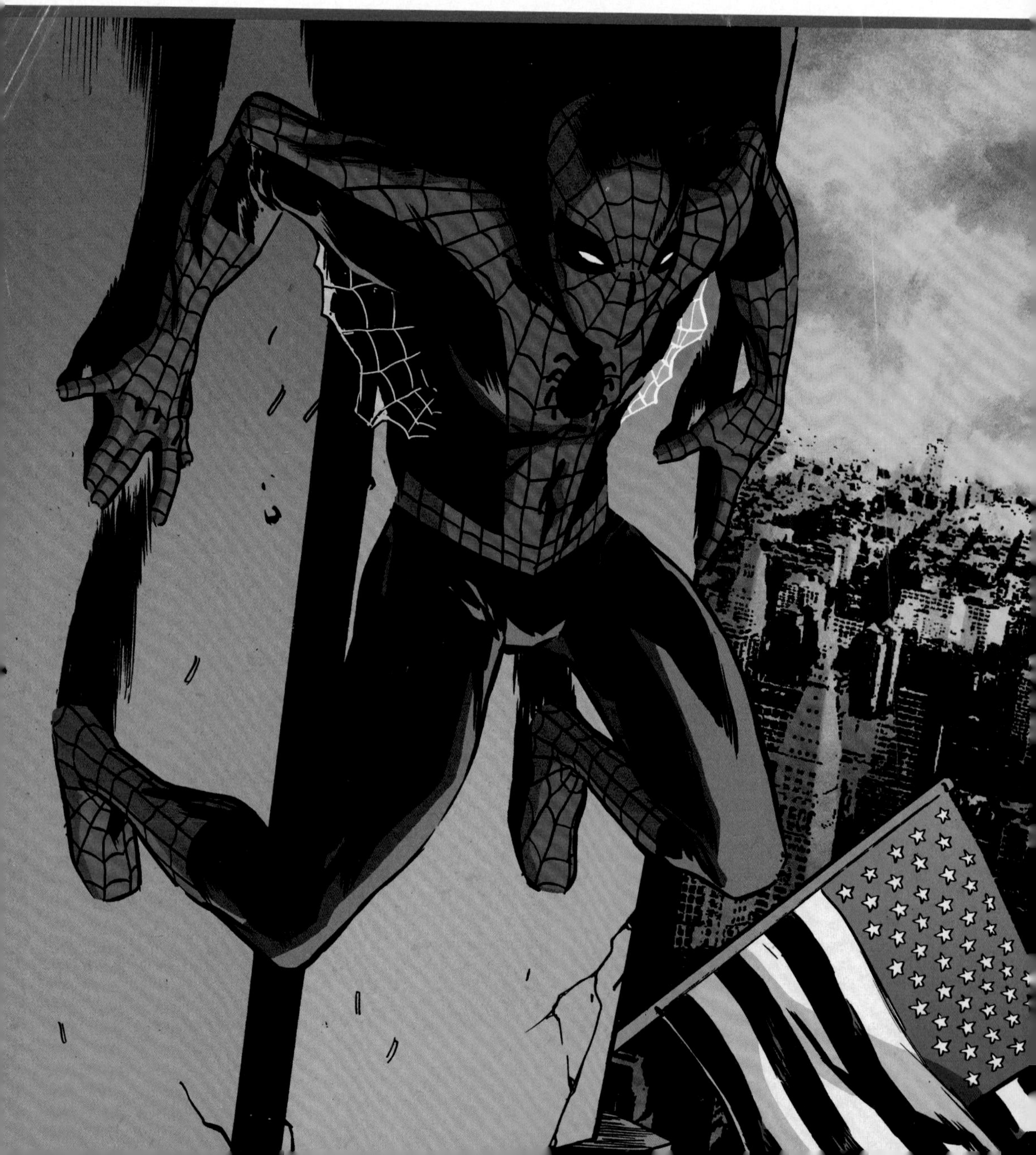

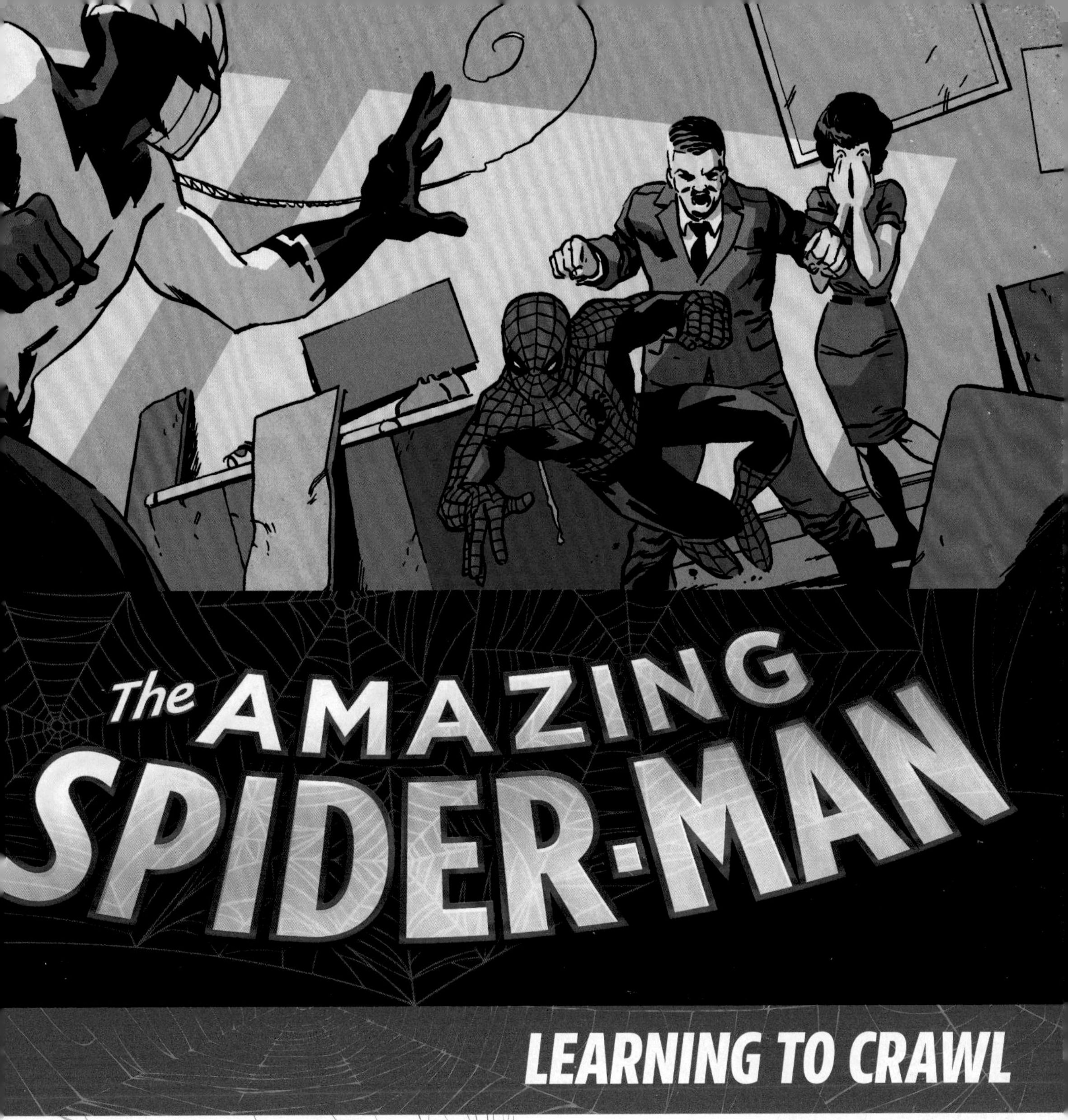

The AMAZING SPIDER-MAN

LEARNING TO CRAWL

YOU KNOW THE STORY...A BITE FROM A RADIOACTIVE SPIDER GAVE TEENAGE SCIENCE WHIZ PETER PARKER POWER; HE COULD LIFT A CAR, STICK TO WALLS AND AVOID IMMINENT DANGER WITH WARNINGS FROM HIS STRANGE SPIDER-SENSE. WHEN HIS UNCLE WAS KILLED BY A CROOK HE HIMSELF COULD HAVE STOPPED EARLIER IN AN UNRELATED CRIME, HE LEARNED THE EFFECTS OF THE SELFISH USE OF HIS NEW ATTRIBUTES AND THE RESPONSIBILITY THAT MUST GO HAND IN HAND WITH HIS POWER.

BUT YOU DON'T KNOW THE WHOLE STORY...

WRITER:
DAN SLOTT

ARTIST:
RAMÓN PÉREZ

COLORIST:
IAN HERRING

LETTERERS: **JOE CARAMAGNA**
WITH **CHRIS ELIOPOULOS**

COVER ART: **ALEX ROSS**

ASSOCIATE EDITOR: **ELLIE PYLE**
EDITOR: **NICK LOWE**

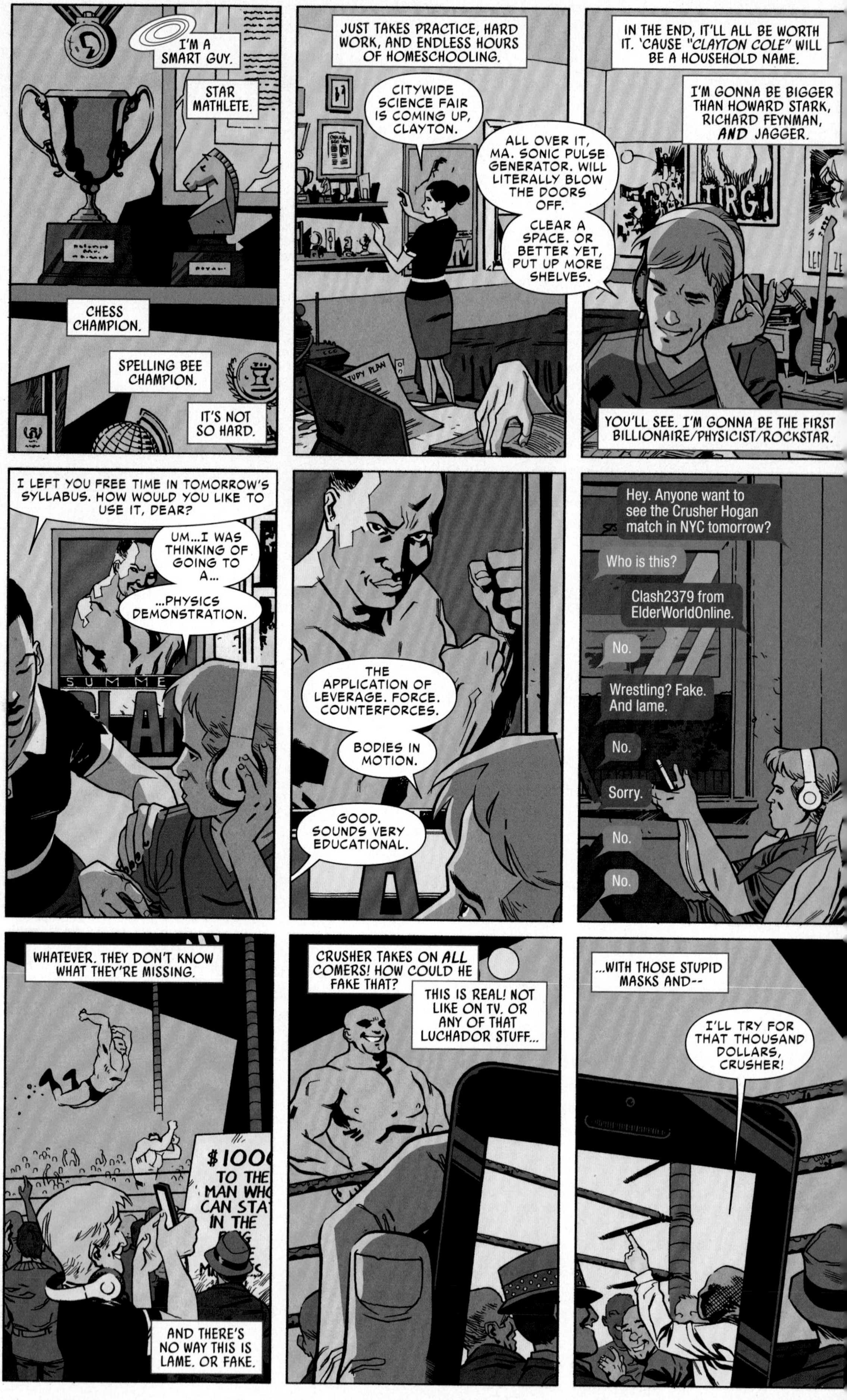
I'M A SMART GUY.
STAR MATHLETE.
CHESS CHAMPION.
SPELLING BEE CHAMPION.
IT'S NOT SO HARD.
JUST TAKES PRACTICE, HARD WORK, AND ENDLESS HOURS OF HOMESCHOOLING.
CITYWIDE SCIENCE FAIR IS COMING UP, CLAYTON.
ALL OVER IT, MA. SONIC PULSE GENERATOR. WILL LITERALLY BLOW THE DOORS OFF.
CLEAR A SPACE. OR BETTER YET, PUT UP MORE SHELVES.
IN THE END, IT'LL ALL BE WORTH IT. 'CAUSE "*CLAYTON COLE*" WILL BE A HOUSEHOLD NAME.
I'M GONNA BE BIGGER THAN HOWARD STARK, RICHARD FEYNMAN, ***AND*** JAGGER.
YOU'LL SEE. I'M GONNA BE THE FIRST BILLIONAIRE/PHYSICIST/ROCKSTAR.
I LEFT YOU FREE TIME IN TOMORROW'S SYLLABUS. HOW WOULD YOU LIKE TO USE IT, DEAR?
UM...I WAS THINKING OF GOING TO A...
...PHYSICS DEMONSTRATION.
THE APPLICATION OF LEVERAGE. FORCE. COUNTERFORCES.
BODIES IN MOTION.
GOOD. SOUNDS VERY EDUCATIONAL.
Hey. Anyone want to see the Crusher Hogan match in NYC tomorrow?
Who is this?
Clash2379 from ElderWorldOnline.
No.
Wrestling? Fake. And lame.
No.
Sorry.
No.
No.
WHATEVER. THEY DON'T KNOW WHAT THEY'RE MISSING.
$100
TO THE
MAN WHO
CAN STA
IN THE
AND THERE'S NO WAY THIS IS LAME. OR FAKE.
CRUSHER TAKES ON *ALL* COMERS! HOW COULD HE FAKE THAT?
THIS IS REAL! NOT LIKE ON TV. OR ANY OF THAT LUCHADOR STUFF...
...WITH THOSE STUPID MASKS AND--
I'LL TRY FOR THAT THOUSAND DOLLARS, CRUSHER!

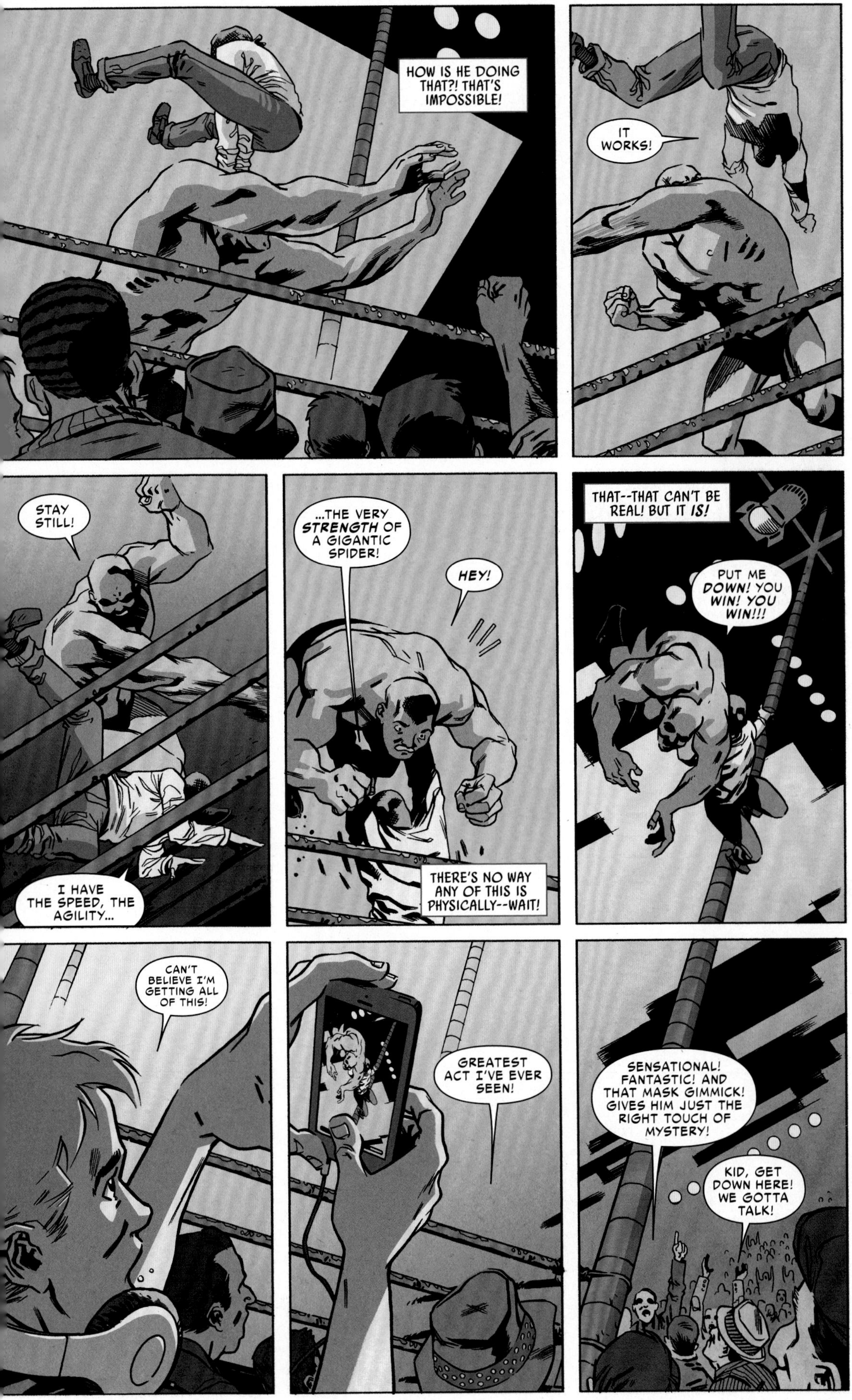
HOW IS HE DOING THAT?! THAT'S IMPOSSIBLE!
IT WORKS!
STAY STILL!
I HAVE THE SPEED, THE AGILITY...
...THE VERY STRENGTH OF A GIGANTIC SPIDER!
HEY!
THERE'S NO WAY ANY OF THIS IS PHYSICALLY--WAIT!
THAT--THAT CAN'T BE REAL! BUT IT IS!
PUT ME DOWN! YOU WIN! YOU WIN!!!
CAN'T BELIEVE I'M GETTING ALL OF THIS!
GREATEST ACT I'VE EVER SEEN!
SENSATIONAL! FANTASTIC! AND THAT MASK GIMMICK! GIVES HIM JUST THE RIGHT TOUCH OF MYSTERY!
KID, GET DOWN HERE! WE GOTTA TALK!

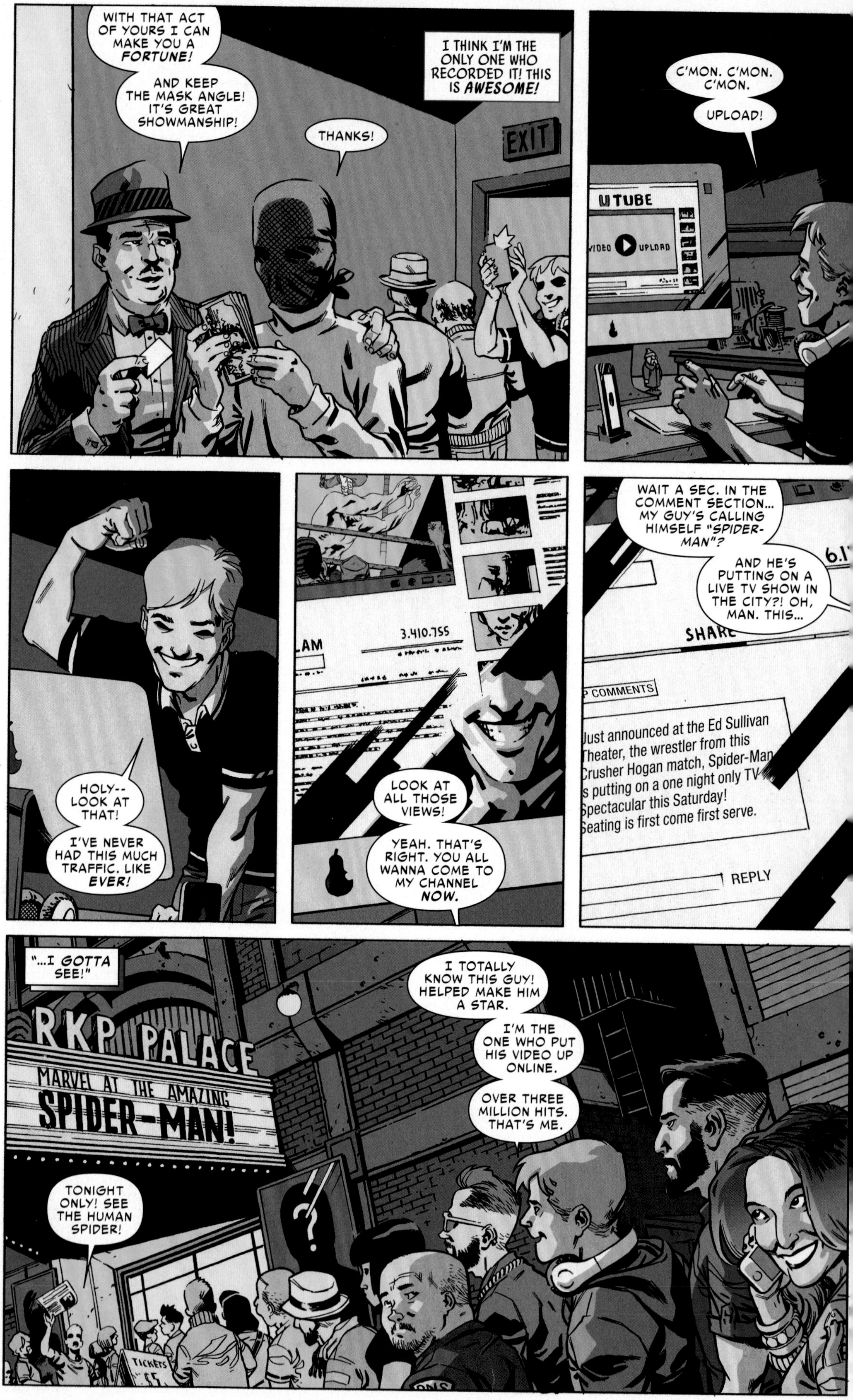
WITH THAT ACT OF YOURS I CAN MAKE YOU A FORTUNE!
AND KEEP THE MASK ANGLE! IT'S GREAT SHOWMANSHIP!
THANKS!
I THINK I'M THE ONLY ONE WHO RECORDED IT! THIS IS AWESOME!
EXIT
C'MON. C'MON. C'MON.
UPLOAD!
U TUBE
VIDEO UPLOAD
HOLY-- LOOK AT THAT!
I'VE NEVER HAD THIS MUCH TRAFFIC. LIKE EVER!
3.410.755
LOOK AT ALL THOSE VIEWS!
YEAH. THAT'S RIGHT. YOU ALL WANNA COME TO MY CHANNEL NOW.
WAIT A SEC. IN THE COMMENT SECTION... MY GUY'S CALLING HIMSELF "SPIDER-MAN"?
AND HE'S PUTTING ON A LIVE TV SHOW IN THE CITY?! OH, MAN. THIS...
SHARE
COMMENTS
Just announced at the Ed Sullivan Theater, the wrestler from this Crusher Hogan match, Spider-Man is putting on a one night only TV Spectacular this Saturday! Seating is first come first serve.
REPLY
"...I GOTTA SEE!"
RKP PALACE
MARVEL AT THE AMAZING SPIDER-MAN!
I TOTALLY KNOW THIS GUY! HELPED MAKE HIM A STAR.
I'M THE ONE WHO PUT HIS VIDEO UP ONLINE.
OVER THREE MILLION HITS. THAT'S ME.
TONIGHT ONLY! SEE THE HUMAN SPIDER!
TICKETS

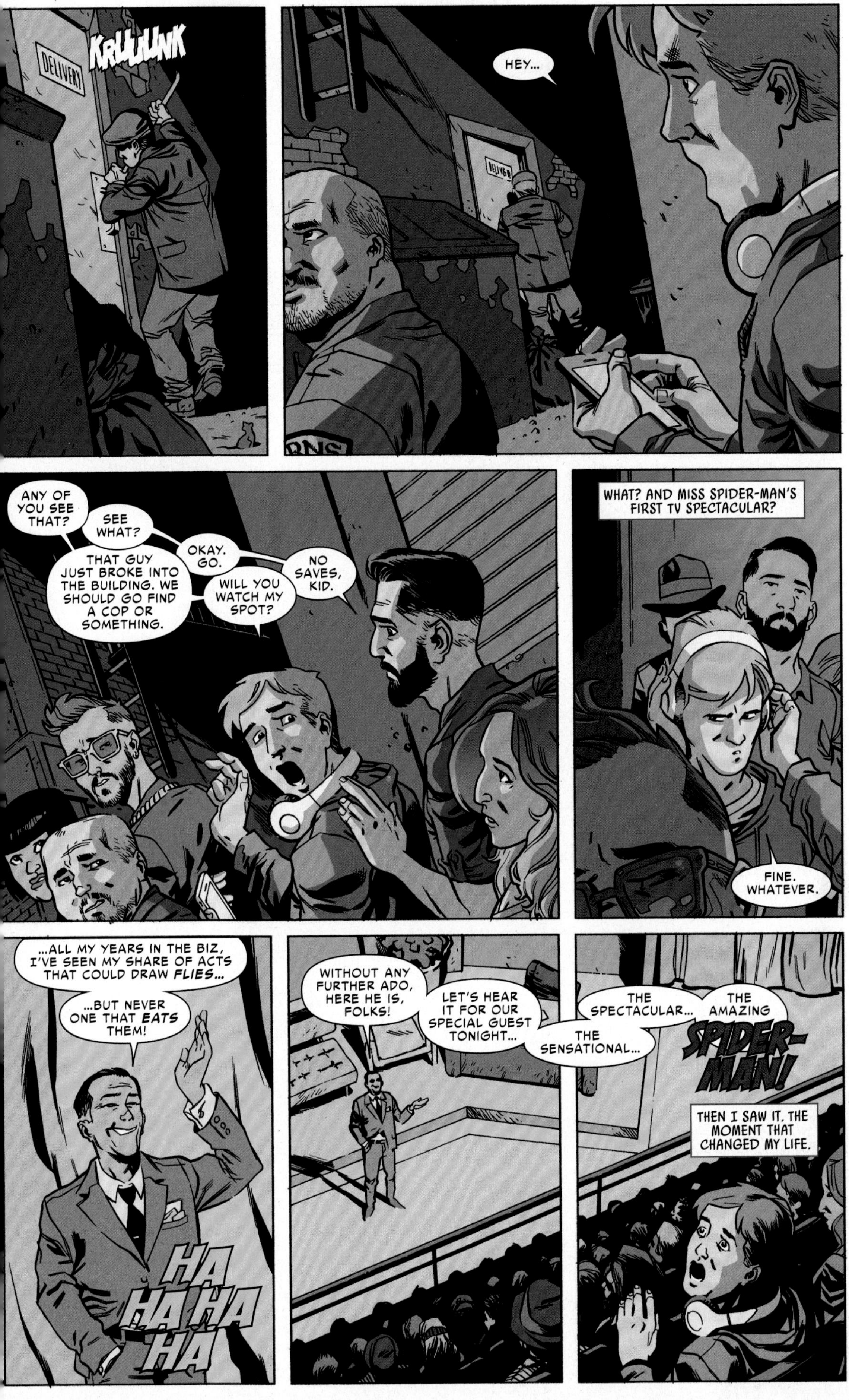
DELIVERY
KRUUUNK
HEY...
ANY OF YOU SEE THAT?
SEE WHAT?
THAT GUY JUST BROKE INTO THE BUILDING. WE SHOULD GO FIND A COP OR SOMETHING.
OKAY. GO.
WILL YOU WATCH MY SPOT?
NO SAVES, KID.
WHAT? AND MISS SPIDER-MAN'S FIRST TV SPECTACULAR?
FINE. WHATEVER.
...ALL MY YEARS IN THE BIZ, I'VE SEEN MY SHARE OF ACTS THAT COULD DRAW FLIES...
...BUT NEVER ONE THAT EATS THEM!
HA HA HA HA HA
WITHOUT ANY FURTHER ADO, HERE HE IS, FOLKS!
LET'S HEAR IT FOR OUR SPECIAL GUEST TONIGHT...
THE SENSATIONAL...
THE SPECTACULAR...
THE AMAZING
SPIDER-MAN!
THEN I SAW IT. THE MOMENT THAT CHANGED MY LIFE.

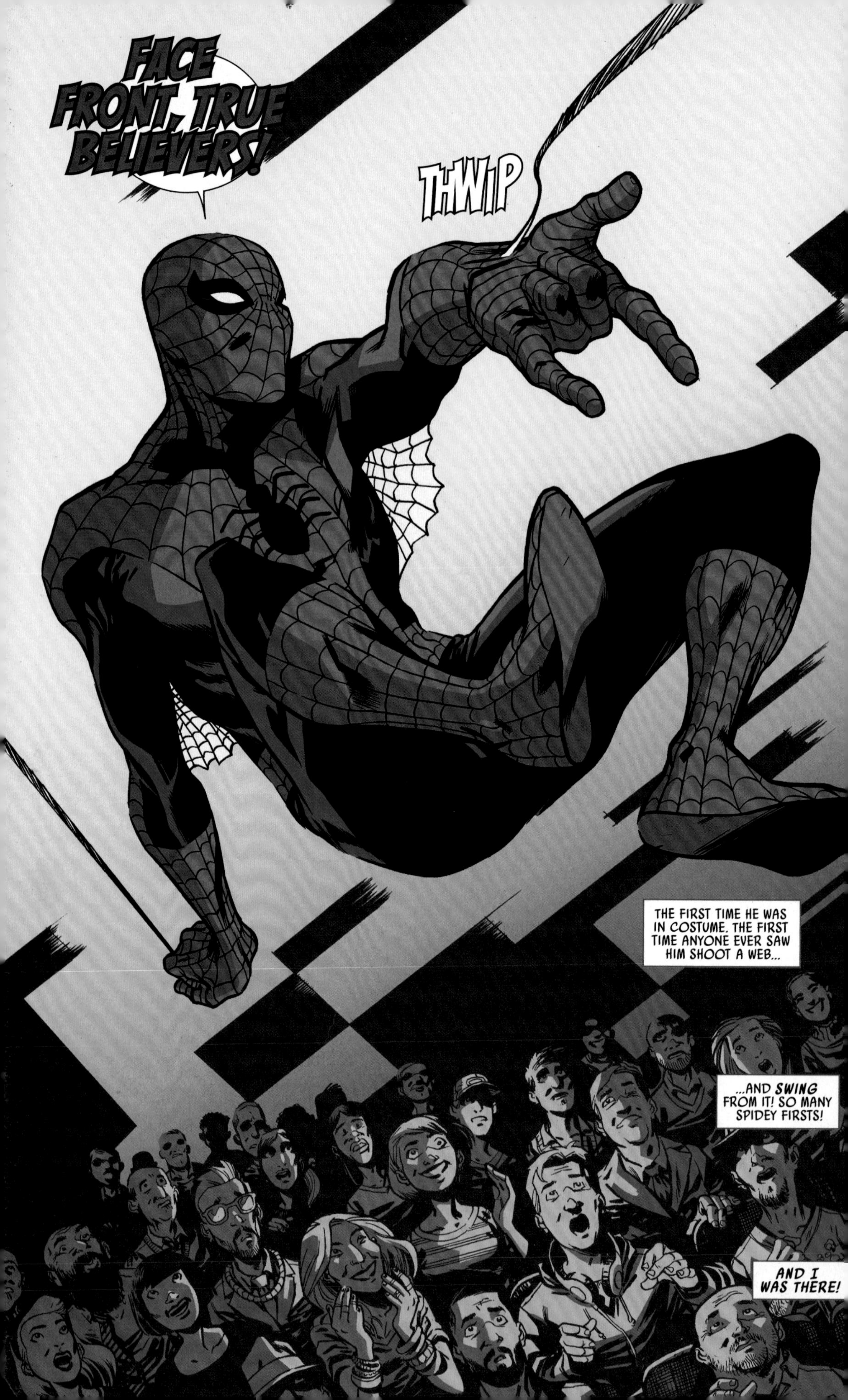
FACE FRONT, TRUE BELIEVERS!
THWIP
THE FIRST TIME HE WAS IN COSTUME. THE FIRST TIME ANYONE EVER SAW HIM SHOOT A WEB...
...AND SWING FROM IT! SO MANY SPIDEY FIRSTS!
AND I WAS THERE!

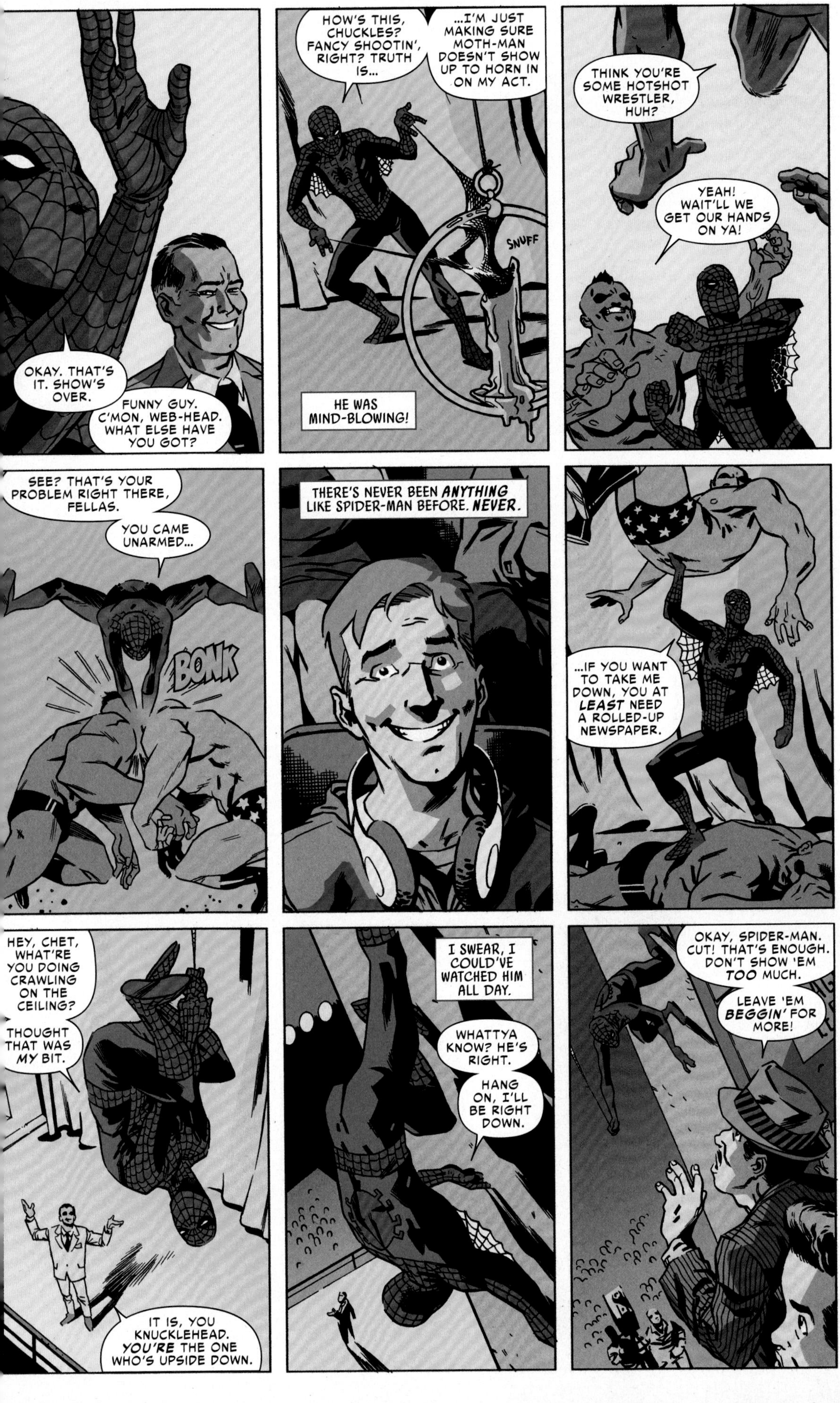

OKAY. THAT'S IT. SHOW'S OVER.
FUNNY GUY. C'MON, WEB-HEAD. WHAT ELSE HAVE YOU GOT?
HOW'S THIS, CHUCKLES? FANCY SHOOTIN', RIGHT? TRUTH IS...
...I'M JUST MAKING SURE MOTH-MAN DOESN'T SHOW UP TO HORN IN ON MY ACT.
SNUFF
HE WAS MIND-BLOWING!
THINK YOU'RE SOME HOTSHOT WRESTLER, HUH?
YEAH! WAIT'LL WE GET OUR HANDS ON YA!
SEE? THAT'S YOUR PROBLEM RIGHT THERE, FELLAS.
YOU CAME UNARMED...
BONK
THERE'S NEVER BEEN ANYTHING LIKE SPIDER-MAN BEFORE. NEVER.
...IF YOU WANT TO TAKE ME DOWN, YOU AT LEAST NEED A ROLLED-UP NEWSPAPER.
HEY, CHET, WHAT'RE YOU DOING CRAWLING ON THE CEILING?
THOUGHT THAT WAS MY BIT.
IT IS, YOU KNUCKLEHEAD. YOU'RE THE ONE WHO'S UPSIDE DOWN.
I SWEAR, I COULD'VE WATCHED HIM ALL DAY.
WHATTYA KNOW? HE'S RIGHT.
HANG ON, I'LL BE RIGHT DOWN.
OKAY, SPIDER-MAN. CUT! THAT'S ENOUGH. DON'T SHOW 'EM TOO MUCH.
LEAVE 'EM BEGGIN' FOR MORE!

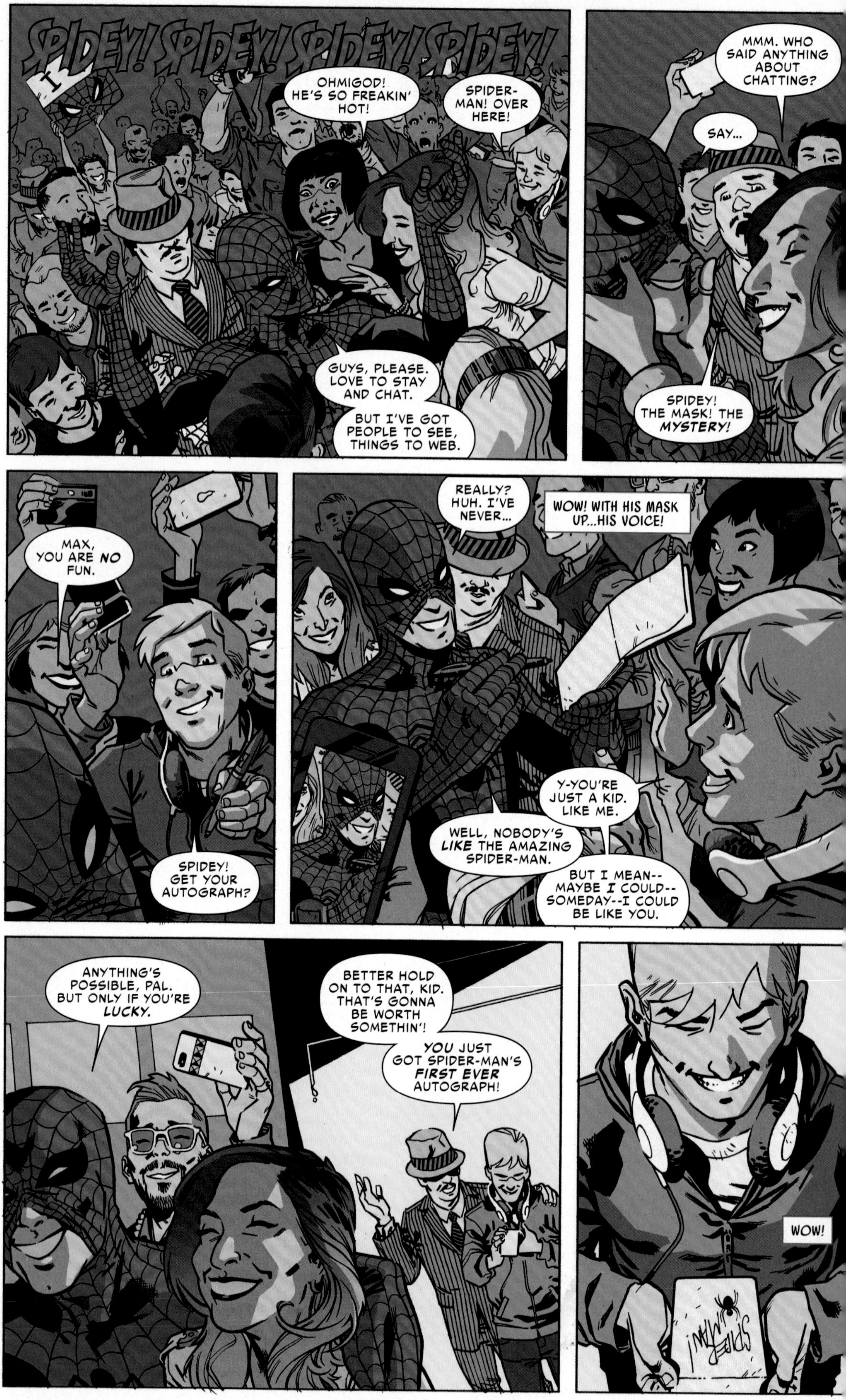
SPIDEY! SPIDEY! SPIDEY! SPIDEY!
OHMIGOD! HE'S SO FREAKIN' HOT!
SPIDER-MAN! OVER HERE!
GUYS, PLEASE. LOVE TO STAY AND CHAT.
BUT I'VE GOT PEOPLE TO SEE, THINGS TO WEB.
MMM. WHO SAID ANYTHING ABOUT CHATTING?
SAY...
SPIDEY! THE MASK! THE MYSTERY!
MAX, YOU ARE NO FUN.
SPIDEY! GET YOUR AUTOGRAPH?
REALLY? HUH. I'VE NEVER...
WOW! WITH HIS MASK UP...HIS VOICE!
Y-YOU'RE JUST A KID. LIKE ME.
WELL, NOBODY'S LIKE THE AMAZING SPIDER-MAN.
BUT I MEAN-- MAYBE I COULD-- SOMEDAY--I COULD BE LIKE YOU.
ANYTHING'S POSSIBLE, PAL. BUT ONLY IF YOU'RE LUCKY.
BETTER HOLD ON TO THAT, KID. THAT'S GONNA BE WORTH SOMETHIN'!
YOU JUST GOT SPIDER-MAN'S FIRST EVER AUTOGRAPH!
WOW!

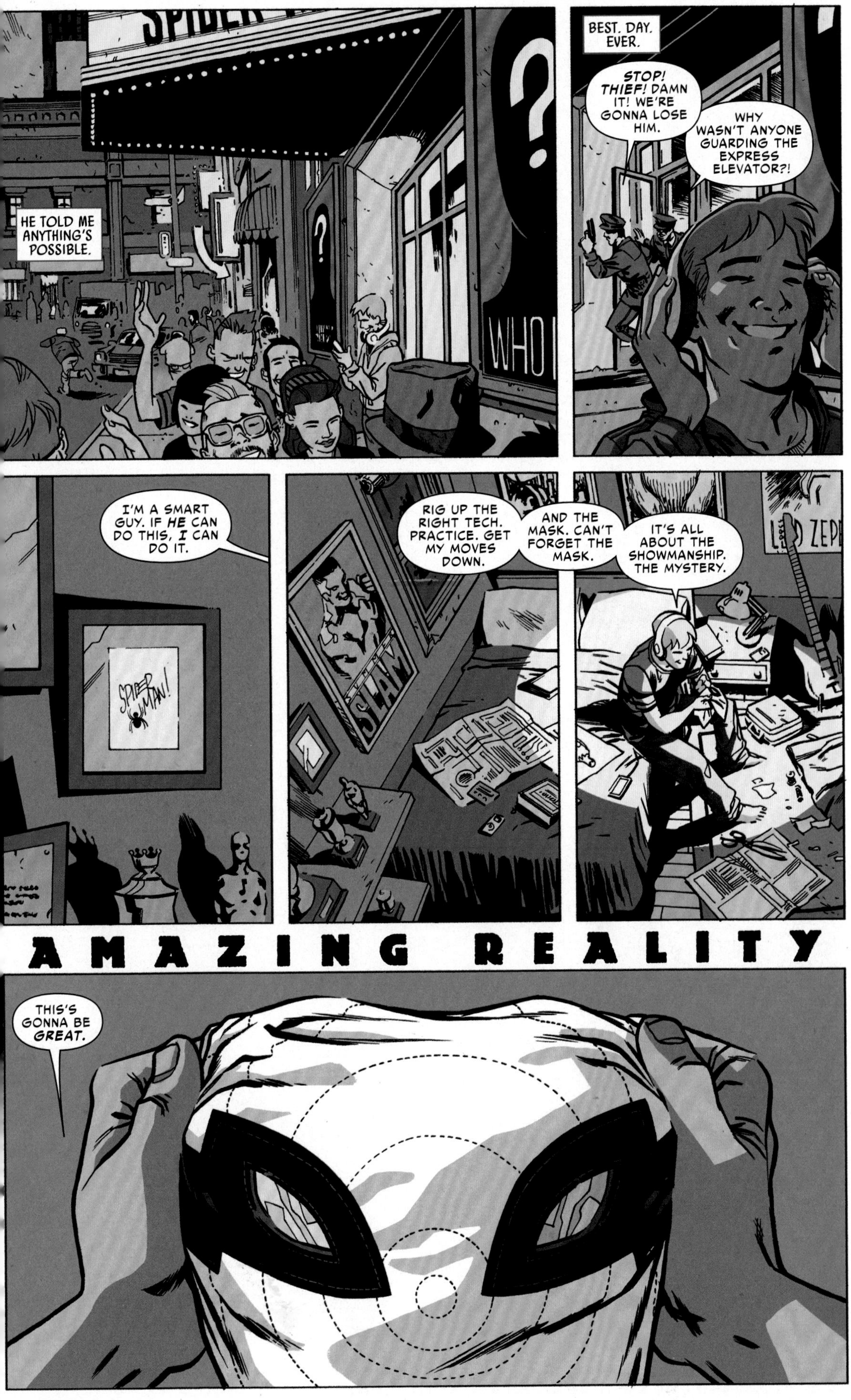
HE TOLD ME ANYTHING'S POSSIBLE.
BEST. DAY. EVER.
STOP! THIEF! DAMN IT! WE'RE GONNA LOSE HIM.
WHY WASN'T ANYONE GUARDING THE EXPRESS ELEVATOR?!
I'M A SMART GUY. IF HE CAN DO THIS, I CAN DO IT.
SPIDER MAN!
RIG UP THE RIGHT TECH. PRACTICE. GET MY MOVES DOWN.
AND THE MASK. CAN'T FORGET THE MASK.
IT'S ALL ABOUT THE SHOWMANSHIP. THE MYSTERY.
AMAZING REALITY
THIS'S GONNA BE GREAT.

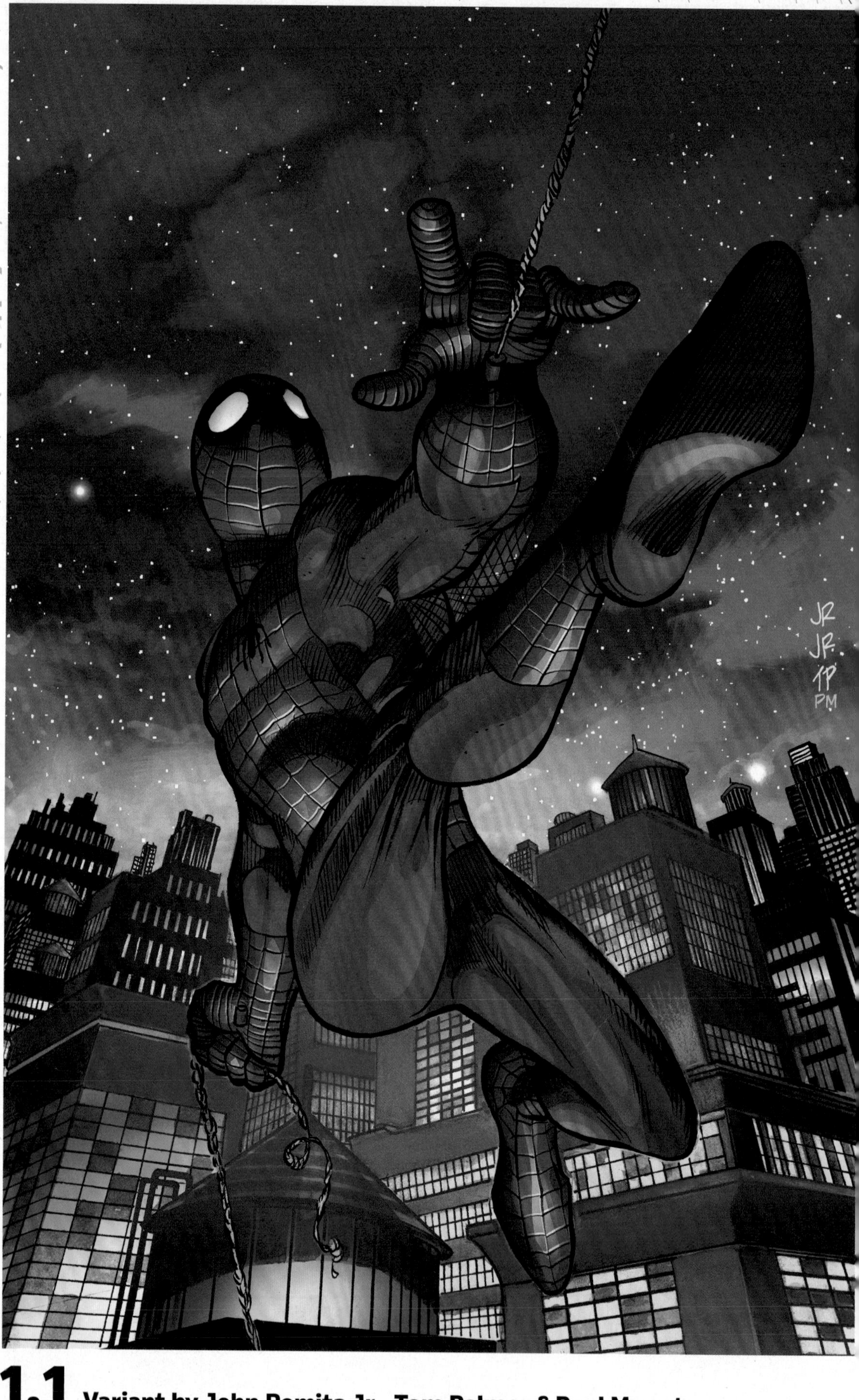
JR
JR.
TP
PM

1.1 **Variant by John Romita Jr., Tom Palmer & Paul Mounts**

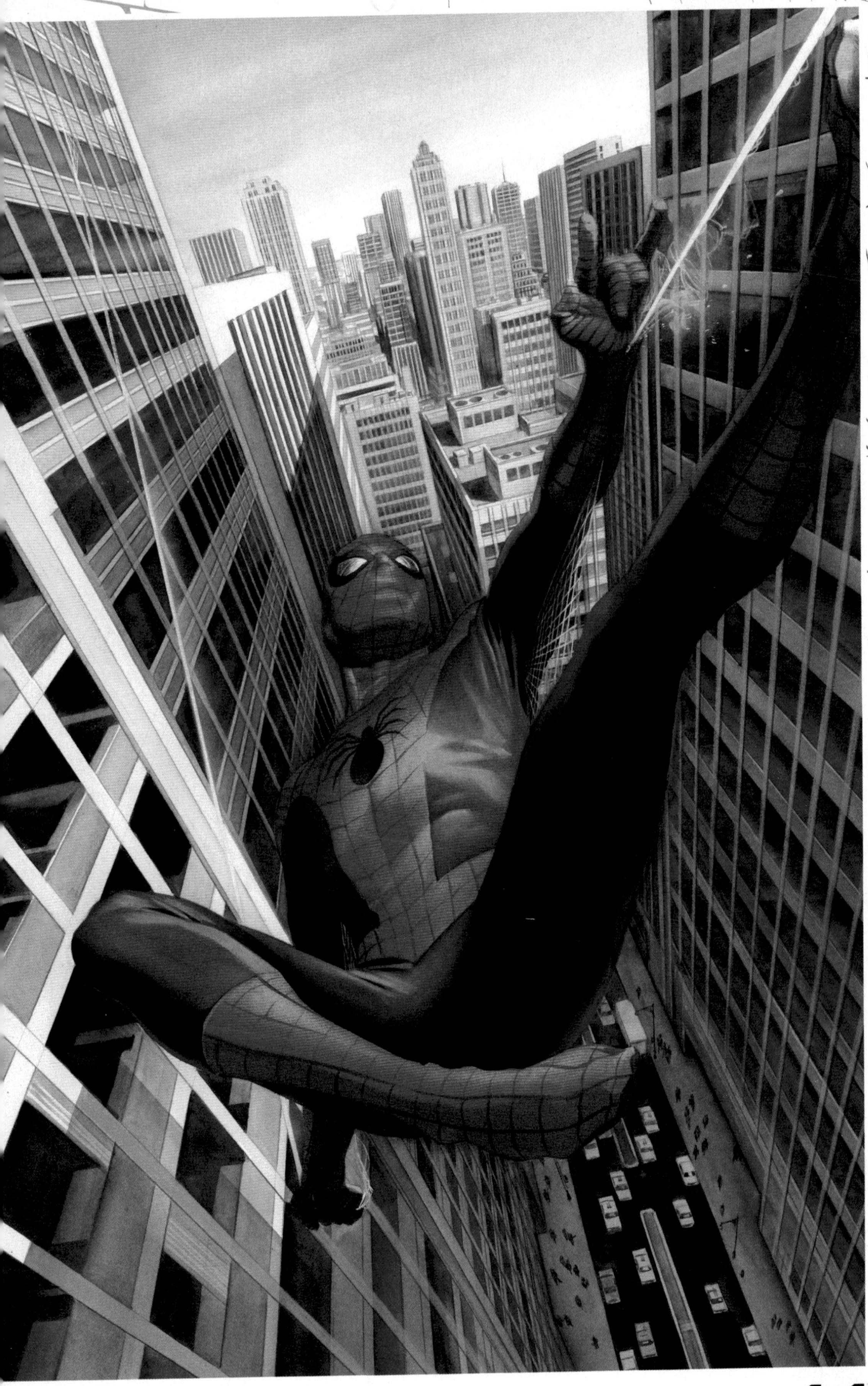

1.1

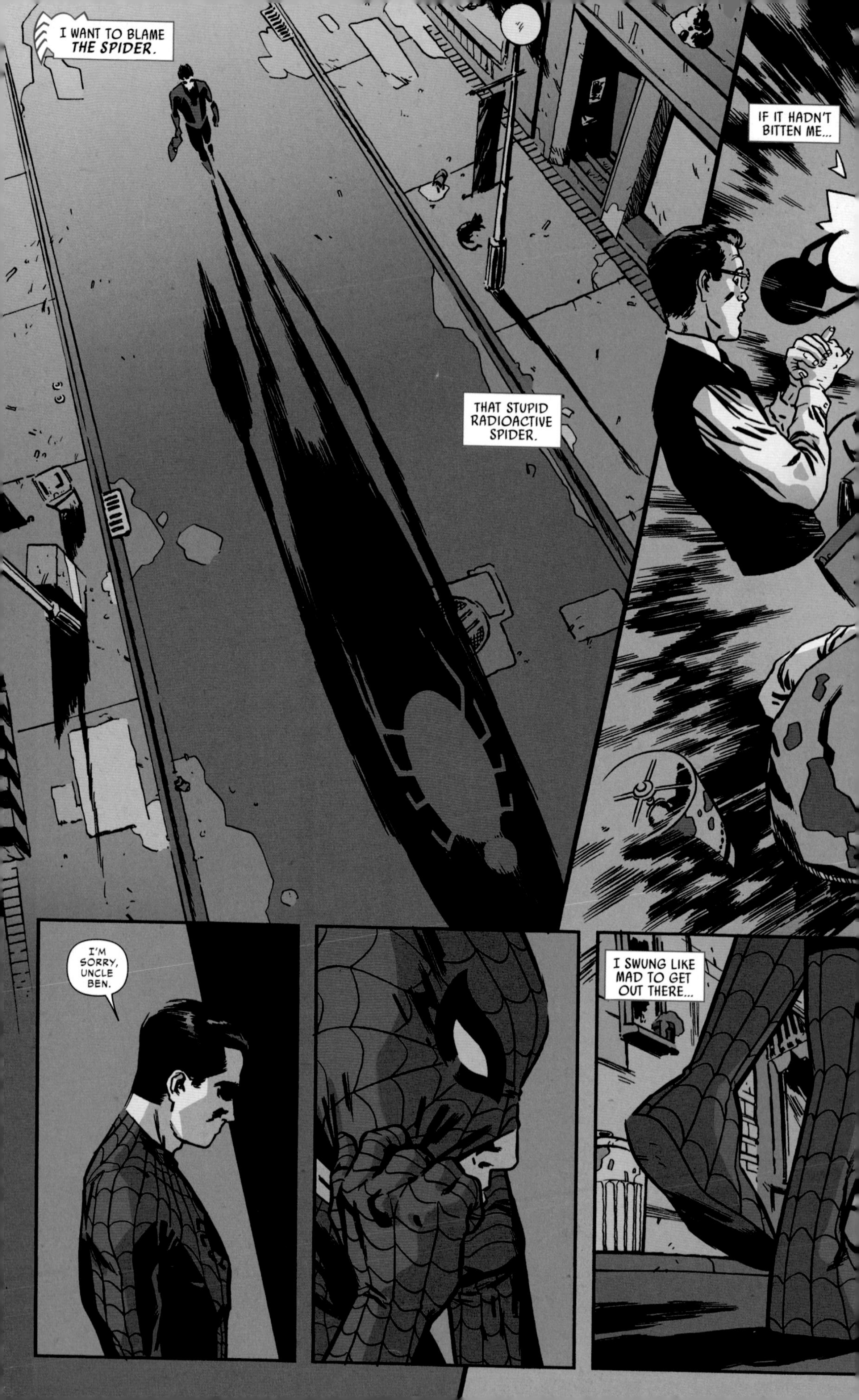
I WANT TO BLAME THE SPIDER.
IF IT HADN'T BITTEN ME...
THAT STUPID RADIOACTIVE SPIDER.
I'M SORRY, UNCLE BEN.
I SWUNG LIKE MAD TO GET OUT THERE...

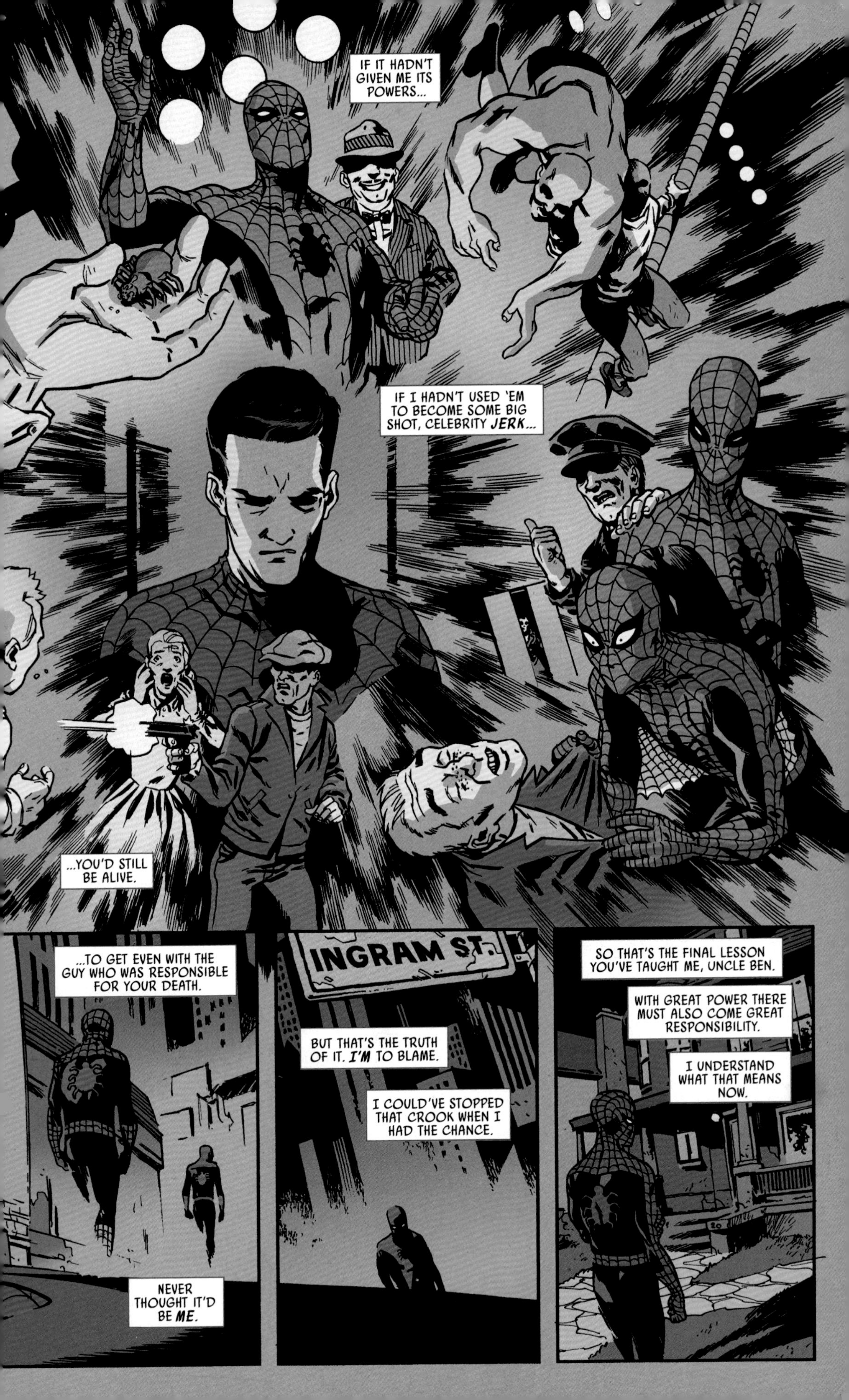
IF IT HADN'T GIVEN ME ITS POWERS...
IF I HADN'T USED 'EM TO BECOME SOME BIG SHOT, CELEBRITY JERK...
...YOU'D STILL BE ALIVE.
...TO GET EVEN WITH THE GUY WHO WAS RESPONSIBLE FOR YOUR DEATH.
NEVER THOUGHT IT'D BE ME.
INGRAM ST.
BUT THAT'S THE TRUTH OF IT. I'M TO BLAME.
I COULD'VE STOPPED THAT CROOK WHEN I HAD THE CHANCE.
SO THAT'S THE FINAL LESSON YOU'VE TAUGHT ME, UNCLE BEN.
WITH GREAT POWER THERE MUST ALSO COME GREAT RESPONSIBILITY.
I UNDERSTAND WHAT THAT MEANS NOW.

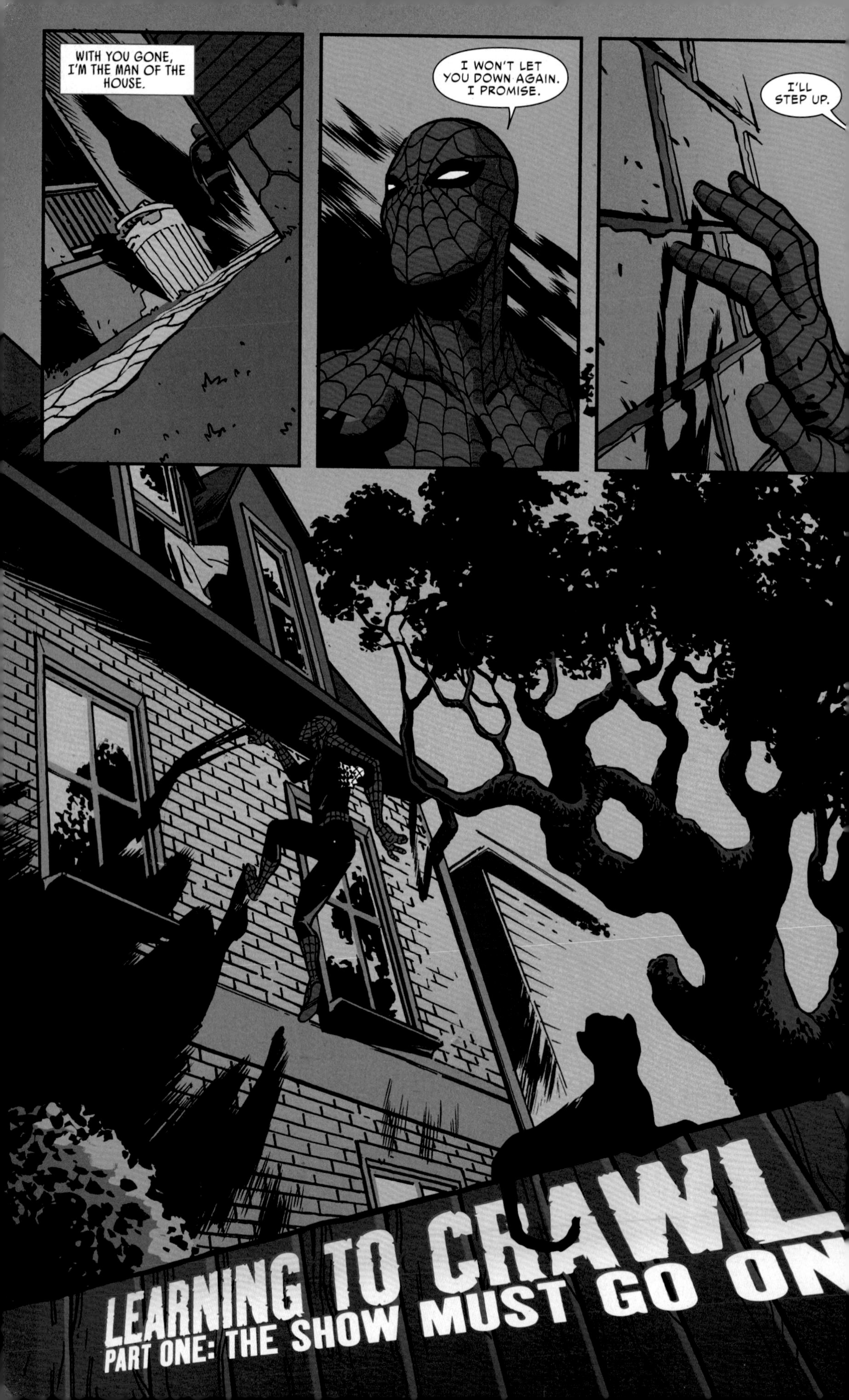
WITH YOU GONE, I'M THE MAN OF THE HOUSE.
I WON'T LET YOU DOWN AGAIN. I PROMISE.
I'LL STEP UP.
LEARNING TO CRAWL
PART ONE: THE SHOW MUST GO ON

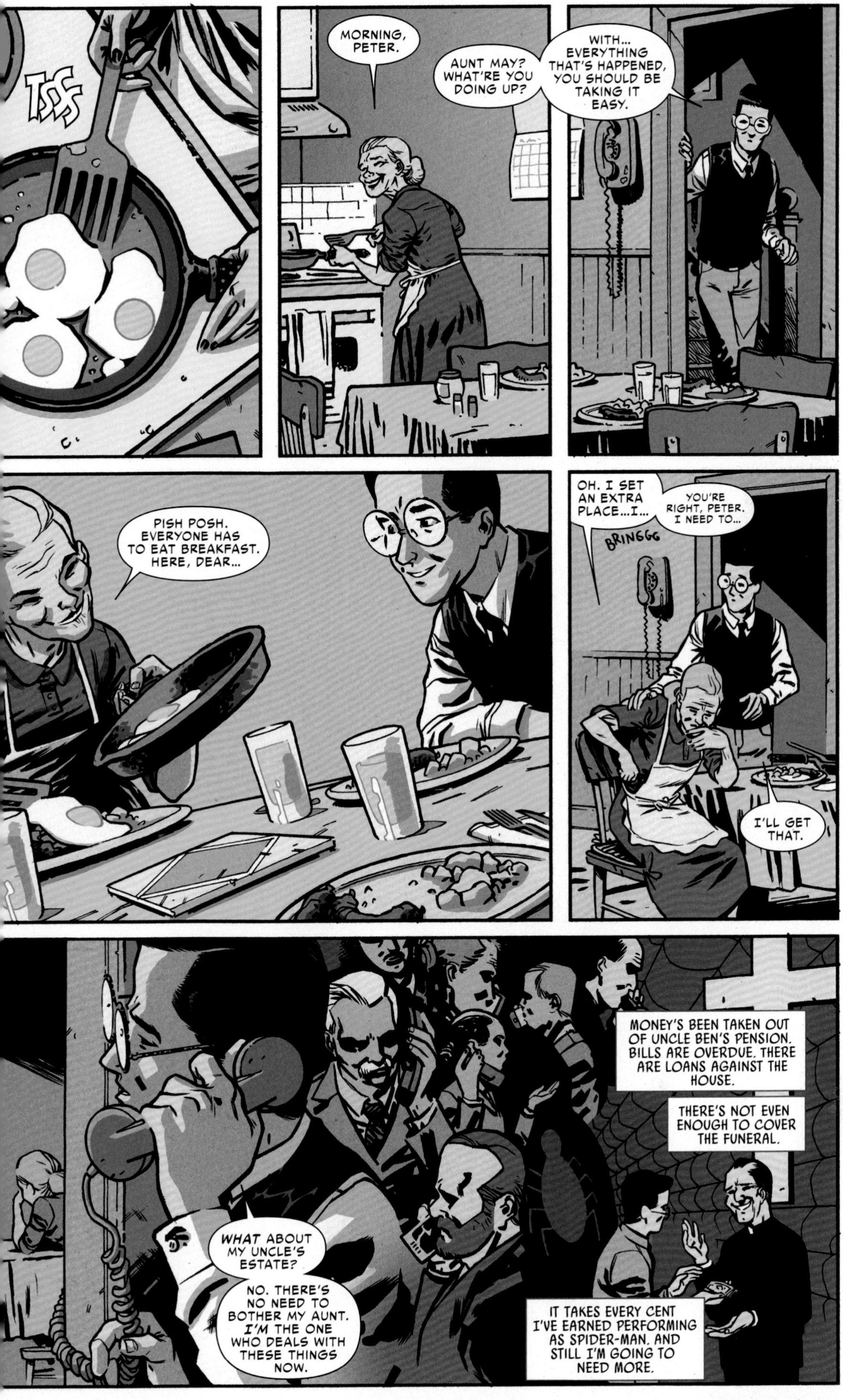
TSSS
MORNING, PETER.
AUNT MAY? WHAT'RE YOU DOING UP?
WITH... EVERYTHING THAT'S HAPPENED, YOU SHOULD BE TAKING IT EASY.
PISH POSH. EVERYONE HAS TO EAT BREAKFAST. HERE, DEAR...
OH. I SET AN EXTRA PLACE...I...
YOU'RE RIGHT, PETER. I NEED TO...
BRINGG
I'LL GET THAT.
MONEY'S BEEN TAKEN OUT OF UNCLE BEN'S PENSION. BILLS ARE OVERDUE. THERE ARE LOANS AGAINST THE HOUSE.
THERE'S NOT EVEN ENOUGH TO COVER THE FUNERAL.
WHAT ABOUT MY UNCLE'S ESTATE?
NO. THERE'S NO NEED TO BOTHER MY AUNT. I'M THE ONE WHO DEALS WITH THESE THINGS NOW.
IT TAKES EVERY CENT I'VE EARNED PERFORMING AS SPIDER-MAN. AND STILL I'M GOING TO NEED MORE.

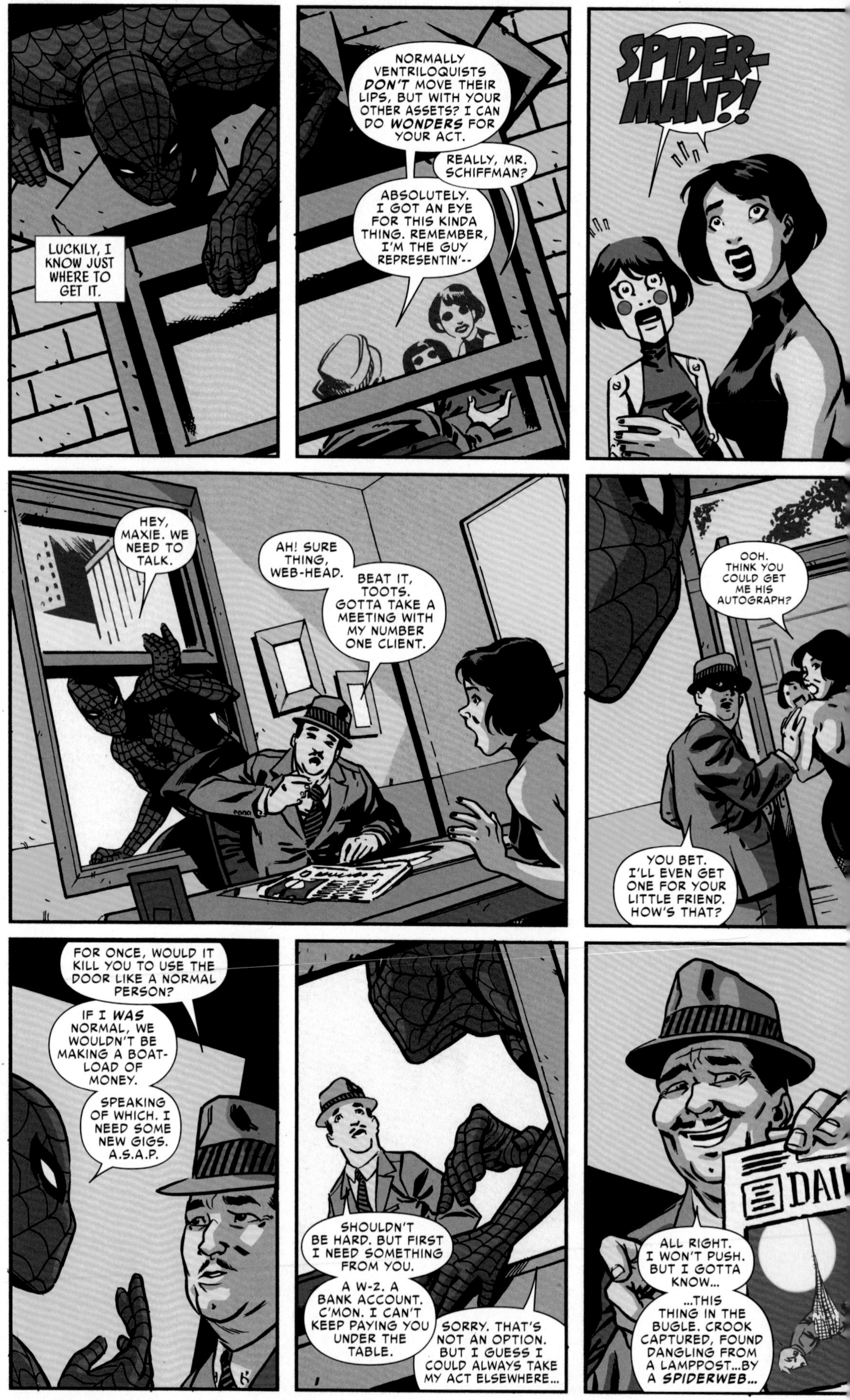

LUCKILY, I KNOW JUST WHERE TO GET IT.
NORMALLY VENTRILOQUISTS DON'T MOVE THEIR LIPS, BUT WITH YOUR OTHER ASSETS? I CAN DO WONDERS FOR YOUR ACT.
REALLY, MR. SCHIFFMAN?
ABSOLUTELY. I GOT AN EYE FOR THIS KINDA THING. REMEMBER, I'M THE GUY REPRESENTIN'--
SPIDER-MAN?!
HEY, MAXIE. WE NEED TO TALK.
AH! SURE THING, WEB-HEAD.
BEAT IT, TOOTS. GOTTA TAKE A MEETING WITH MY NUMBER ONE CLIENT.
OOH. THINK YOU COULD GET ME HIS AUTOGRAPH?
YOU BET. I'LL EVEN GET ONE FOR YOUR LITTLE FRIEND. HOW'S THAT?
FOR ONCE, WOULD IT KILL YOU TO USE THE DOOR LIKE A NORMAL PERSON?
IF I WAS NORMAL, WE WOULDN'T BE MAKING A BOAT-LOAD OF MONEY.
SPEAKING OF WHICH. I NEED SOME NEW GIGS. A.S.A.P.
SHOULDN'T BE HARD. BUT FIRST I NEED SOMETHING FROM YOU.
A W-2. A BANK ACCOUNT. C'MON. I CAN'T KEEP PAYING YOU UNDER THE TABLE.
SORRY. THAT'S NOT AN OPTION. BUT I GUESS I COULD ALWAYS TAKE MY ACT ELSEWHERE...
ALL RIGHT. I WON'T PUSH. BUT I GOTTA KNOW...
...THIS THING IN THE BUGLE. CROOK CAPTURED, FOUND DANGLING FROM A LAMPPOST...BY A SPIDERWEB...

DID YOU DO THAT? I-- UHH...

I KNEW IT WAS YOU! THIS IS GREAT!

ONE OF MY CLIENTS CAPTURED A DANGEROUS CRIMINAL?! IMAGINE THE HEADLINES: "WEB-HEADED HERO HANGS UP HOODLUMS!"

THINK OF THE PRESS WE'RE GONNA GET FOR THIS! NATIONWIDE FOR SURE!

WHAP!

NO. I-- I'M NO HERO.

AND I WILL NOT PROFIT OFF OF THIS! IN ANY WAY!

DO YOU UNDERSTAND?!

SURE. SURE. WHATEVER YOU SAY! NO PROBLEM!

LOOK, JUST LINE ME UP SOME MORE SHOWS! OKAY?!

THIS USED TO BE THE FUN PART. PERFORMING IN THIS SUIT. BEING A STAR.

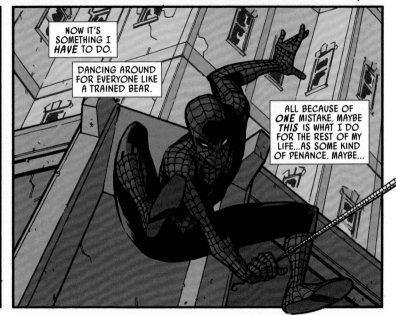

NOW IT'S SOMETHING I HAVE TO DO.

DANCING AROUND FOR EVERYONE LIKE A TRAINED BEAR.

ALL BECAUSE OF ONE MISTAKE. MAYBE THIS IS WHAT I DO FOR THE REST OF MY LIFE...AS SOME KIND OF PENANCE. MAYBE...

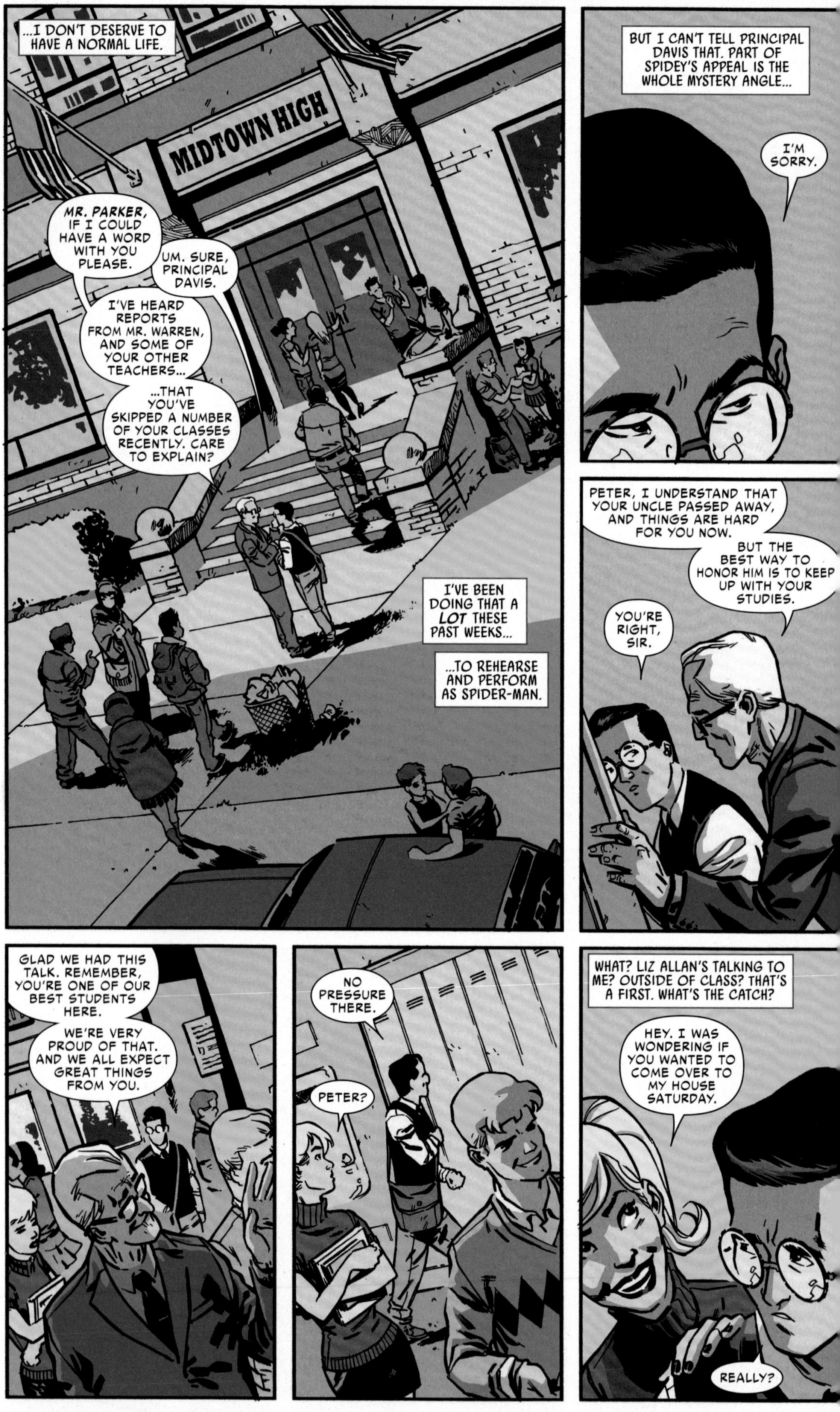
...I DON'T DESERVE TO HAVE A NORMAL LIFE.
MIDTOWN HIGH
MR. PARKER, IF I COULD HAVE A WORD WITH YOU PLEASE.
UM. SURE, PRINCIPAL DAVIS.
I'VE HEARD REPORTS FROM MR. WARREN, AND SOME OF YOUR OTHER TEACHERS...
...THAT YOU'VE SKIPPED A NUMBER OF YOUR CLASSES RECENTLY. CARE TO EXPLAIN?
I'VE BEEN DOING THAT A LOT THESE PAST WEEKS...
...TO REHEARSE AND PERFORM AS SPIDER-MAN.
BUT I CAN'T TELL PRINCIPAL DAVIS THAT. PART OF SPIDEY'S APPEAL IS THE WHOLE MYSTERY ANGLE...
I'M SORRY.
PETER, I UNDERSTAND THAT YOUR UNCLE PASSED AWAY, AND THINGS ARE HARD FOR YOU NOW.
BUT THE BEST WAY TO HONOR HIM IS TO KEEP UP WITH YOUR STUDIES.
YOU'RE RIGHT, SIR.
GLAD WE HAD THIS TALK. REMEMBER, YOU'RE ONE OF OUR BEST STUDENTS HERE.
WE'RE VERY PROUD OF THAT. AND WE ALL EXPECT GREAT THINGS FROM YOU.
NO PRESSURE THERE.
PETER?
WHAT? LIZ ALLAN'S TALKING TO ME? OUTSIDE OF CLASS? THAT'S A FIRST. WHAT'S THE CATCH?
HEY. I WAS WONDERING IF YOU WANTED TO COME OVER TO MY HOUSE SATURDAY.
REALLY?

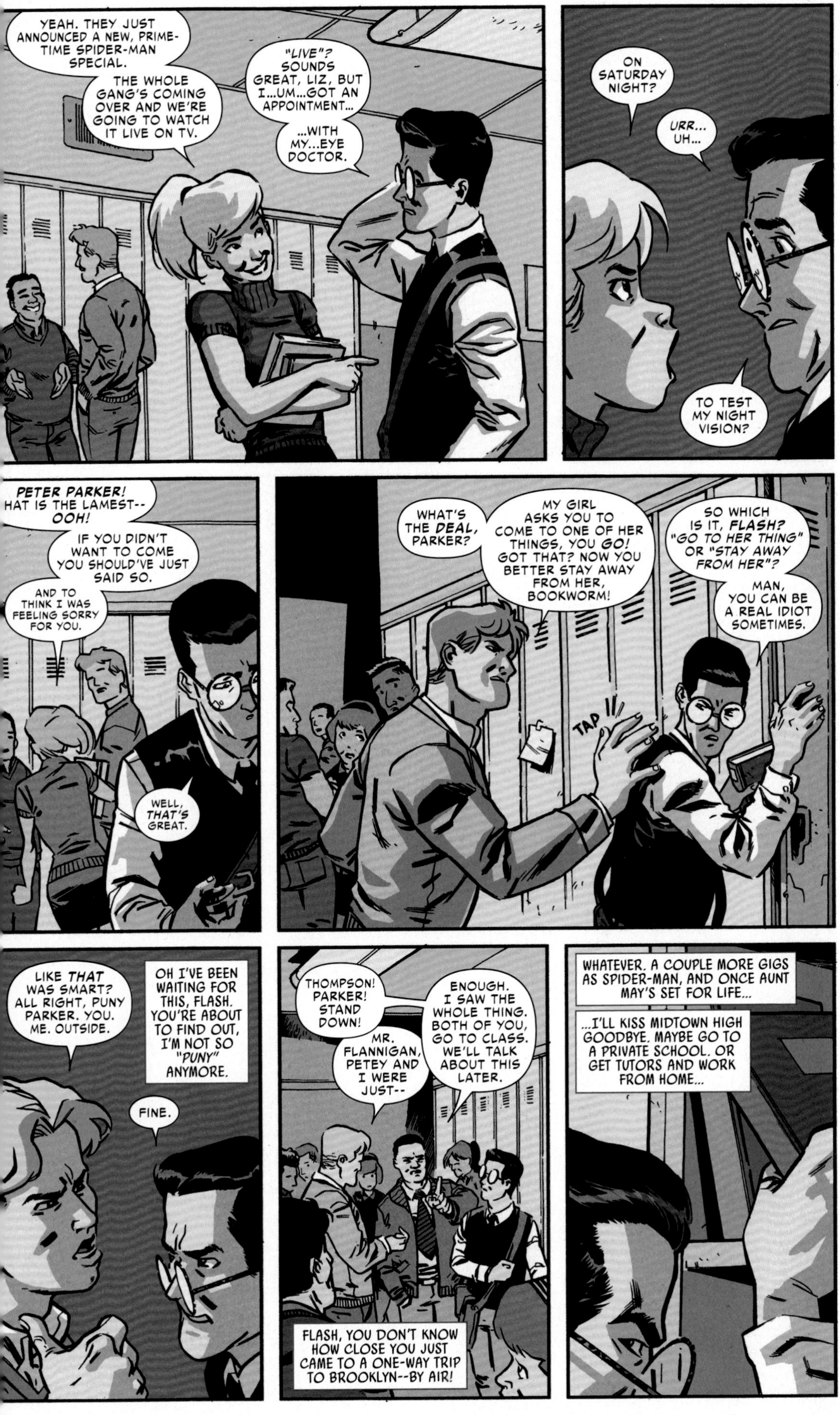

YEAH. THEY JUST ANNOUNCED A NEW, PRIME-TIME SPIDER-MAN SPECIAL.
THE WHOLE GANG'S COMING OVER AND WE'RE GOING TO WATCH IT LIVE ON TV.
"LIVE"? SOUNDS GREAT, LIZ, BUT I...UM...GOT AN APPOINTMENT...
...WITH MY...EYE DOCTOR.
ON SATURDAY NIGHT?
URR... UH...
TO TEST MY NIGHT VISION?
PETER PARKER! HAT IS THE LAMEST-- OOH!
IF YOU DIDN'T WANT TO COME YOU SHOULD'VE JUST SAID SO.
AND TO THINK I WAS FEELING SORRY FOR YOU.
WELL, THAT'S GREAT.
WHAT'S THE DEAL, PARKER?
MY GIRL ASKS YOU TO COME TO ONE OF HER THINGS, YOU GO! GOT THAT? NOW YOU BETTER STAY AWAY FROM HER, BOOKWORM!
TAP
SO WHICH IS IT, FLASH? "GO TO HER THING" OR "STAY AWAY FROM HER"?
MAN, YOU CAN BE A REAL IDIOT SOMETIMES.
LIKE THAT WAS SMART? ALL RIGHT, PUNY PARKER. YOU. ME. OUTSIDE.
OH I'VE BEEN WAITING FOR THIS, FLASH. YOU'RE ABOUT TO FIND OUT, I'M NOT SO "PUNY" ANYMORE.
FINE.
THOMPSON! PARKER! STAND DOWN!
MR. FLANNIGAN, PETEY AND I WERE JUST--
ENOUGH. I SAW THE WHOLE THING. BOTH OF YOU, GO TO CLASS. WE'LL TALK ABOUT THIS LATER.
FLASH, YOU DON'T KNOW HOW CLOSE YOU JUST CAME TO A ONE-WAY TRIP TO BROOKLYN--BY AIR!
WHATEVER. A COUPLE MORE GIGS AS SPIDER-MAN, AND ONCE AUNT MAY'S SET FOR LIFE...
...I'LL KISS MIDTOWN HIGH GOODBYE. MAYBE GO TO A PRIVATE SCHOOL. OR GET TUTORS AND WORK FROM HOME...

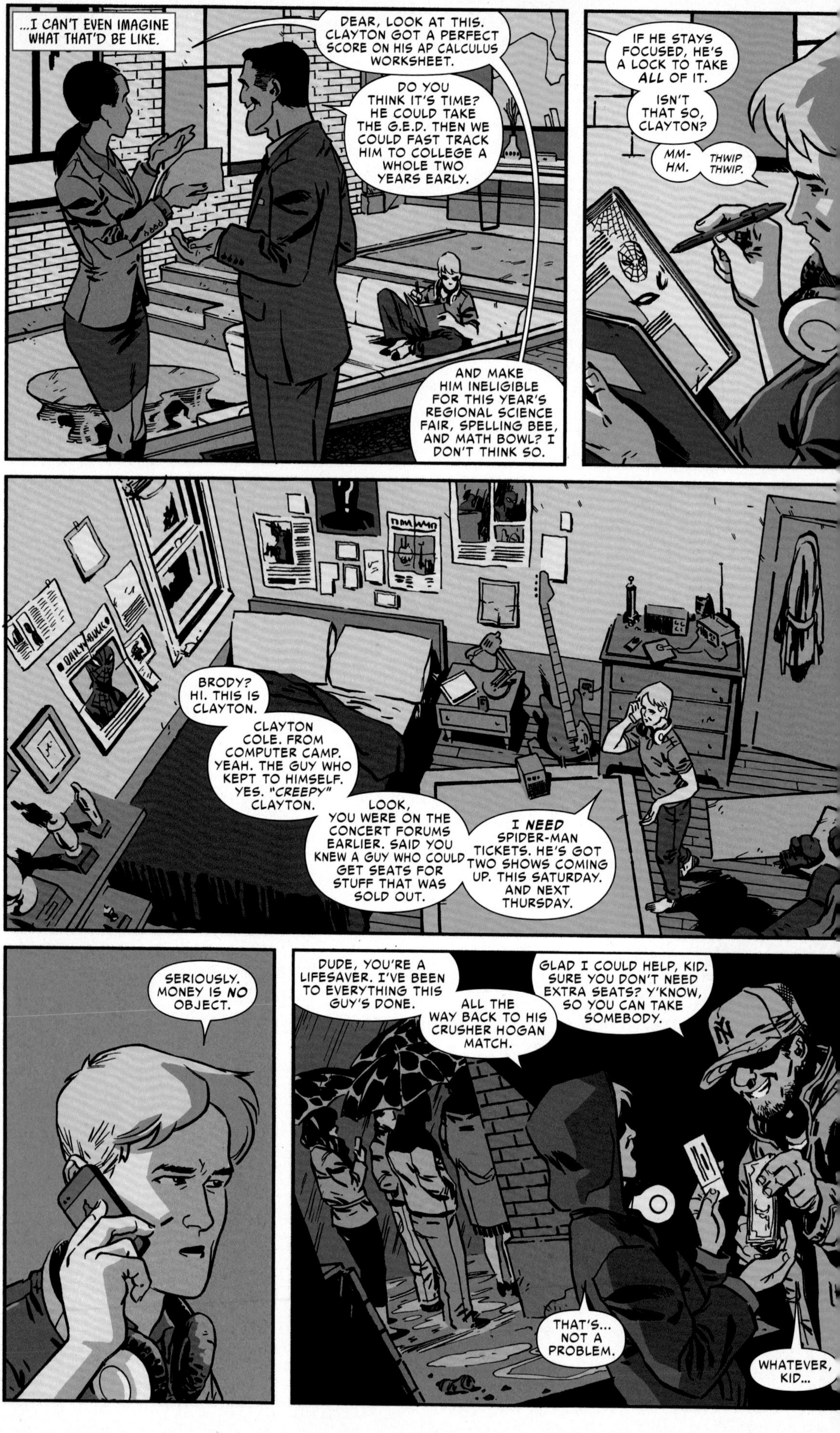
...I CAN'T EVEN IMAGINE WHAT THAT'D BE LIKE.
DEAR, LOOK AT THIS. CLAYTON GOT A PERFECT SCORE ON HIS AP CALCULUS WORKSHEET.
DO YOU THINK IT'S TIME? HE COULD TAKE THE G.E.D. THEN WE COULD FAST TRACK HIM TO COLLEGE A WHOLE TWO YEARS EARLY.
AND MAKE HIM INELIGIBLE FOR THIS YEAR'S REGIONAL SCIENCE FAIR, SPELLING BEE, AND MATH BOWL? I DON'T THINK SO.
IF HE STAYS FOCUSED, HE'S A LOCK TO TAKE ALL OF IT.
ISN'T THAT SO, CLAYTON?
MM-HM.
THWIP THWIP.
BRODY? HI. THIS IS CLAYTON.
CLAYTON COLE. FROM COMPUTER CAMP. YEAH. THE GUY WHO KEPT TO HIMSELF. YES. "CREEPY" CLAYTON.
LOOK, YOU WERE ON THE CONCERT FORUMS EARLIER. SAID YOU KNEW A GUY WHO COULD GET SEATS FOR STUFF THAT WAS SOLD OUT.
I NEED SPIDER-MAN TICKETS. HE'S GOT TWO SHOWS COMING UP. THIS SATURDAY. AND NEXT THURSDAY.
SERIOUSLY. MONEY IS NO OBJECT.
DUDE, YOU'RE A LIFESAVER. I'VE BEEN TO EVERYTHING THIS GUY'S DONE.
ALL THE WAY BACK TO HIS CRUSHER HOGAN MATCH.
GLAD I COULD HELP, KID. SURE YOU DON'T NEED EXTRA SEATS? Y'KNOW, SO YOU CAN TAKE SOMEBODY.
THAT'S... NOT A PROBLEM.
WHATEVER, KID...

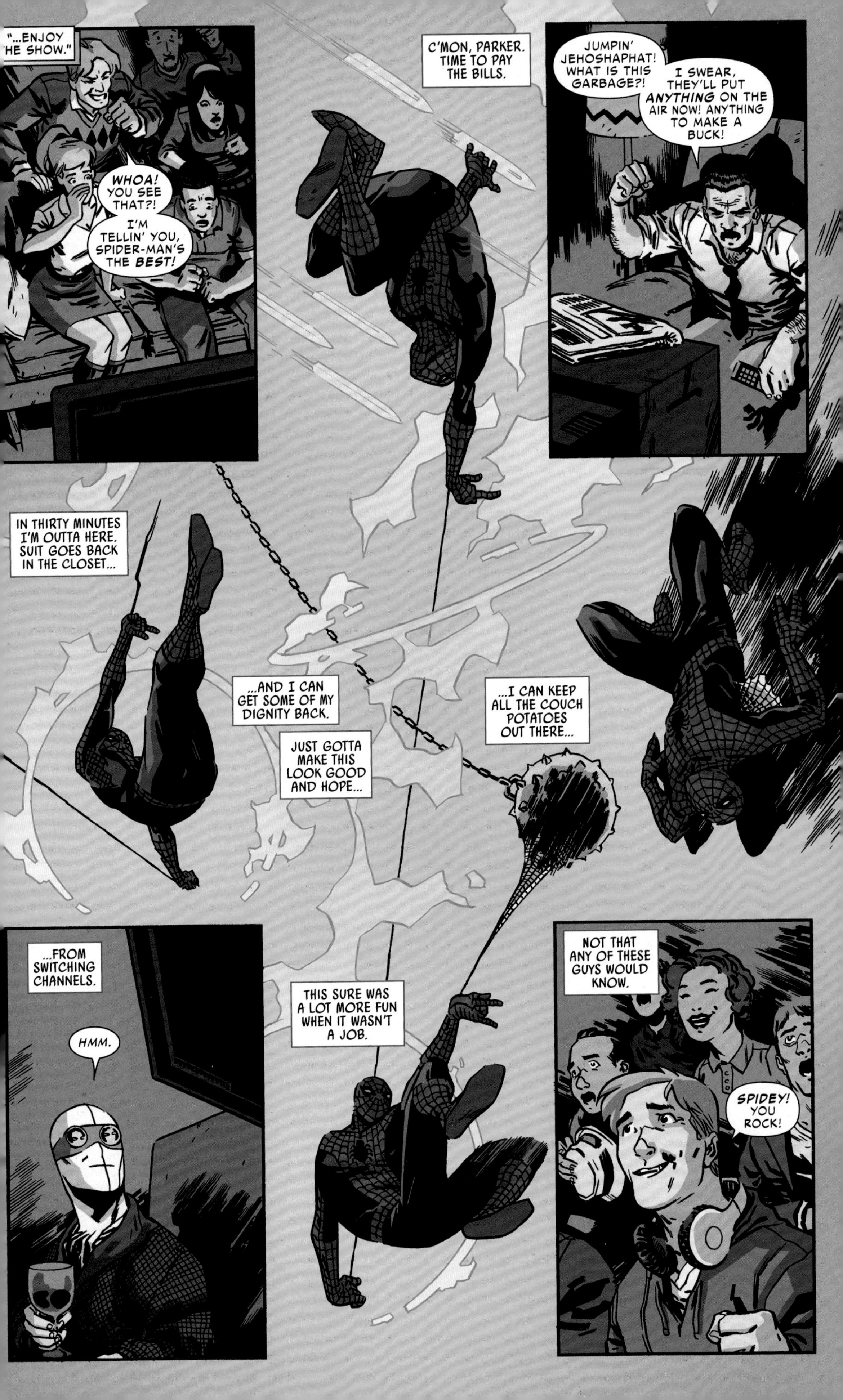

"...ENJOY
HE SHOW."
WHOA! YOU SEE THAT?!
I'M TELLIN' YOU, SPIDER-MAN'S THE BEST!
C'MON, PARKER. TIME TO PAY THE BILLS.
JUMPIN' JEHOSHAPHAT! WHAT IS THIS GARBAGE?!
I SWEAR, THEY'LL PUT ANYTHING ON THE AIR NOW! ANYTHING TO MAKE A BUCK!
IN THIRTY MINUTES I'M OUTTA HERE. SUIT GOES BACK IN THE CLOSET...
...AND I CAN GET SOME OF MY DIGNITY BACK.
JUST GOTTA MAKE THIS LOOK GOOD AND HOPE...
...I CAN KEEP ALL THE COUCH POTATOES OUT THERE...
...FROM SWITCHING CHANNELS.
HMM.
THIS SURE WAS A LOT MORE FUN WHEN IT WASN'T A JOB.
NOT THAT ANY OF THESE GUYS WOULD KNOW.
SPIDEY! YOU ROCK!

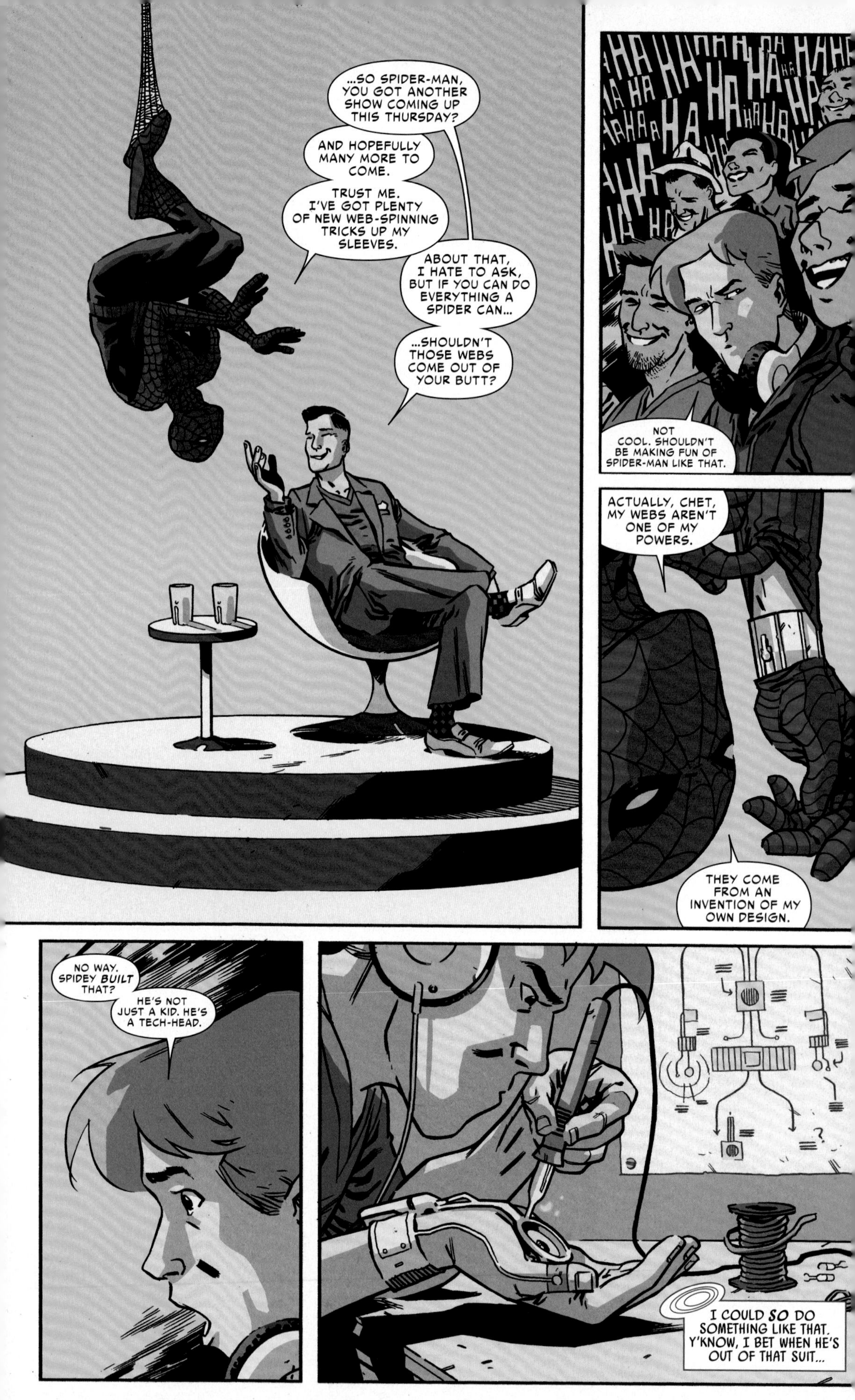
...SO SPIDER-MAN, YOU GOT ANOTHER SHOW COMING UP THIS THURSDAY?
AND HOPEFULLY MANY MORE TO COME.
TRUST ME. I'VE GOT PLENTY OF NEW WEB-SPINNING TRICKS UP MY SLEEVES.
ABOUT THAT, I HATE TO ASK, BUT IF YOU CAN DO EVERYTHING A SPIDER CAN...
...SHOULDN'T THOSE WEBS COME OUT OF YOUR BUTT?
HAHAHA HA HA HA HA
NOT COOL. SHOULDN'T BE MAKING FUN OF SPIDER-MAN LIKE THAT.
ACTUALLY, CHET, MY WEBS AREN'T ONE OF MY POWERS.
THEY COME FROM AN INVENTION OF MY OWN DESIGN.
NO WAY. SPIDEY BUILT THAT?
HE'S NOT JUST A KID. HE'S A TECH-HEAD.
I COULD SO DO SOMETHING LIKE THAT. Y'KNOW, I BET WHEN HE'S OUT OF THAT SUIT...

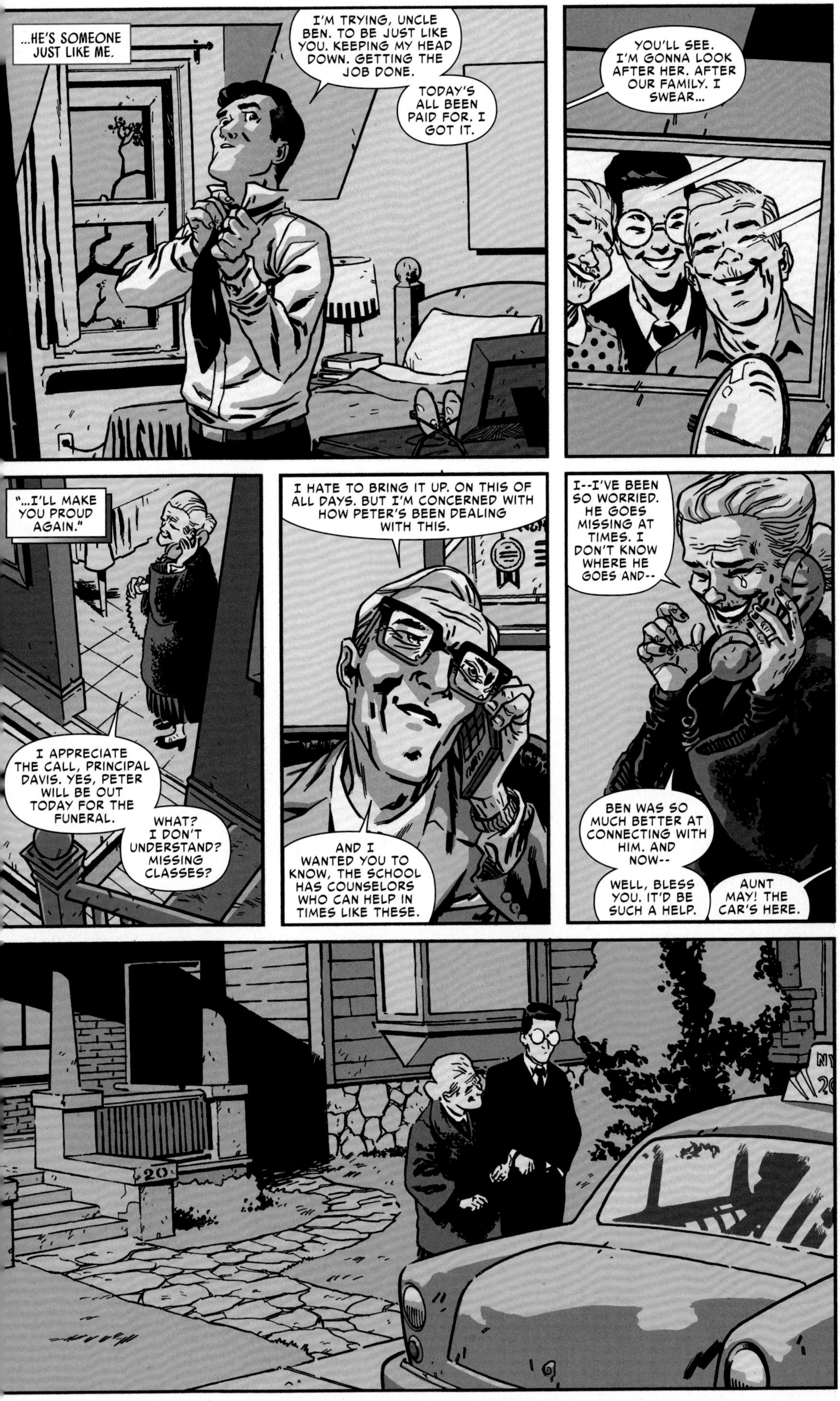
...HE'S SOMEONE JUST LIKE ME.
I'M TRYING, UNCLE BEN. TO BE JUST LIKE YOU. KEEPING MY HEAD DOWN. GETTING THE JOB DONE.
TODAY'S ALL BEEN PAID FOR. I GOT IT.
YOU'LL SEE. I'M GONNA LOOK AFTER HER. AFTER OUR FAMILY. I SWEAR...
"...I'LL MAKE YOU PROUD AGAIN."
I APPRECIATE THE CALL, PRINCIPAL DAVIS. YES, PETER WILL BE OUT TODAY FOR THE FUNERAL.
WHAT? I DON'T UNDERSTAND? MISSING CLASSES?
I HATE TO BRING IT UP. ON THIS OF ALL DAYS. BUT I'M CONCERNED WITH HOW PETER'S BEEN DEALING WITH THIS.
AND I WANTED YOU TO KNOW, THE SCHOOL HAS COUNSELORS WHO CAN HELP IN TIMES LIKE THESE.
I--I'VE BEEN SO WORRIED. HE GOES MISSING AT TIMES. I DON'T KNOW WHERE HE GOES AND--
BEN WAS SO MUCH BETTER AT CONNECTING WITH HIM. AND NOW--
WELL, BLESS YOU. IT'D BE SUCH A HELP.
AUNT MAY! THE CAR'S HERE.
20

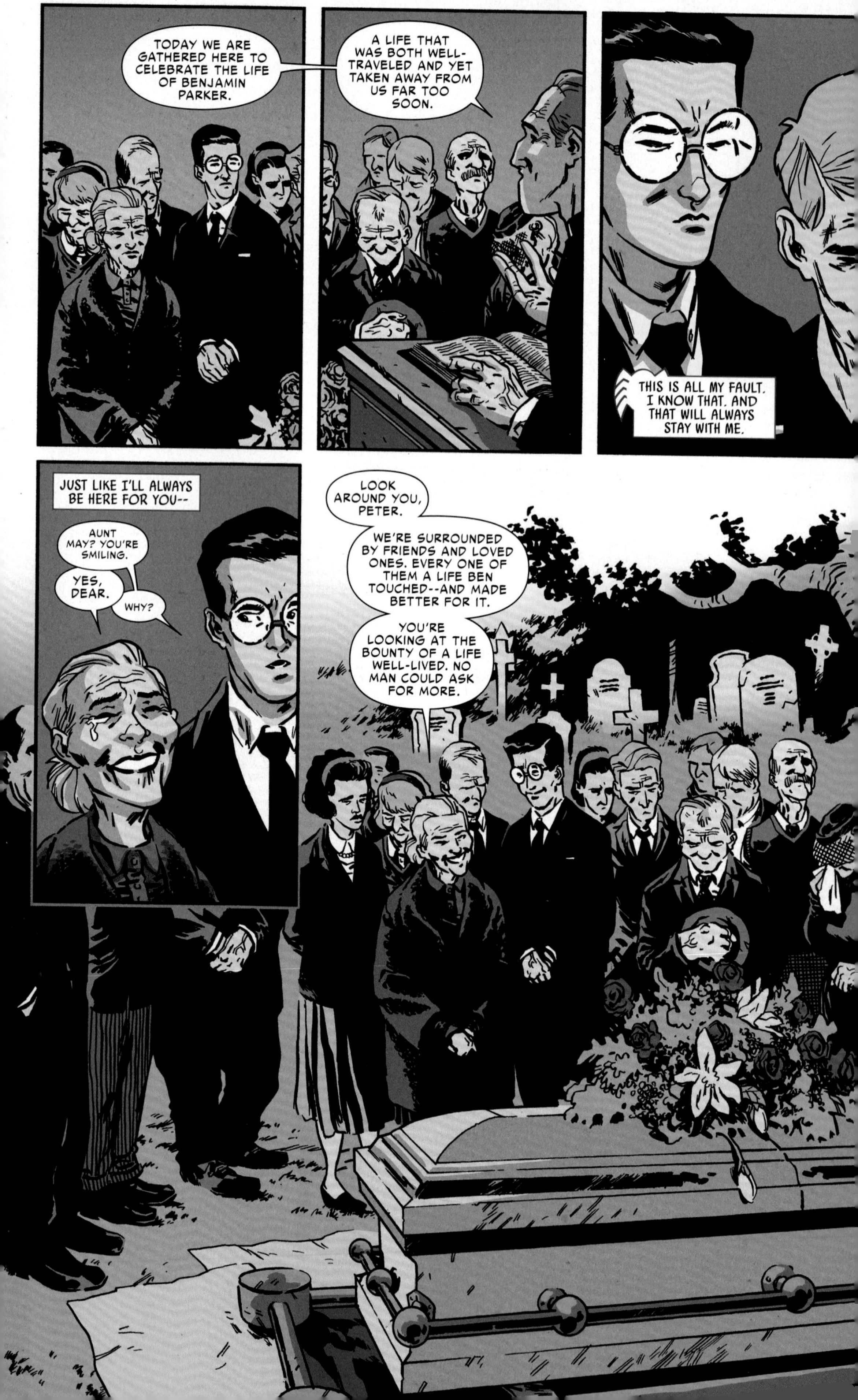
TODAY WE ARE GATHERED HERE TO CELEBRATE THE LIFE OF BENJAMIN PARKER.
A LIFE THAT WAS BOTH WELL-TRAVELED AND YET TAKEN AWAY FROM US FAR TOO SOON.
THIS IS ALL MY FAULT. I KNOW THAT. AND THAT WILL ALWAYS STAY WITH ME.
JUST LIKE I'LL ALWAYS BE HERE FOR YOU--
AUNT MAY? YOU'RE SMILING.
YES, DEAR.
WHY?
LOOK AROUND YOU, PETER.
WE'RE SURROUNDED BY FRIENDS AND LOVED ONES. EVERY ONE OF THEM A LIFE BEN TOUCHED--AND MADE BETTER FOR IT.
YOU'RE LOOKING AT THE BOUNTY OF A LIFE WELL-LIVED. NO MAN COULD ASK FOR MORE.

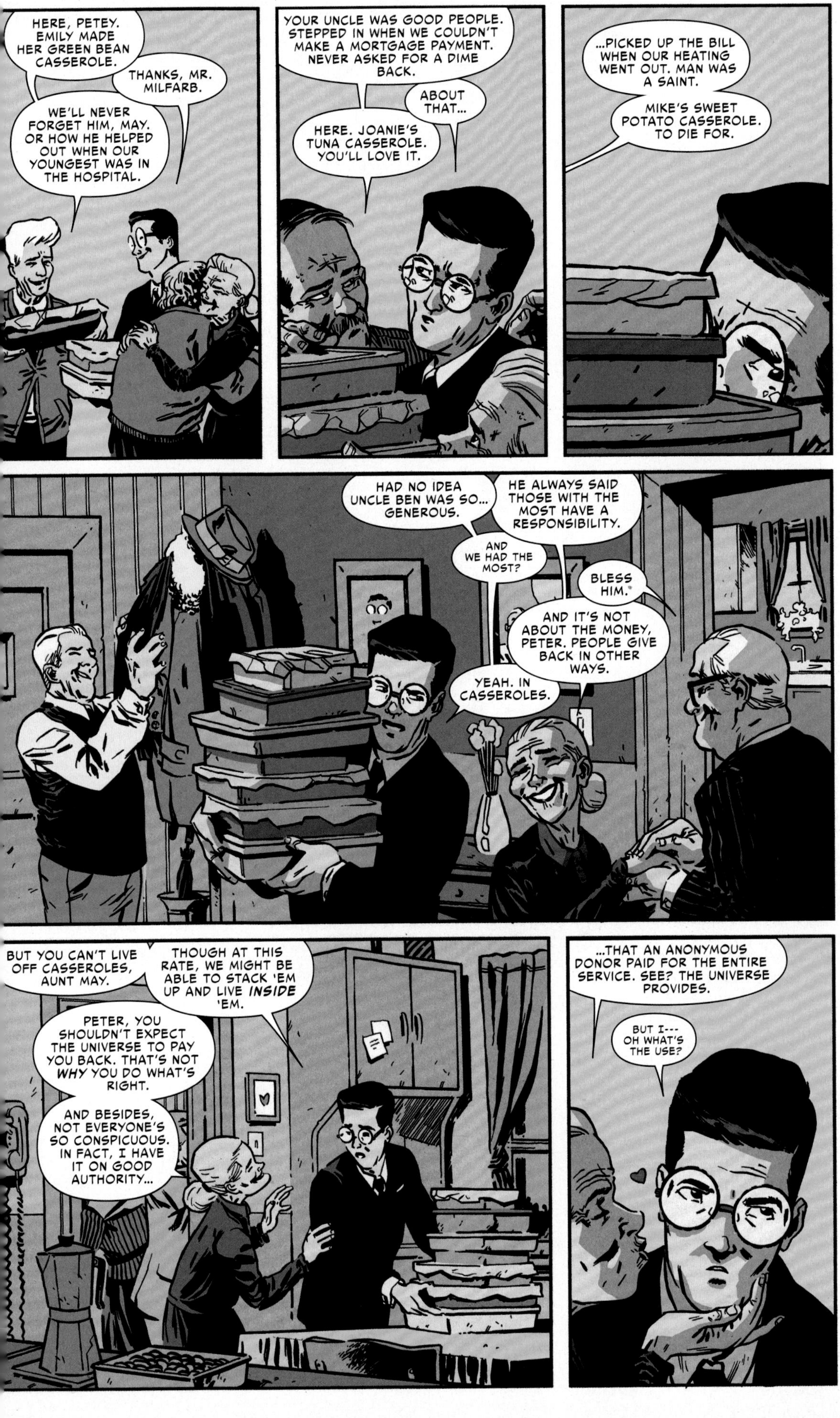
HERE, PETEY. EMILY MADE HER GREEN BEAN CASSEROLE.
THANKS, MR. MILFARB.
WE'LL NEVER FORGET HIM, MAY. OR HOW HE HELPED OUT WHEN OUR YOUNGEST WAS IN THE HOSPITAL.
YOUR UNCLE WAS GOOD PEOPLE. STEPPED IN WHEN WE COULDN'T MAKE A MORTGAGE PAYMENT. NEVER ASKED FOR A DIME BACK.
ABOUT THAT...
HERE. JOANIE'S TUNA CASSEROLE. YOU'LL LOVE IT.
...PICKED UP THE BILL WHEN OUR HEATING WENT OUT. MAN WAS A SAINT.
MIKE'S SWEET POTATO CASSEROLE. TO DIE FOR.
HAD NO IDEA UNCLE BEN WAS SO... GENEROUS.
HE ALWAYS SAID THOSE WITH THE MOST HAVE A RESPONSIBILITY.
AND WE HAD THE MOST?
BLESS HIM.
AND IT'S NOT ABOUT THE MONEY, PETER. PEOPLE GIVE BACK IN OTHER WAYS.
YEAH. IN CASSEROLES.
BUT YOU CAN'T LIVE OFF CASSEROLES, AUNT MAY.
THOUGH AT THIS RATE, WE MIGHT BE ABLE TO STACK 'EM UP AND LIVE *INSIDE* 'EM.
PETER, YOU SHOULDN'T EXPECT THE UNIVERSE TO PAY YOU BACK. THAT'S NOT *WHY* YOU DO WHAT'S RIGHT.
AND BESIDES, NOT EVERYONE'S SO CONSPICUOUS. IN FACT, I HAVE IT ON GOOD AUTHORITY...
...THAT AN ANONYMOUS DONOR PAID FOR THE ENTIRE SERVICE. SEE? THE UNIVERSE PROVIDES.
BUT I--- OH WHAT'S THE USE?

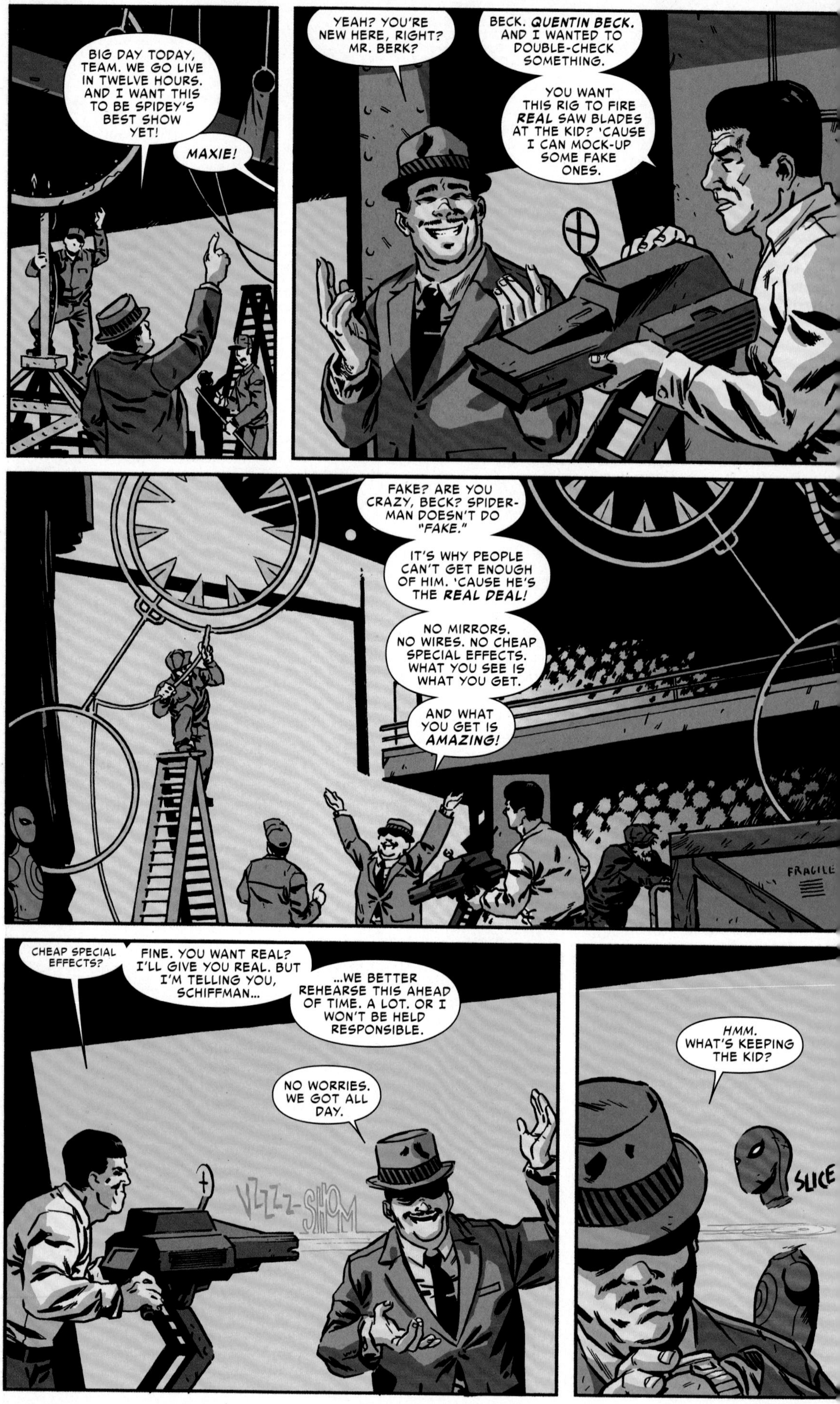
BIG DAY TODAY, TEAM. WE GO LIVE IN TWELVE HOURS. AND I WANT THIS TO BE SPIDEY'S BEST SHOW YET!
MAXIE!
YEAH? YOU'RE NEW HERE, RIGHT? MR. BERK?
BECK. QUENTIN BECK. AND I WANTED TO DOUBLE-CHECK SOMETHING.
YOU WANT THIS RIG TO FIRE REAL SAW BLADES AT THE KID? 'CAUSE I CAN MOCK-UP SOME FAKE ONES.
FAKE? ARE YOU CRAZY, BECK? SPIDER-MAN DOESN'T DO "FAKE."
IT'S WHY PEOPLE CAN'T GET ENOUGH OF HIM. 'CAUSE HE'S THE REAL DEAL!
NO MIRRORS. NO WIRES. NO CHEAP SPECIAL EFFECTS. WHAT YOU SEE IS WHAT YOU GET.
AND WHAT YOU GET IS AMAZING!
FRAGILE
CHEAP SPECIAL EFFECTS?
FINE. YOU WANT REAL? I'LL GIVE YOU REAL. BUT I'M TELLING YOU, SCHIFFMAN...
...WE BETTER REHEARSE THIS AHEAD OF TIME. A LOT. OR I WON'T BE HELD RESPONSIBLE.
NO WORRIES. WE GOT ALL DAY.
VZZZZ-SHOOM
HMM. WHAT'S KEEPING THE KID?
SLICE

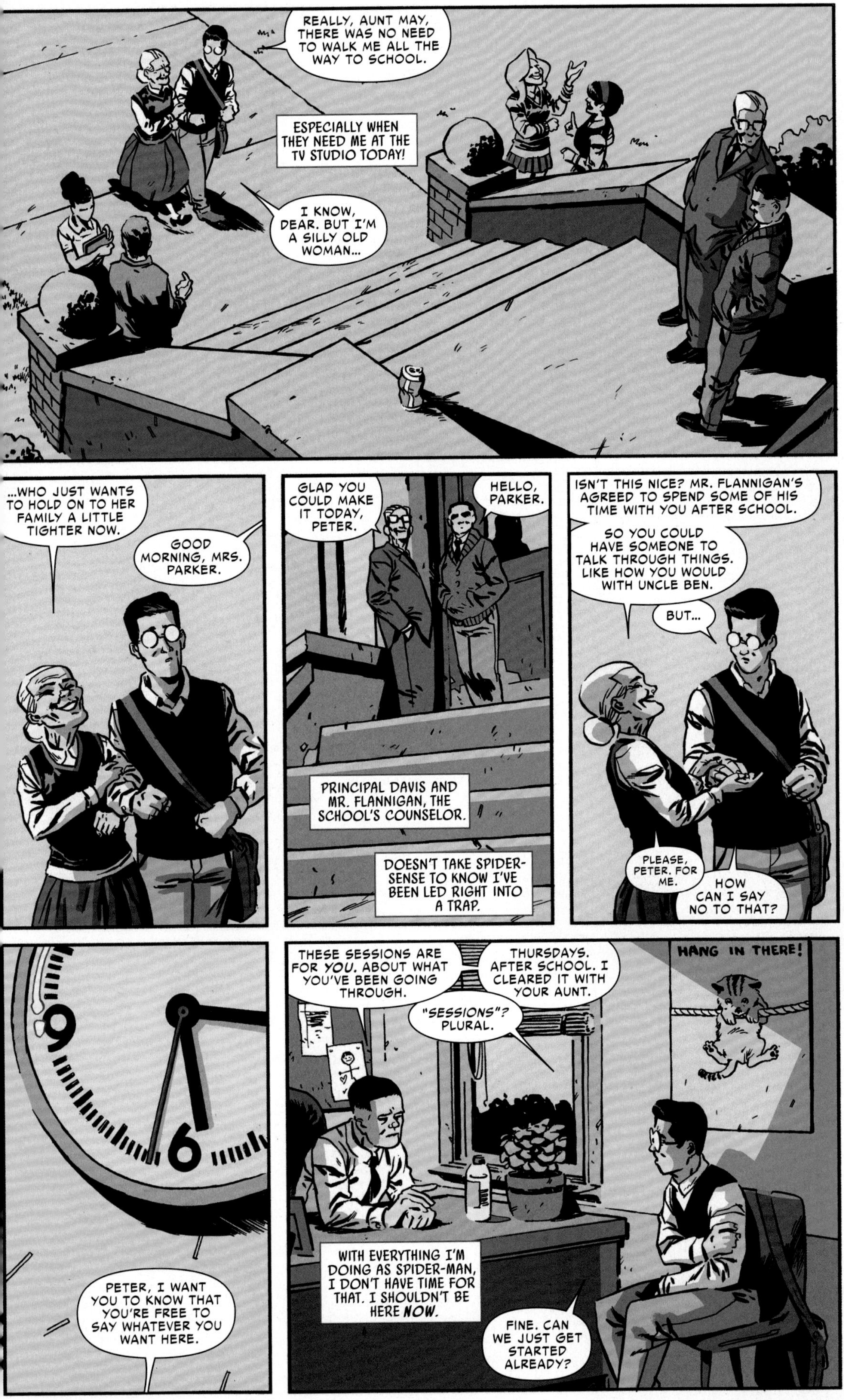

REALLY, AUNT MAY, THERE WAS NO NEED TO WALK ME ALL THE WAY TO SCHOOL.
ESPECIALLY WHEN THEY NEED ME AT THE TV STUDIO TODAY!
I KNOW, DEAR. BUT I'M A SILLY OLD WOMAN...
...WHO JUST WANTS TO HOLD ON TO HER FAMILY A LITTLE TIGHTER NOW.
GOOD MORNING, MRS. PARKER.
GLAD YOU COULD MAKE IT TODAY, PETER.
HELLO, PARKER.
PRINCIPAL DAVIS AND MR. FLANNIGAN, THE SCHOOL'S COUNSELOR.
DOESN'T TAKE SPIDER-SENSE TO KNOW I'VE BEEN LED RIGHT INTO A TRAP.
ISN'T THIS NICE? MR. FLANNIGAN'S AGREED TO SPEND SOME OF HIS TIME WITH YOU AFTER SCHOOL.
SO YOU COULD HAVE SOMEONE TO TALK THROUGH THINGS. LIKE HOW YOU WOULD WITH UNCLE BEN.
BUT...
PLEASE, PETER. FOR ME.
HOW CAN I SAY NO TO THAT?
PETER, I WANT YOU TO KNOW THAT YOU'RE FREE TO SAY WHATEVER YOU WANT HERE.
THESE SESSIONS ARE FOR *YOU*. ABOUT WHAT YOU'VE BEEN GOING THROUGH.
THURSDAYS. AFTER SCHOOL. I CLEARED IT WITH YOUR AUNT.
"SESSIONS"? PLURAL.
HANG IN THERE!
WITH EVERYTHING I'M DOING AS SPIDER-MAN, I DON'T HAVE TIME FOR THAT. I SHOULDN'T BE HERE ***NOW***.
FINE. CAN WE JUST GET STARTED ALREADY?

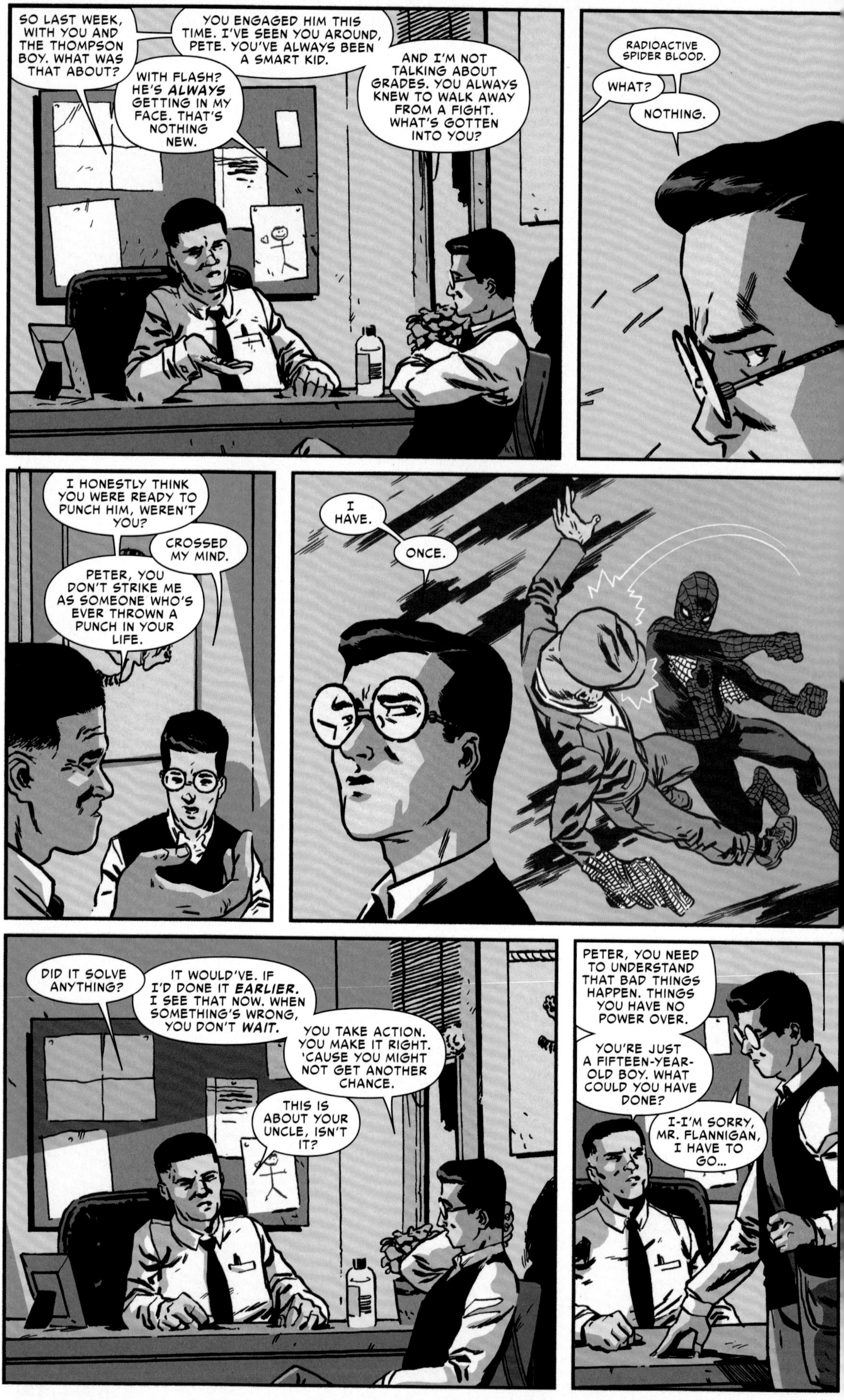
SO LAST WEEK, WITH YOU AND THE THOMPSON BOY. WHAT WAS THAT ABOUT?
YOU ENGAGED HIM THIS TIME. I'VE SEEN YOU AROUND, PETE. YOU'VE ALWAYS BEEN A SMART KID.
WITH FLASH? HE'S *ALWAYS* GETTING IN MY FACE. THAT'S NOTHING NEW.
AND I'M NOT TALKING ABOUT GRADES. YOU ALWAYS KNEW TO WALK AWAY FROM A FIGHT. WHAT'S GOTTEN INTO YOU?
RADIOACTIVE SPIDER BLOOD.
WHAT?
NOTHING.
I HONESTLY THINK YOU WERE READY TO PUNCH HIM, WEREN'T YOU?
CROSSED MY MIND.
PETER, YOU DON'T STRIKE ME AS SOMEONE WHO'S EVER THROWN A PUNCH IN YOUR LIFE.
I HAVE.
ONCE.
DID IT SOLVE ANYTHING?
IT WOULD'VE. IF I'D DONE IT *EARLIER.* I SEE THAT NOW. WHEN SOMETHING'S WRONG, YOU DON'T *WAIT.*
YOU TAKE ACTION. YOU MAKE IT RIGHT. 'CAUSE YOU MIGHT NOT GET ANOTHER CHANCE.
THIS IS ABOUT YOUR UNCLE, ISN'T IT?
PETER, YOU NEED TO UNDERSTAND THAT BAD THINGS HAPPEN. THINGS YOU HAVE NO POWER OVER.
YOU'RE JUST A FIFTEEN-YEAR-OLD BOY. WHAT COULD YOU HAVE DONE?
I-I'M SORRY, MR. FLANNIGAN, I HAVE TO GO...

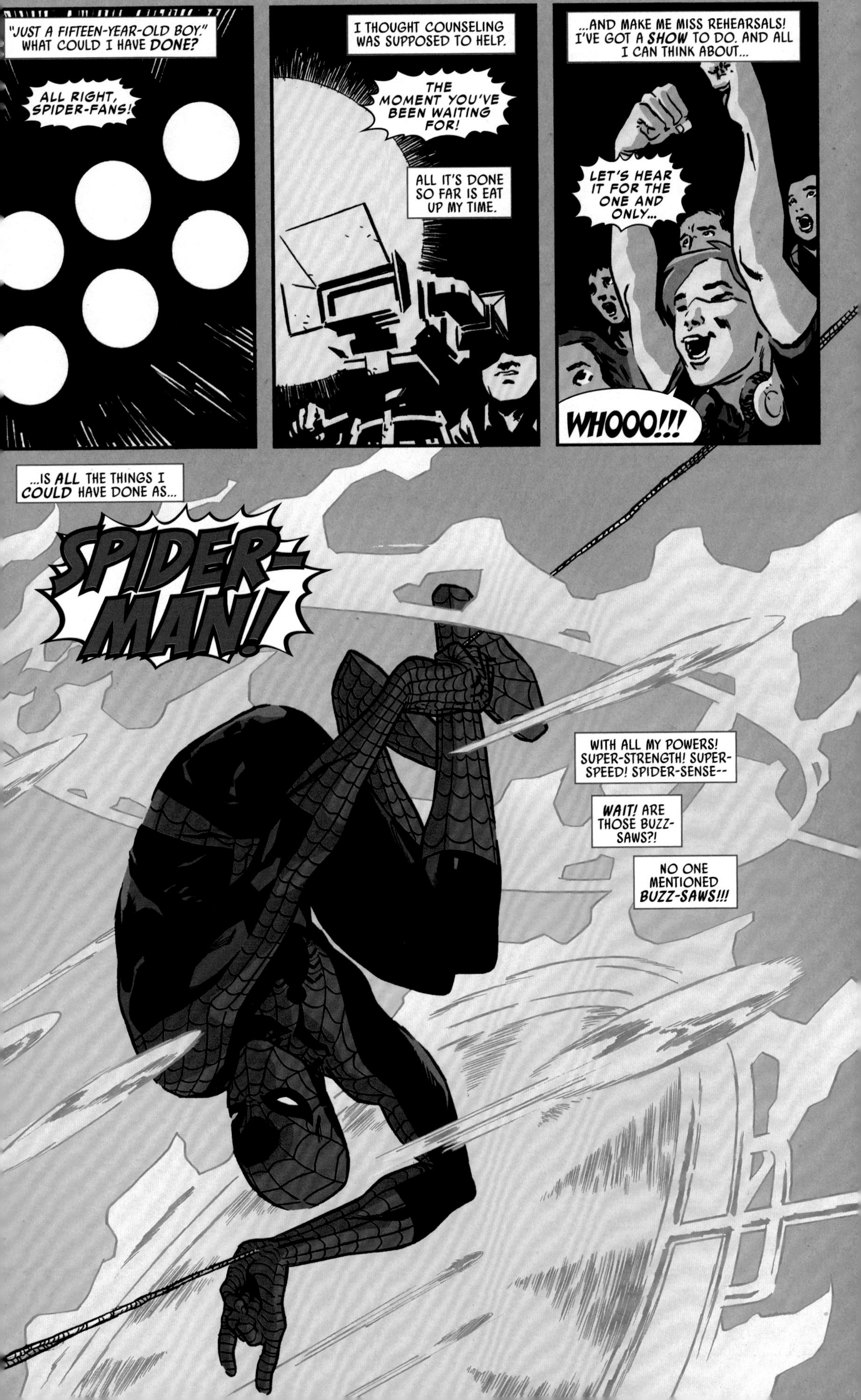
"JUST A FIFTEEN-YEAR-OLD BOY." WHAT COULD I HAVE DONE?
ALL RIGHT, SPIDER-FANS!
I THOUGHT COUNSELING WAS SUPPOSED TO HELP.
THE MOMENT YOU'VE BEEN WAITING FOR!
ALL IT'S DONE SO FAR IS EAT UP MY TIME.
...AND MAKE ME MISS REHEARSALS! I'VE GOT A SHOW TO DO. AND ALL I CAN THINK ABOUT...
LET'S HEAR IT FOR THE ONE AND ONLY...
WHOOO!!!
...IS ALL THE THINGS I COULD HAVE DONE AS...
SPIDER-MAN!
WITH ALL MY POWERS! SUPER-STRENGTH! SUPER-SPEED! SPIDER-SENSE--
WAIT! ARE THOSE BUZZ-SAWS?!
NO ONE MENTIONED BUZZ-SAWS!!!

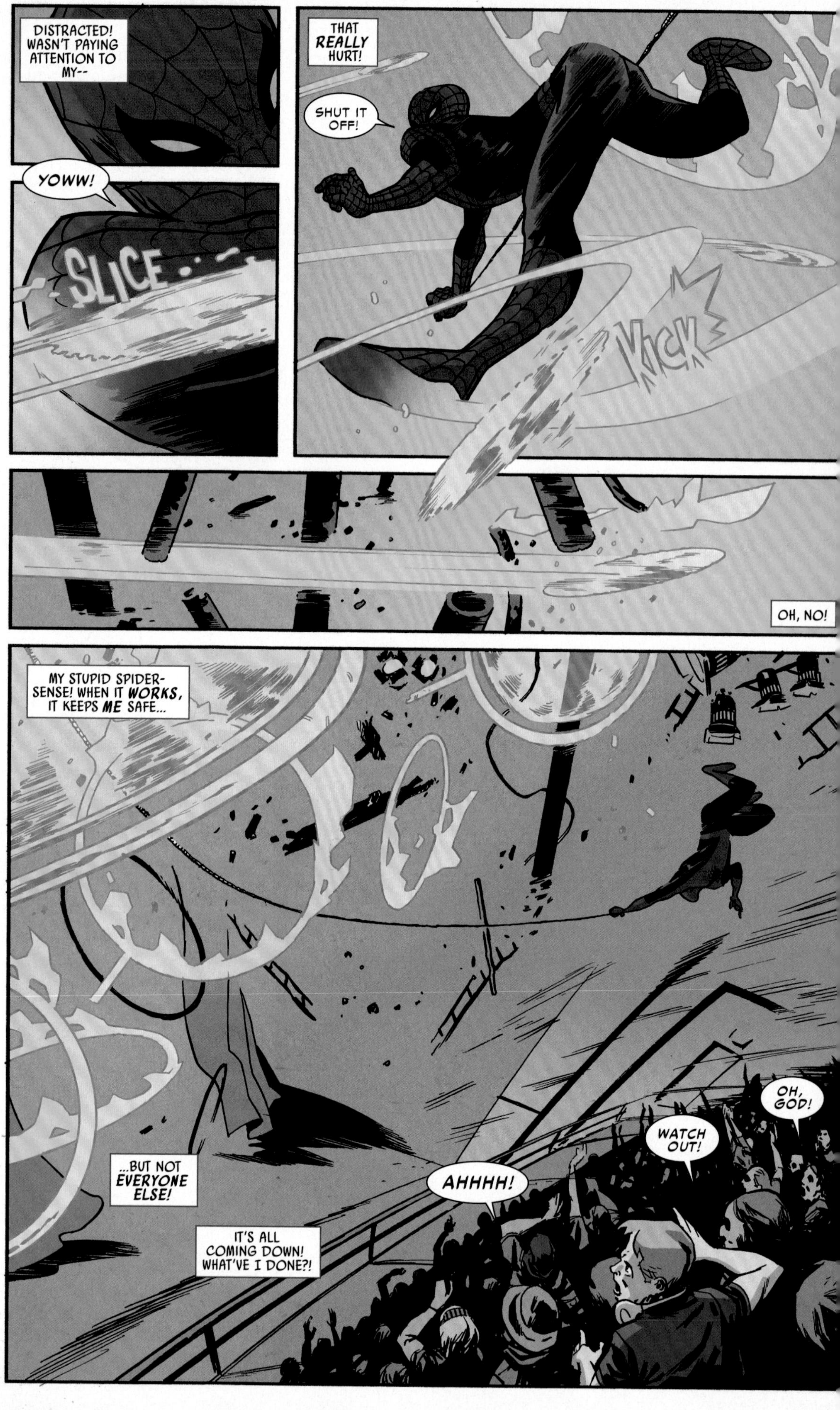
DISTRACTED! WASN'T PAYING ATTENTION TO MY--
YOWW!
SLICE
THAT REALLY HURT!
SHUT IT OFF!
KICK
OH, NO!
MY STUPID SPIDER-SENSE! WHEN IT WORKS, IT KEEPS ME SAFE...
...BUT NOT EVERYONE ELSE!
IT'S ALL COMING DOWN! WHAT'VE I DONE?!
AHHHH!
WATCH OUT!
OH, GOD!

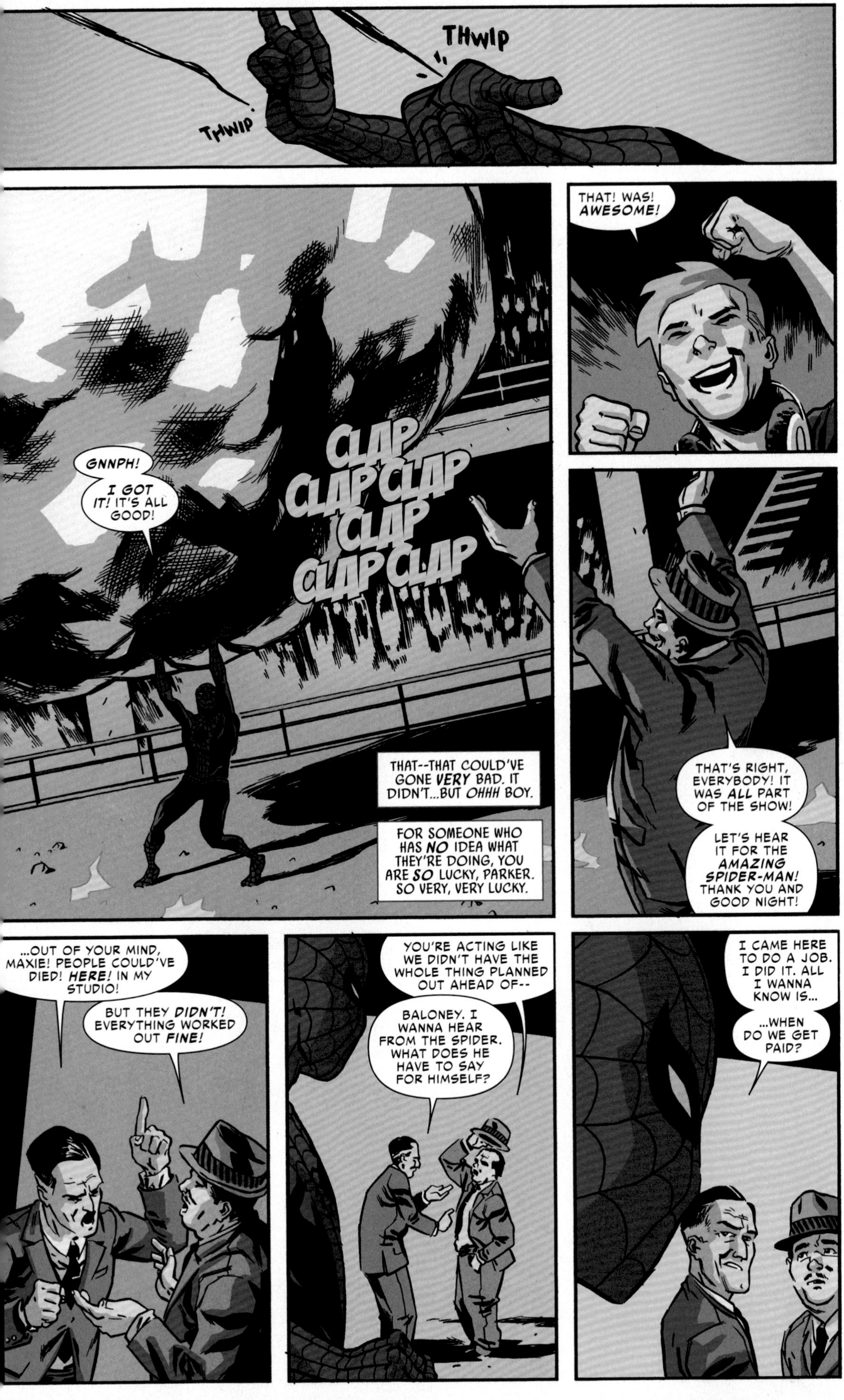
THWIP
THWIP
GNNPH!
I GOT IT! IT'S ALL GOOD!
CLAP CLAP CLAP CLAP CLAP CLAP
THAT--THAT COULD'VE GONE VERY BAD. IT DIDN'T...BUT OHHH BOY.
FOR SOMEONE WHO HAS NO IDEA WHAT THEY'RE DOING, YOU ARE SO LUCKY, PARKER. SO VERY, VERY LUCKY.
THAT! WAS! AWESOME!
THAT'S RIGHT, EVERYBODY! IT WAS ALL PART OF THE SHOW!
LET'S HEAR IT FOR THE AMAZING SPIDER-MAN! THANK YOU AND GOOD NIGHT!
...OUT OF YOUR MIND, MAXIE! PEOPLE COULD'VE DIED! HERE! IN MY STUDIO!
BUT THEY DIDN'T! EVERYTHING WORKED OUT FINE!
YOU'RE ACTING LIKE WE DIDN'T HAVE THE WHOLE THING PLANNED OUT AHEAD OF--
BALONEY. I WANNA HEAR FROM THE SPIDER. WHAT DOES HE HAVE TO SAY FOR HIMSELF?
I CAME HERE TO DO A JOB. I DID IT. ALL I WANNA KNOW IS...
...WHEN DO WE GET PAID?

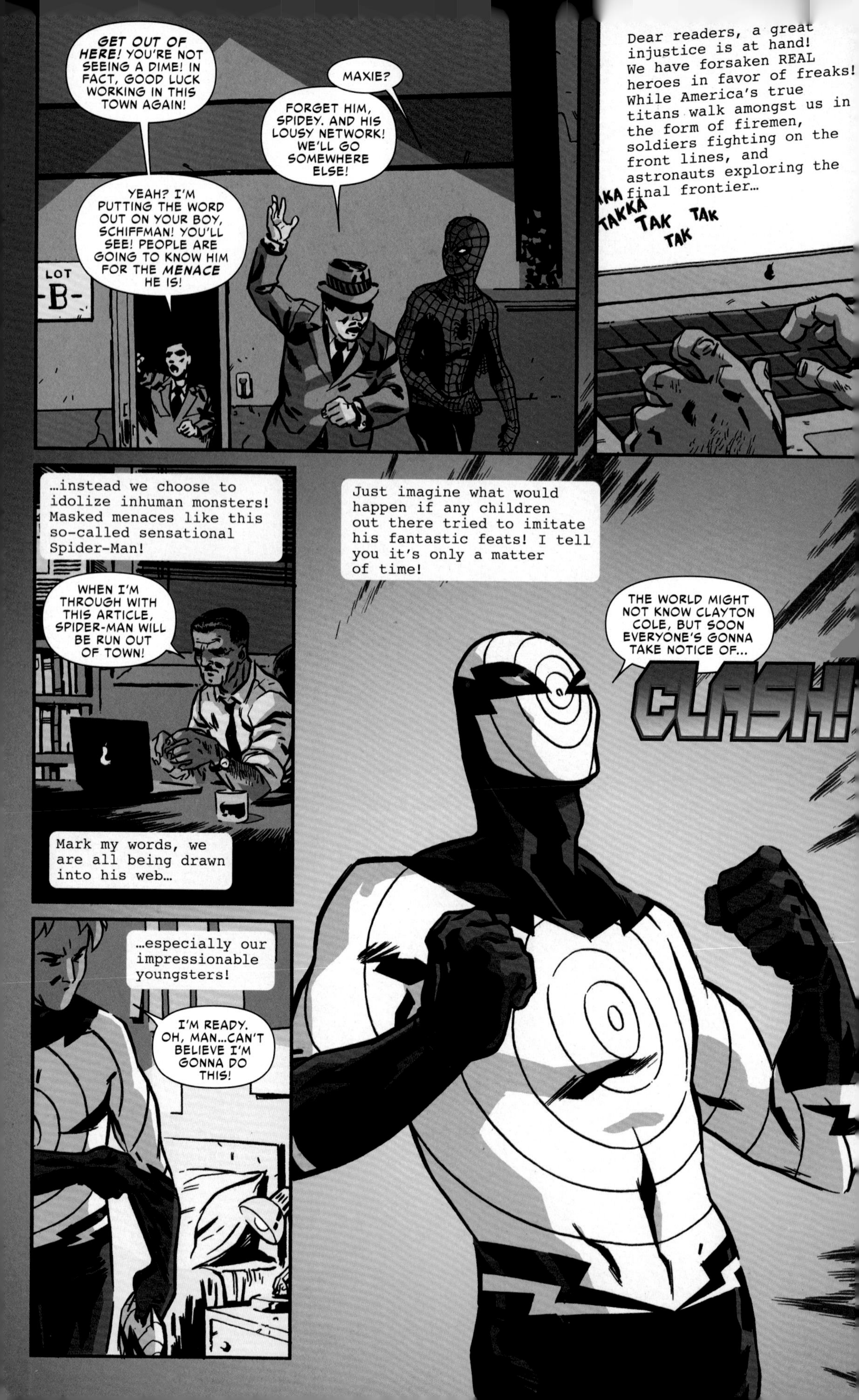
GET OUT OF HERE! YOU'RE NOT SEEING A DIME! IN FACT, GOOD LUCK WORKING IN THIS TOWN AGAIN!
MAXIE?
FORGET HIM, SPIDEY. AND HIS LOUSY NETWORK! WE'LL GO SOMEWHERE ELSE!
YEAH? I'M PUTTING THE WORD OUT ON YOUR BOY, SCHIFFMAN! YOU'LL SEE! PEOPLE ARE GOING TO KNOW HIM FOR THE MENACE HE IS!
LOT -B-
Dear readers, a great injustice is at hand! We have forsaken REAL heroes in favor of freaks! While America's true titans walk amongst us in the form of firemen, soldiers fighting on the front lines, and astronauts exploring the final frontier...
TAKKA TAKKA TAK TAK TAK
...instead we choose to idolize inhuman monsters! Masked menaces like this so-called sensational Spider-Man!
WHEN I'M THROUGH WITH THIS ARTICLE, SPIDER-MAN WILL BE RUN OUT OF TOWN!
Mark my words, we are all being drawn into his web...
Just imagine what would happen if any children out there tried to imitate his fantastic feats! I tell you it's only a matter of time!
THE WORLD MIGHT NOT KNOW CLAYTON COLE, BUT SOON EVERYONE'S GONNA TAKE NOTICE OF...
CLASH!
...especially our impressionable youngsters!
I'M READY. OH, MAN...CAN'T BELIEVE I'M GONNA DO THIS!

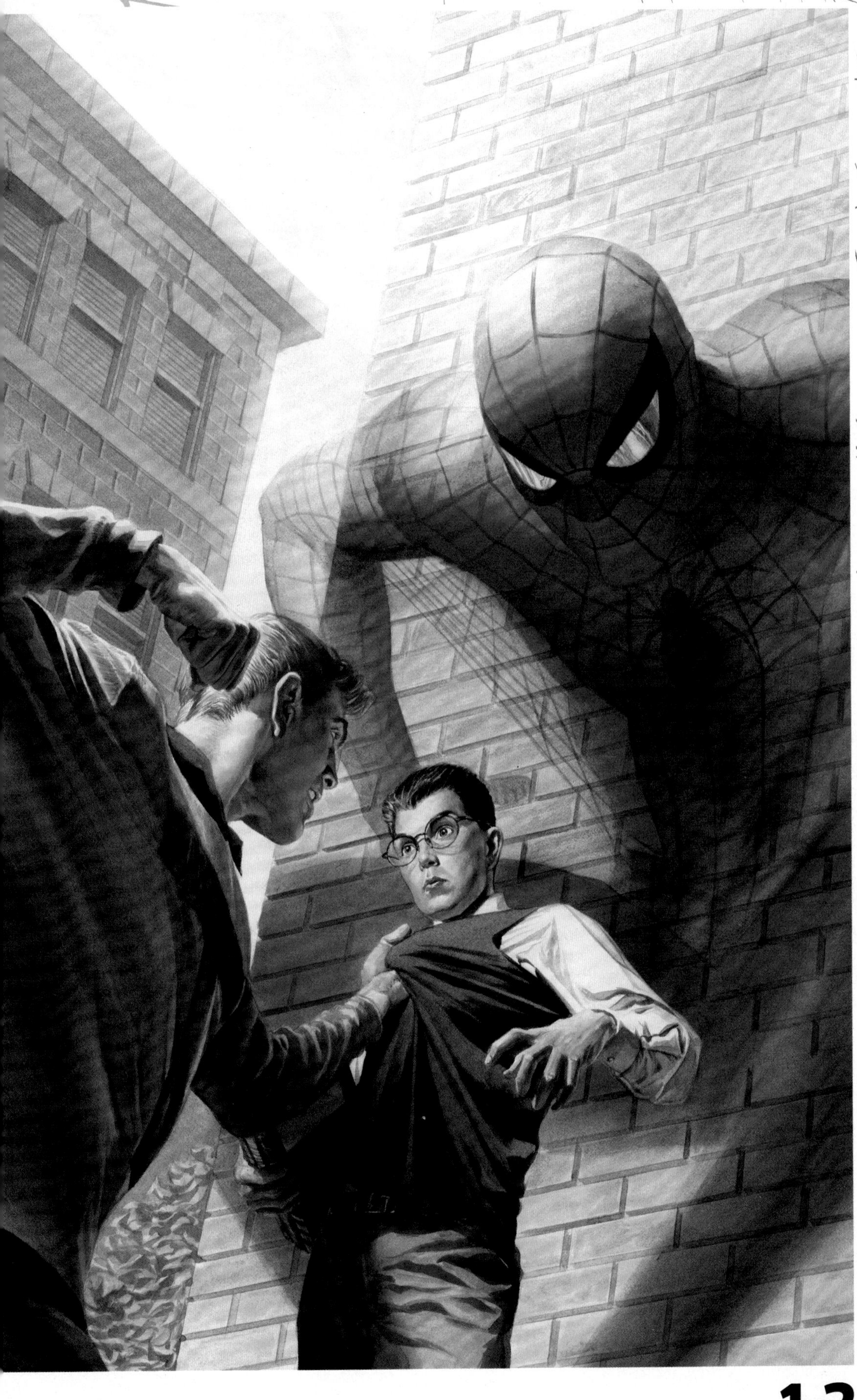

1.2

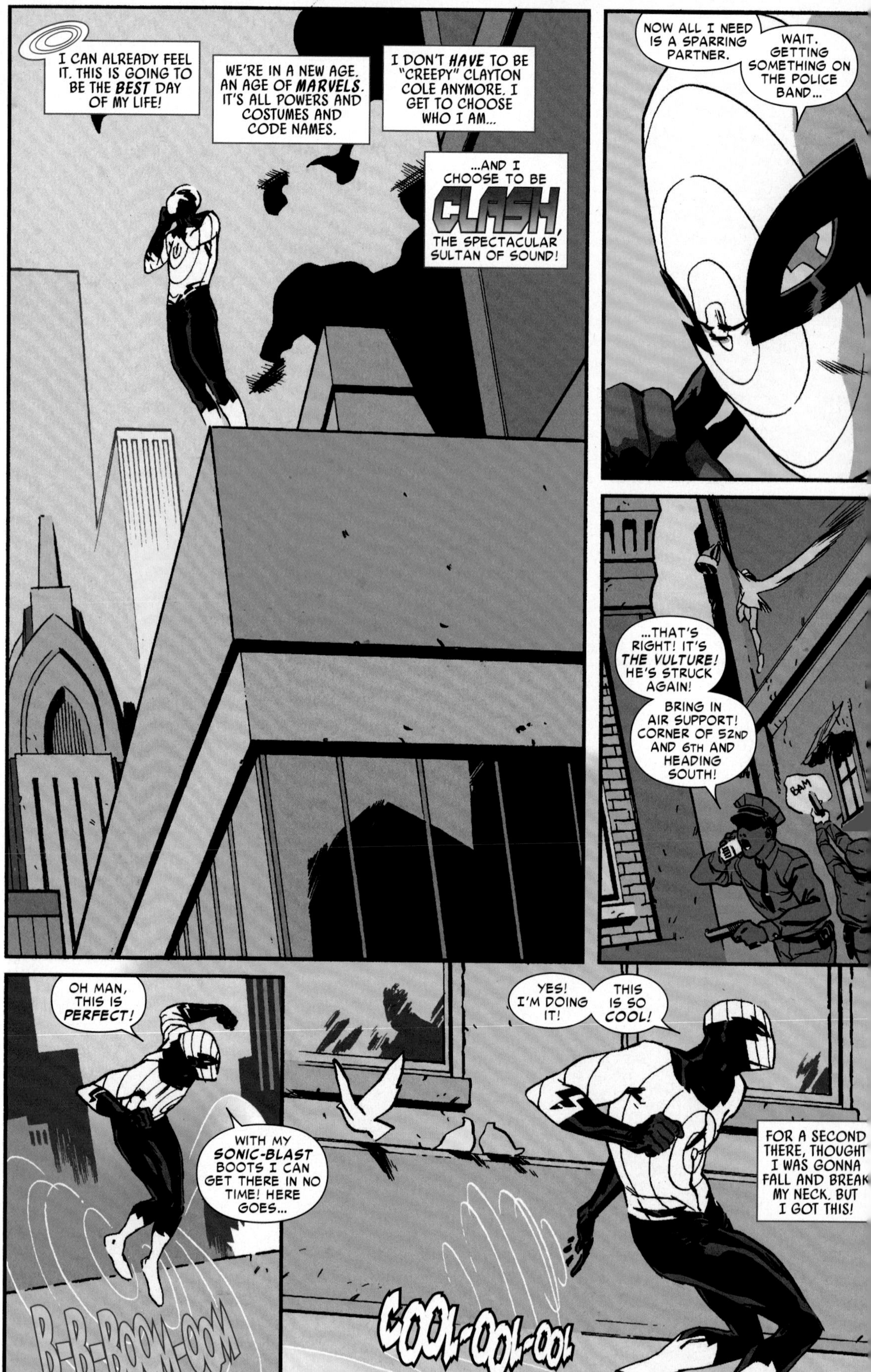

I CAN ALREADY FEEL IT. THIS IS GOING TO BE THE BEST DAY OF MY LIFE!
WE'RE IN A NEW AGE. AN AGE OF MARVELS. IT'S ALL POWERS AND COSTUMES AND CODE NAMES.
I DON'T HAVE TO BE "CREEPY" CLAYTON COLE ANYMORE. I GET TO CHOOSE WHO I AM...
...AND I CHOOSE TO BE CLASH, THE SPECTACULAR SULTAN OF SOUND!
NOW ALL I NEED IS A SPARRING PARTNER.
WAIT. GETTING SOMETHING ON THE POLICE BAND...
...THAT'S RIGHT! IT'S THE VULTURE! HE'S STRUCK AGAIN!
BRING IN AIR SUPPORT! CORNER OF 52ND AND 6TH AND HEADING SOUTH!
BAM
OH MAN, THIS IS PERFECT!
WITH MY SONIC-BLAST BOOTS I CAN GET THERE IN NO TIME! HERE GOES...
B-B-BOOM-OOM
YES! I'M DOING IT!
THIS IS SO COOL!
COOL-OOL-OOL
FOR A SECOND THERE, THOUGHT I WAS GONNA FALL AND BREAK MY NECK. BUT I GOT THIS!

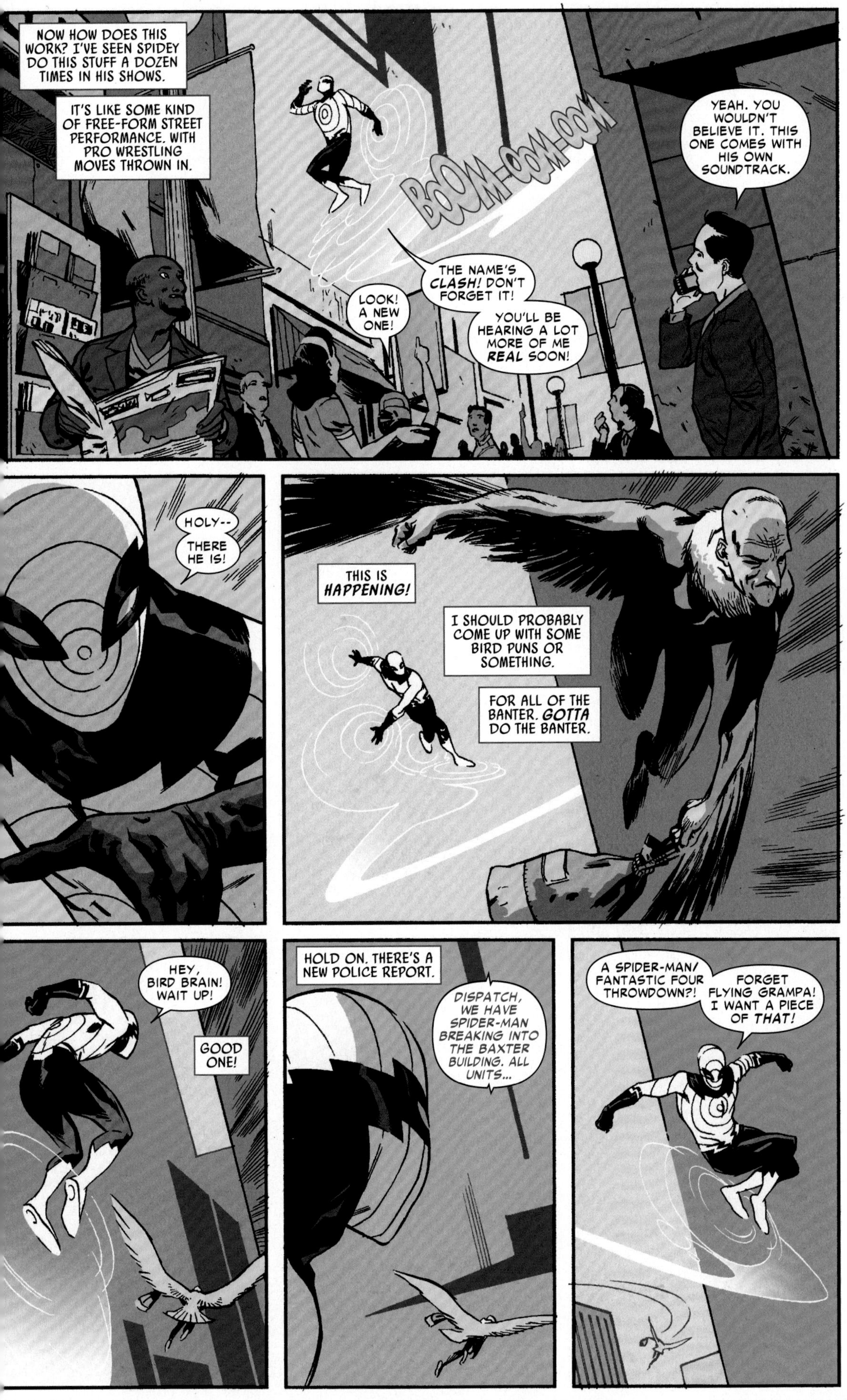
NOW HOW DOES THIS WORK? I'VE SEEN SPIDEY DO THIS STUFF A DOZEN TIMES IN HIS SHOWS.
IT'S LIKE SOME KIND OF FREE-FORM STREET PERFORMANCE. WITH PRO WRESTLING MOVES THROWN IN.
BOOM-OOM-OOM
YEAH. YOU WOULDN'T BELIEVE IT. THIS ONE COMES WITH HIS OWN SOUNDTRACK.
THE NAME'S CLASH! DON'T FORGET IT!
LOOK! A NEW ONE!
YOU'LL BE HEARING A LOT MORE OF ME REAL SOON!
HOLY--
THERE HE IS!
THIS IS HAPPENING!
I SHOULD PROBABLY COME UP WITH SOME BIRD PUNS OR SOMETHING.
FOR ALL OF THE BANTER. GOTTA DO THE BANTER.
HEY, BIRD BRAIN! WAIT UP!
GOOD ONE!
HOLD ON. THERE'S A NEW POLICE REPORT.
DISPATCH, WE HAVE SPIDER-MAN BREAKING INTO THE BAXTER BUILDING. ALL UNITS...
A SPIDER-MAN/ FANTASTIC FOUR THROWDOWN?!
FORGET FLYING GRAMPA! I WANT A PIECE OF THAT!

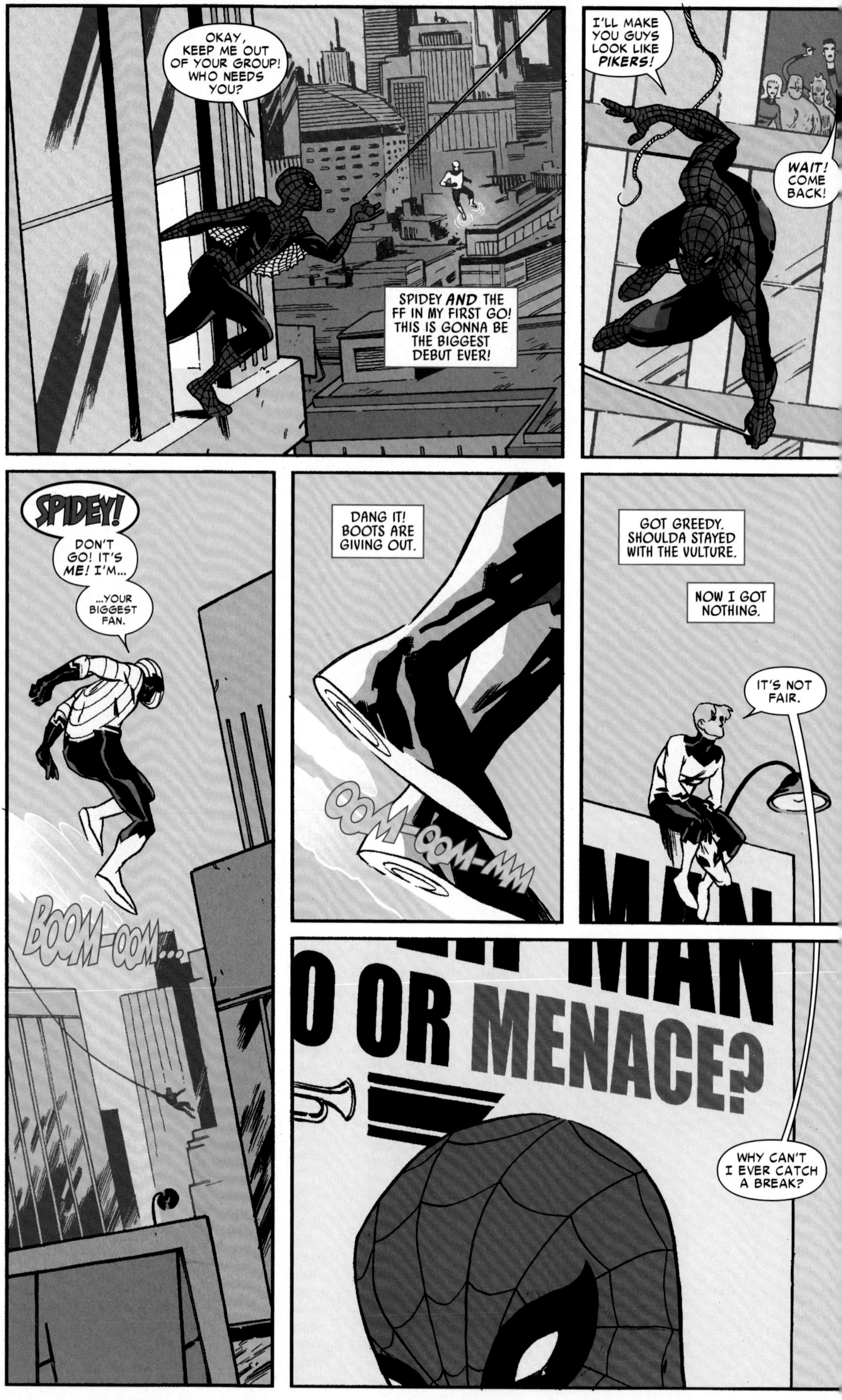
OKAY, KEEP ME OUT OF YOUR GROUP! WHO NEEDS YOU?
SPIDEY AND THE FF IN MY FIRST GO! THIS IS GONNA BE THE BIGGEST DEBUT EVER!
I'LL MAKE YOU GUYS LOOK LIKE PIKERS!
WAIT! COME BACK!
SPIDEY!
DON'T GO! IT'S ME! I'M...
...YOUR BIGGEST FAN.
BOOM-OOM...
DANG IT! BOOTS ARE GIVING OUT.
OOM-OOM-OOM-MM
GOT GREEDY. SHOULDA STAYED WITH THE VULTURE.
NOW I GOT NOTHING.
IT'S NOT FAIR.
MAN
MAN
O OR MENACE?
WHY CAN'T I EVER CATCH A BREAK?

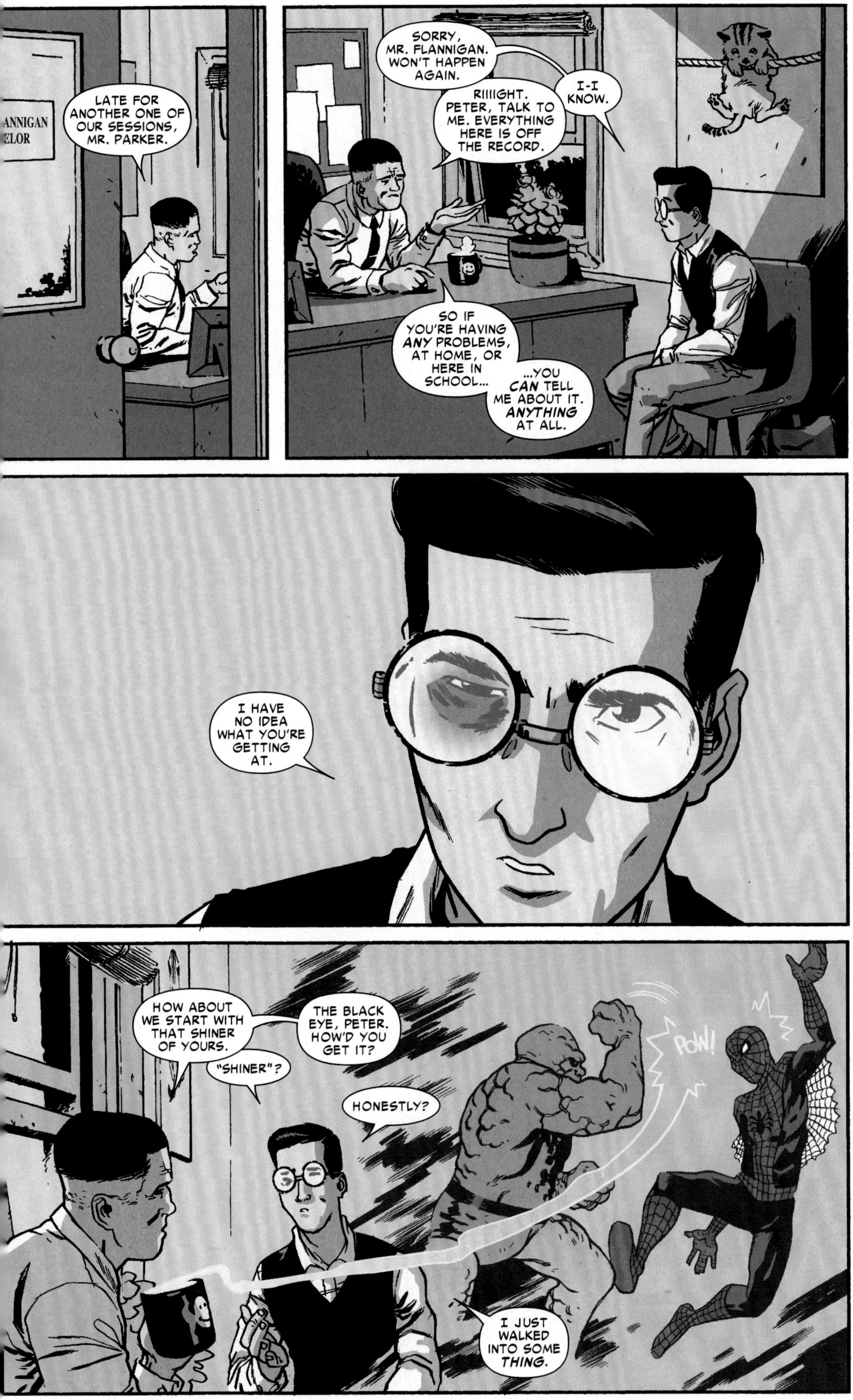
ANNIGAN
ELOR
LATE FOR ANOTHER ONE OF OUR SESSIONS, MR. PARKER.
SORRY, MR. FLANNIGAN. WON'T HAPPEN AGAIN.
I-I KNOW.
RIIIIGHT. PETER, TALK TO ME. EVERYTHING HERE IS OFF THE RECORD.
SO IF YOU'RE HAVING *ANY* PROBLEMS, AT HOME, OR HERE IN SCHOOL...
...YOU *CAN* TELL ME ABOUT IT. *ANYTHING* AT ALL.
I HAVE NO IDEA WHAT YOU'RE GETTING AT.
HOW ABOUT WE START WITH THAT SHINER OF YOURS.
"SHINER"?
THE BLACK EYE, PETER. HOW'D YOU GET IT?
HONESTLY?
POW!
I JUST WALKED INTO SOME *THING*.

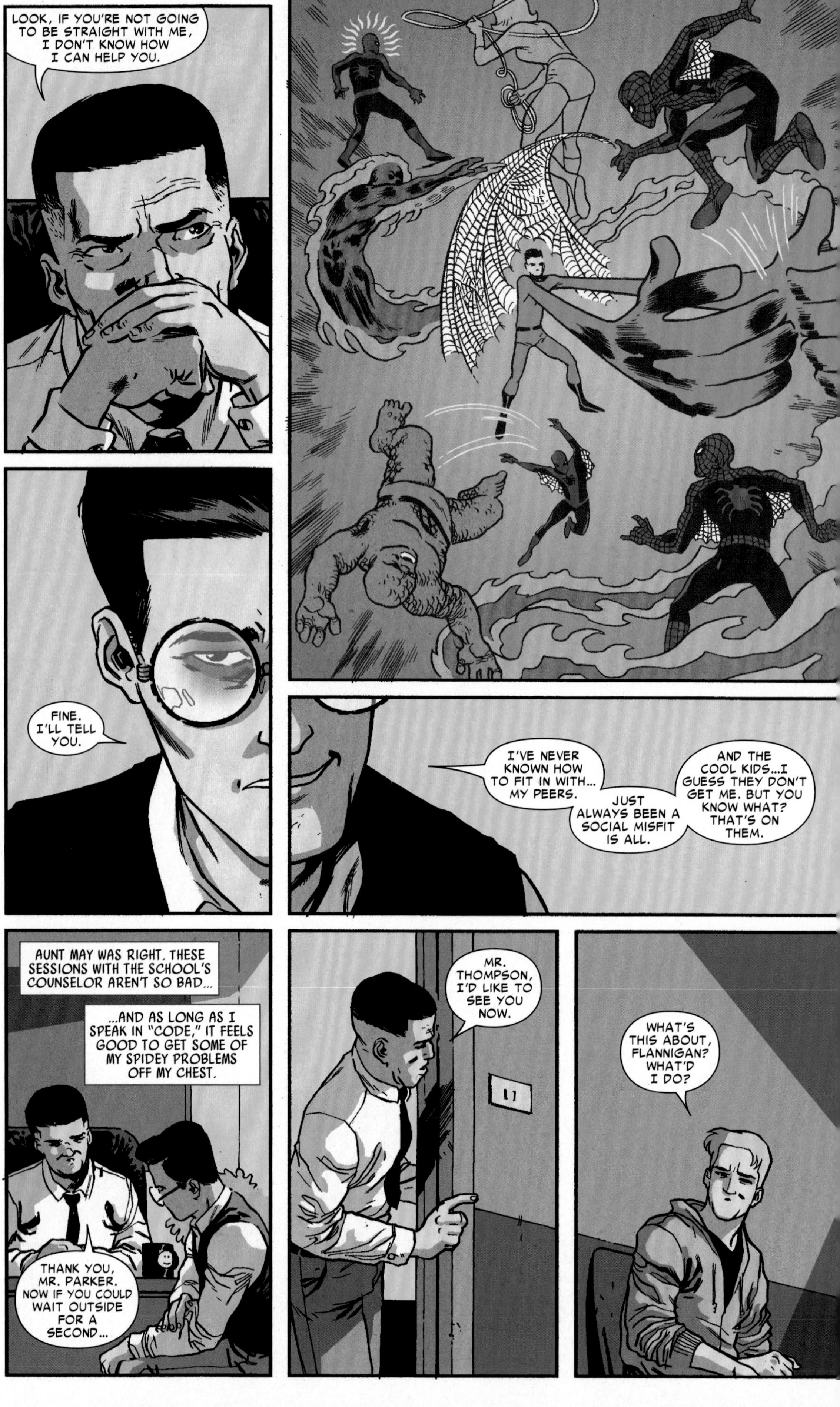
LOOK, IF YOU'RE NOT GOING TO BE STRAIGHT WITH ME, I DON'T KNOW HOW I CAN HELP YOU.
FINE. I'LL TELL YOU.
I'VE NEVER KNOWN HOW TO FIT IN WITH... MY PEERS.
JUST ALWAYS BEEN A SOCIAL MISFIT IS ALL.
AND THE COOL KIDS...I GUESS THEY DON'T GET ME. BUT YOU KNOW WHAT? THAT'S ON THEM.
AUNT MAY WAS RIGHT. THESE SESSIONS WITH THE SCHOOL'S COUNSELOR AREN'T SO BAD...
...AND AS LONG AS I SPEAK IN "CODE," IT FEELS GOOD TO GET SOME OF MY SPIDEY PROBLEMS OFF MY CHEST.
THANK YOU, MR. PARKER. NOW IF YOU COULD WAIT OUTSIDE FOR A SECOND...
MR. THOMPSON, I'D LIKE TO SEE YOU NOW.
WHAT'S THIS ABOUT, FLANNIGAN? WHAT'D I DO?

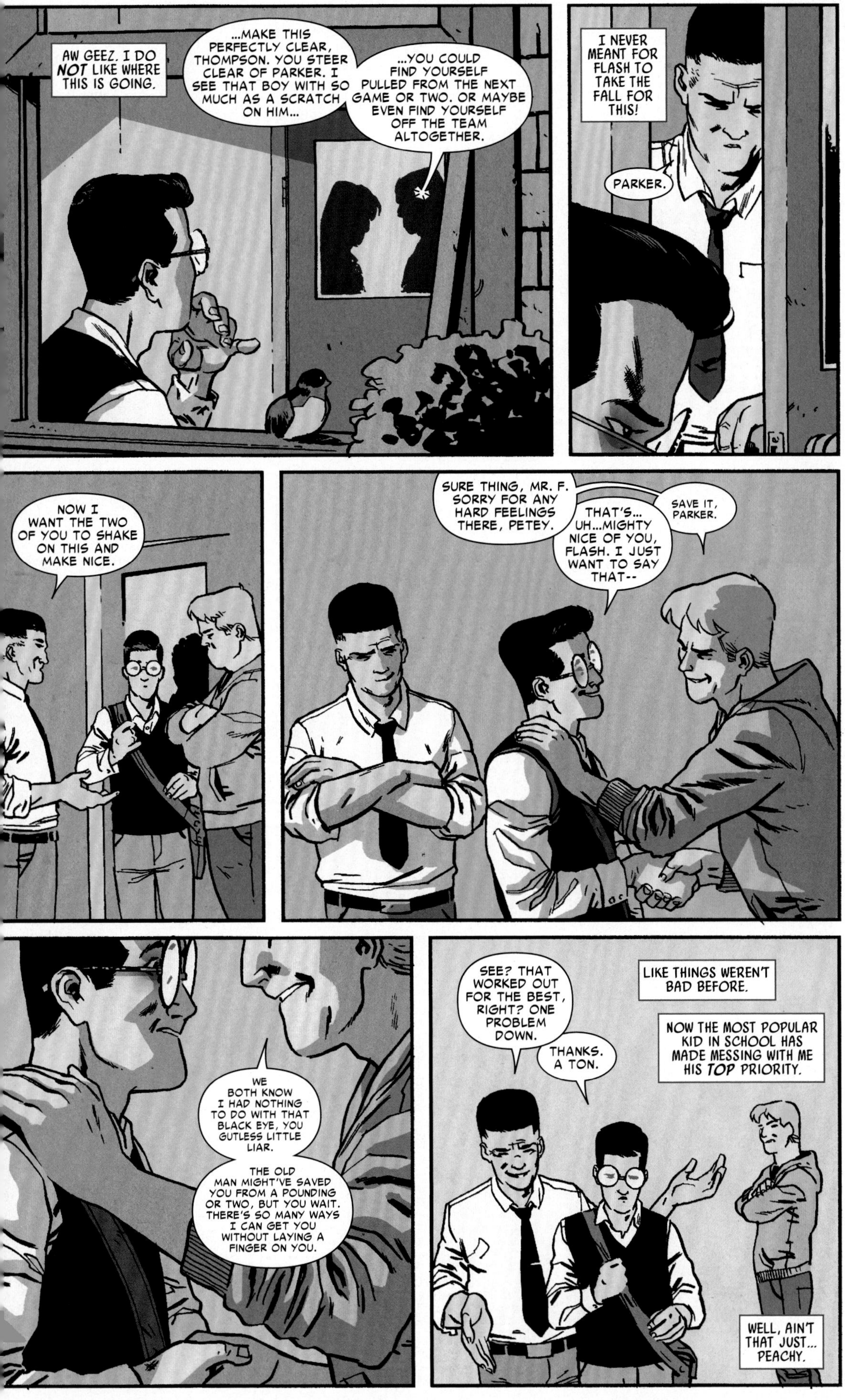
AW GEEZ. I DO NOT LIKE WHERE THIS IS GOING.
...MAKE THIS PERFECTLY CLEAR, THOMPSON. YOU STEER CLEAR OF PARKER. I SEE THAT BOY WITH SO MUCH AS A SCRATCH ON HIM...
...YOU COULD FIND YOURSELF PULLED FROM THE NEXT GAME OR TWO. OR MAYBE EVEN FIND YOURSELF OFF THE TEAM ALTOGETHER.
I NEVER MEANT FOR FLASH TO TAKE THE FALL FOR THIS!
PARKER.
NOW I WANT THE TWO OF YOU TO SHAKE ON THIS AND MAKE NICE.
SURE THING, MR. F. SORRY FOR ANY HARD FEELINGS THERE, PETEY.
THAT'S... UH...MIGHTY NICE OF YOU, FLASH. I JUST WANT TO SAY THAT--
SAVE IT, PARKER.
WE BOTH KNOW I HAD NOTHING TO DO WITH THAT BLACK EYE, YOU GUTLESS LITTLE LIAR.
THE OLD MAN MIGHT'VE SAVED YOU FROM A POUNDING OR TWO, BUT YOU WAIT. THERE'S SO MANY WAYS I CAN GET YOU WITHOUT LAYING A FINGER ON YOU.
SEE? THAT WORKED OUT FOR THE BEST, RIGHT? ONE PROBLEM DOWN.
THANKS. A TON.
LIKE THINGS WEREN'T BAD BEFORE.
NOW THE MOST POPULAR KID IN SCHOOL HAS MADE MESSING WITH ME HIS TOP PRIORITY.
WELL, AIN'T THAT JUST... PEACHY.

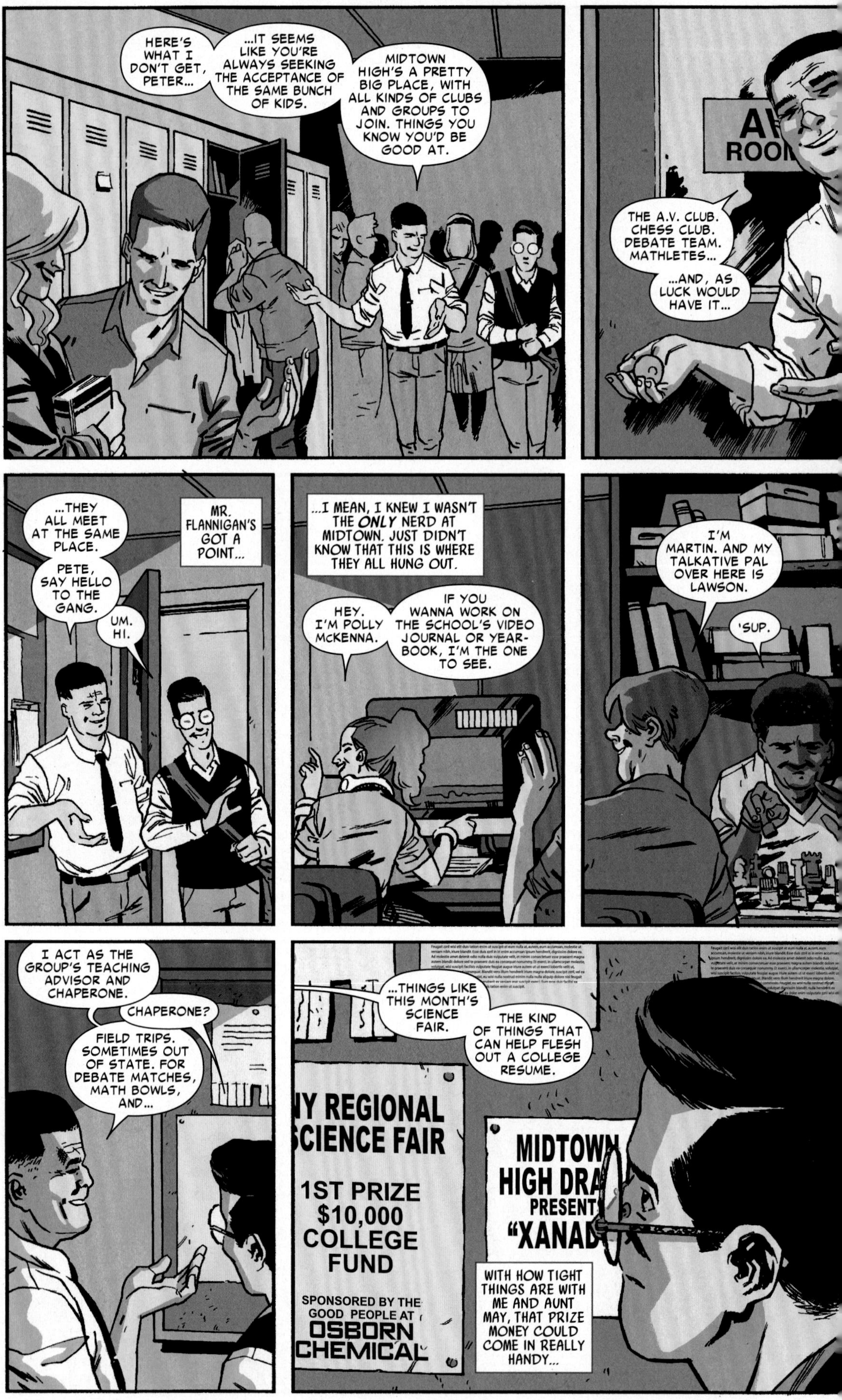
HERE'S WHAT I DON'T GET, PETER...
...IT SEEMS LIKE YOU'RE ALWAYS SEEKING THE ACCEPTANCE OF THE SAME BUNCH OF KIDS.
MIDTOWN HIGH'S A PRETTY BIG PLACE, WITH ALL KINDS OF CLUBS AND GROUPS TO JOIN. THINGS YOU KNOW YOU'D BE GOOD AT.
AV ROO
THE A.V. CLUB. CHESS CLUB. DEBATE TEAM. MATHLETES...
...AND, AS LUCK WOULD HAVE IT...
...THEY ALL MEET AT THE SAME PLACE.
MR. FLANNIGAN'S GOT A POINT...
PETE, SAY HELLO TO THE GANG.
UM. HI.
...I MEAN, I KNEW I WASN'T THE *ONLY* NERD AT MIDTOWN. JUST DIDN'T KNOW THAT THIS IS WHERE THEY ALL HUNG OUT.
HEY. I'M POLLY McKENNA.
IF YOU WANNA WORK ON THE SCHOOL'S VIDEO JOURNAL OR YEAR-BOOK, I'M THE ONE TO SEE.
I'M MARTIN. AND MY TALKATIVE PAL OVER HERE IS LAWSON.
'SUP.
I ACT AS THE GROUP'S TEACHING ADVISOR AND CHAPERONE.
CHAPERONE?
FIELD TRIPS. SOMETIMES OUT OF STATE. FOR DEBATE MATCHES, MATH BOWLS, AND...
...THINGS LIKE THIS MONTH'S SCIENCE FAIR.
THE KIND OF THINGS THAT CAN HELP FLESH OUT A COLLEGE RESUME.
NY REGIONAL
SCIENCE FAIR
1ST PRIZE $10,000 COLLEGE FUND
SPONSORED BY THE GOOD PEOPLE AT
OSBORN CHEMICAL
MIDTOWN HIGH DRA PRESENT "XANAD
WITH HOW TIGHT THINGS ARE WITH ME AND AUNT MAY, THAT PRIZE MONEY COULD COME IN REALLY HANDY...

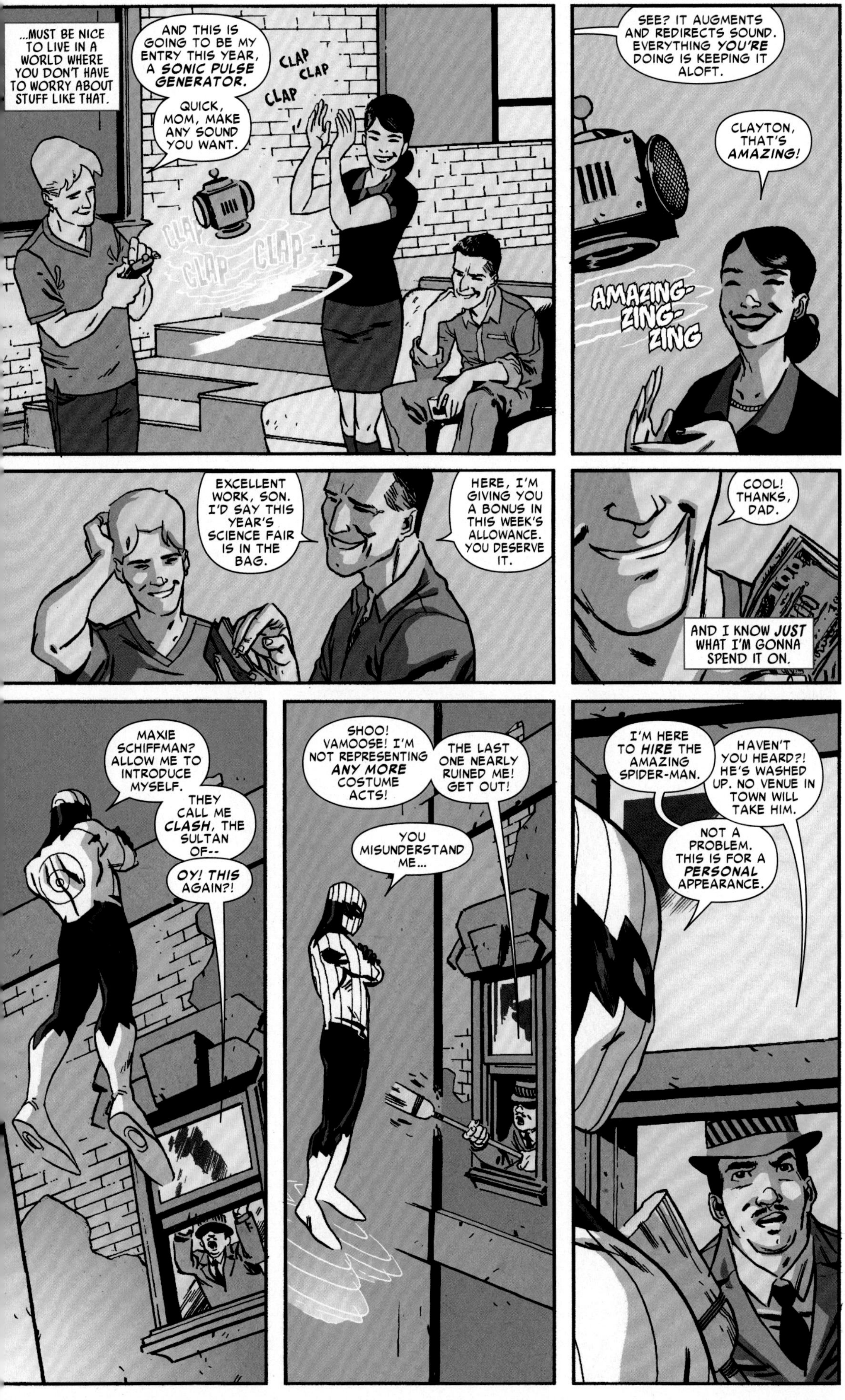
...MUST BE NICE TO LIVE IN A WORLD WHERE YOU DON'T HAVE TO WORRY ABOUT STUFF LIKE THAT.
AND THIS IS GOING TO BE MY ENTRY THIS YEAR, A SONIC PULSE GENERATOR.
QUICK, MOM, MAKE ANY SOUND YOU WANT.
CLAP CLAP CLAP
CLAP CLAP CLAP
SEE? IT AUGMENTS AND REDIRECTS SOUND. EVERYTHING YOU'RE DOING IS KEEPING IT ALOFT.
CLAYTON, THAT'S AMAZING!
AMAZING-ZING-ZING
EXCELLENT WORK, SON. I'D SAY THIS YEAR'S SCIENCE FAIR IS IN THE BAG.
HERE, I'M GIVING YOU A BONUS IN THIS WEEK'S ALLOWANCE. YOU DESERVE IT.
COOL! THANKS, DAD.
AND I KNOW JUST WHAT I'M GONNA SPEND IT ON.
MAXIE SCHIFFMAN? ALLOW ME TO INTRODUCE MYSELF.
THEY CALL ME CLASH, THE SULTAN OF--
OY! THIS AGAIN?!
SHOO! VAMOOSE! I'M NOT REPRESENTING ANY MORE COSTUME ACTS!
THE LAST ONE NEARLY RUINED ME! GET OUT!
YOU MISUNDERSTAND ME...
I'M HERE TO HIRE THE AMAZING SPIDER-MAN.
HAVEN'T YOU HEARD?! HE'S WASHED UP. NO VENUE IN TOWN WILL TAKE HIM.
NOT A PROBLEM. THIS IS FOR A PERSONAL APPEARANCE.

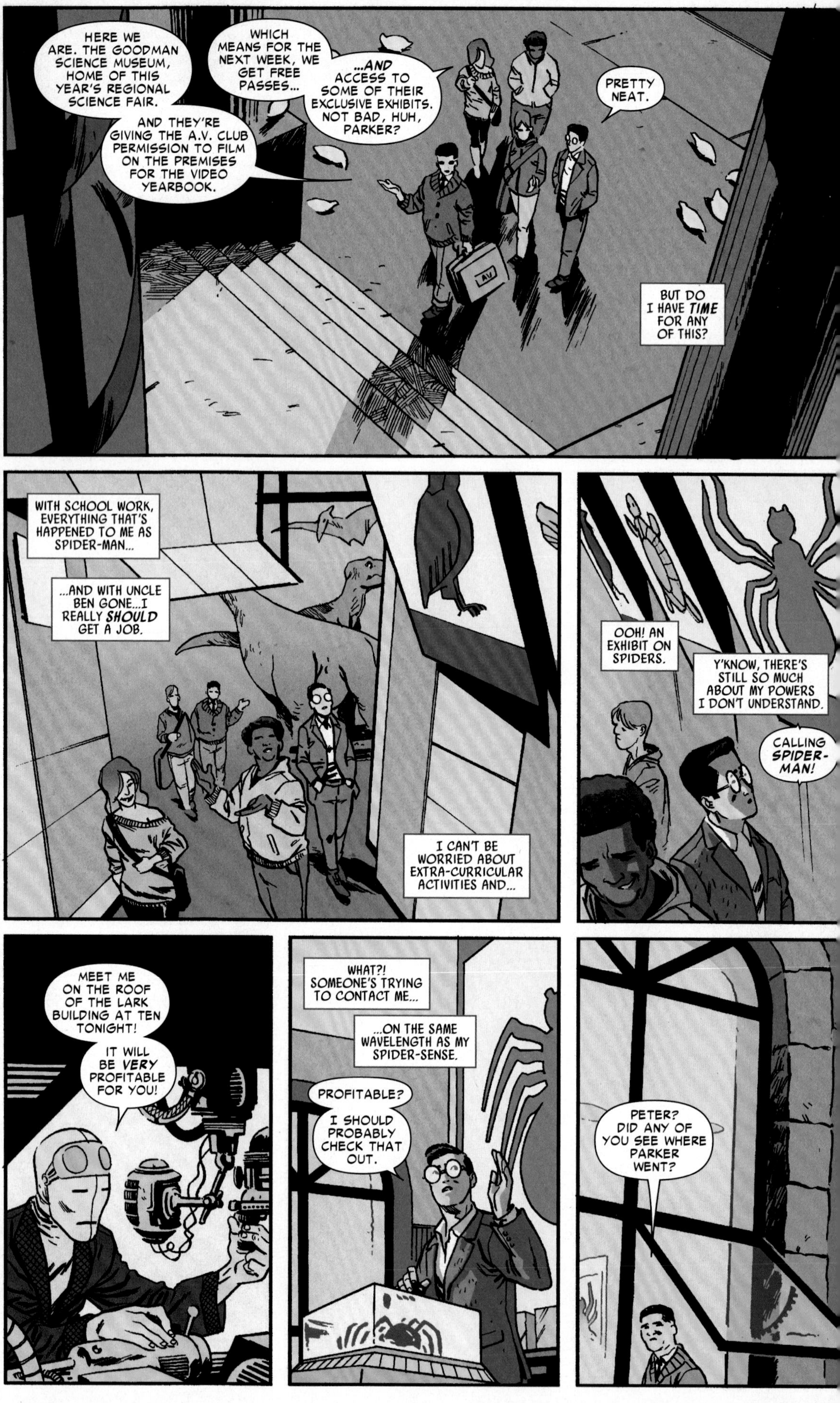
HERE WE ARE. THE GOODMAN SCIENCE MUSEUM, HOME OF THIS YEAR'S REGIONAL SCIENCE FAIR.
AND THEY'RE GIVING THE A.V. CLUB PERMISSION TO FILM ON THE PREMISES FOR THE VIDEO YEARBOOK.
WHICH MEANS FOR THE NEXT WEEK, WE GET FREE PASSES...
...AND ACCESS TO SOME OF THEIR EXCLUSIVE EXHIBITS. NOT BAD, HUH, PARKER?
PRETTY NEAT.
AV
BUT DO I HAVE TIME FOR ANY OF THIS?
WITH SCHOOL WORK, EVERYTHING THAT'S HAPPENED TO ME AS SPIDER-MAN...
...AND WITH UNCLE BEN GONE...I REALLY SHOULD GET A JOB.
I CAN'T BE WORRIED ABOUT EXTRA-CURRICULAR ACTIVITIES AND...
OOH! AN EXHIBIT ON SPIDERS.
Y'KNOW, THERE'S STILL SO MUCH ABOUT MY POWERS I DON'T UNDERSTAND.
CALLING SPIDER-MAN!
MEET ME ON THE ROOF OF THE LARK BUILDING AT TEN TONIGHT!
IT WILL BE VERY PROFITABLE FOR YOU!
WHAT?! SOMEONE'S TRYING TO CONTACT ME...
...ON THE SAME WAVELENGTH AS MY SPIDER-SENSE.
PROFITABLE?
I SHOULD PROBABLY CHECK THAT OUT.
PETER? DID ANY OF YOU SEE WHERE PARKER WENT?

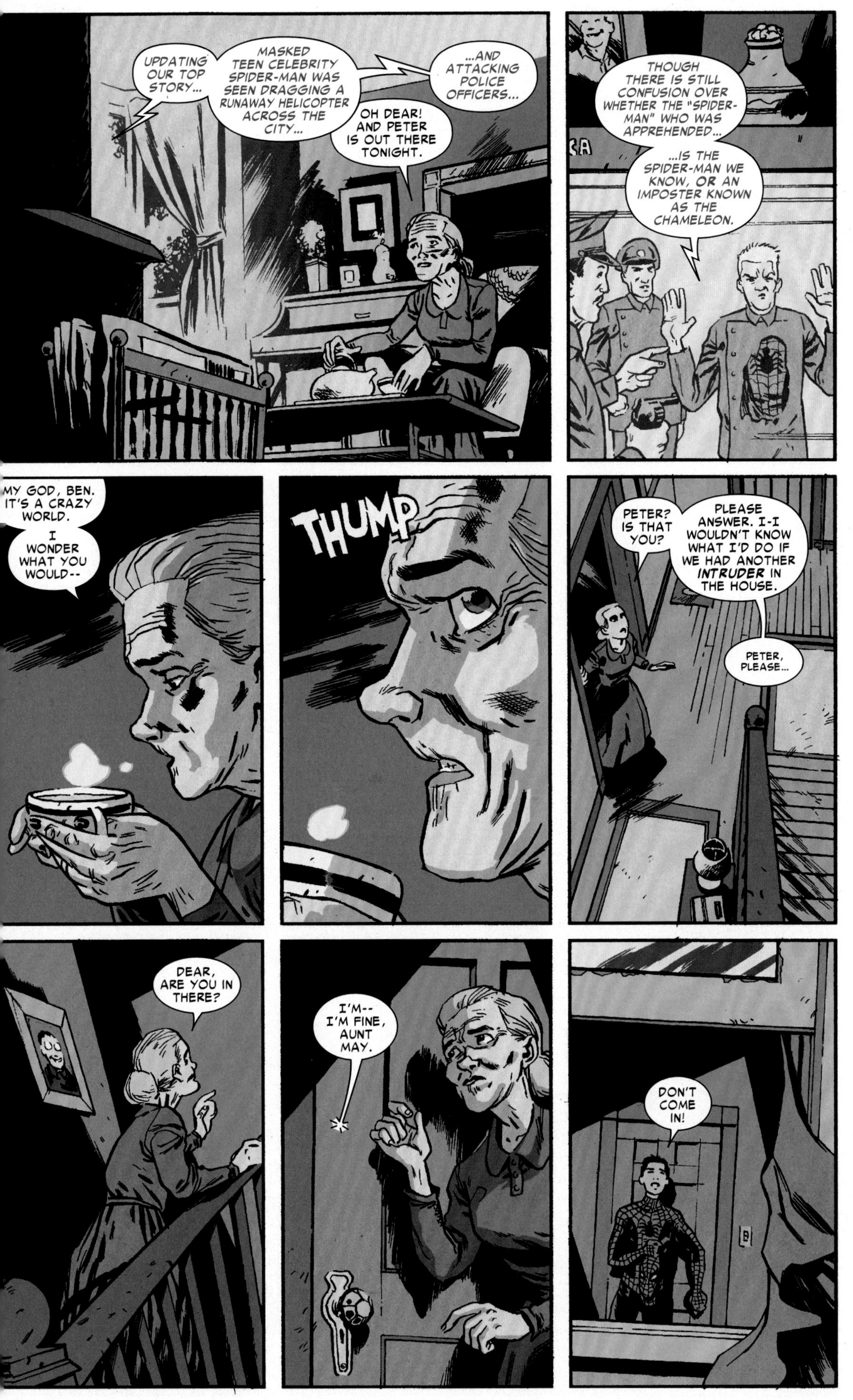
UPDATING OUR TOP STORY...
MASKED TEEN CELEBRITY SPIDER-MAN WAS SEEN DRAGGING A RUNAWAY HELICOPTER ACROSS THE CITY...
...AND ATTACKING POLICE OFFICERS...
OH DEAR! AND PETER IS OUT THERE TONIGHT.
THOUGH THERE IS STILL CONFUSION OVER WHETHER THE "SPIDER-MAN" WHO WAS APPREHENDED...
...IS THE SPIDER-MAN WE KNOW, OR AN IMPOSTER KNOWN AS THE CHAMELEON.
MY GOD, BEN. IT'S A CRAZY WORLD.
I WONDER WHAT YOU WOULD--
THUMP
PETER? IS THAT YOU?
PLEASE ANSWER. I-I WOULDN'T KNOW WHAT I'D DO IF WE HAD ANOTHER INTRUDER IN THE HOUSE.
PETER, PLEASE...
DEAR, ARE YOU IN THERE?
I'M-- I'M FINE, AUNT MAY.
DON'T COME IN!

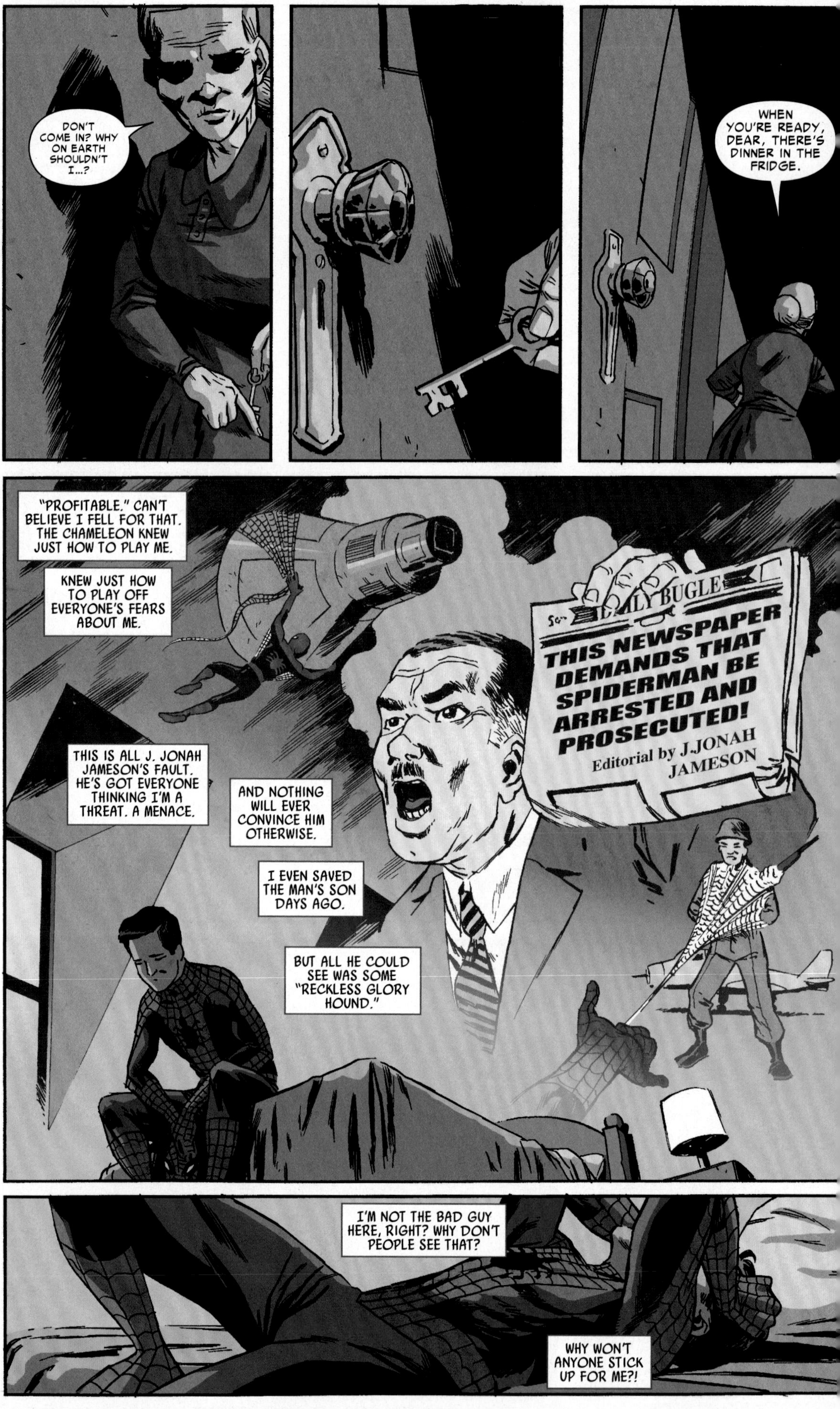
DON'T COME IN? WHY ON EARTH SHOULDN'T I...?
WHEN YOU'RE READY, DEAR, THERE'S DINNER IN THE FRIDGE.
"PROFITABLE." CAN'T BELIEVE I FELL FOR THAT. THE CHAMELEON KNEW JUST HOW TO PLAY ME.
KNEW JUST HOW TO PLAY OFF EVERYONE'S FEARS ABOUT ME.
DAILY BUGLE
THIS NEWSPAPER DEMANDS THAT SPIDERMAN BE ARRESTED AND PROSECUTED!
Editorial by J.JONAH JAMESON
THIS IS ALL J. JONAH JAMESON'S FAULT. HE'S GOT EVERYONE THINKING I'M A THREAT. A MENACE.
AND NOTHING WILL EVER CONVINCE HIM OTHERWISE.
I EVEN SAVED THE MAN'S SON DAYS AGO.
BUT ALL HE COULD SEE WAS SOME "RECKLESS GLORY HOUND."
I'M NOT THE BAD GUY HERE, RIGHT? WHY DON'T PEOPLE SEE THAT?
WHY WON'T ANYONE STICK UP FOR ME?!

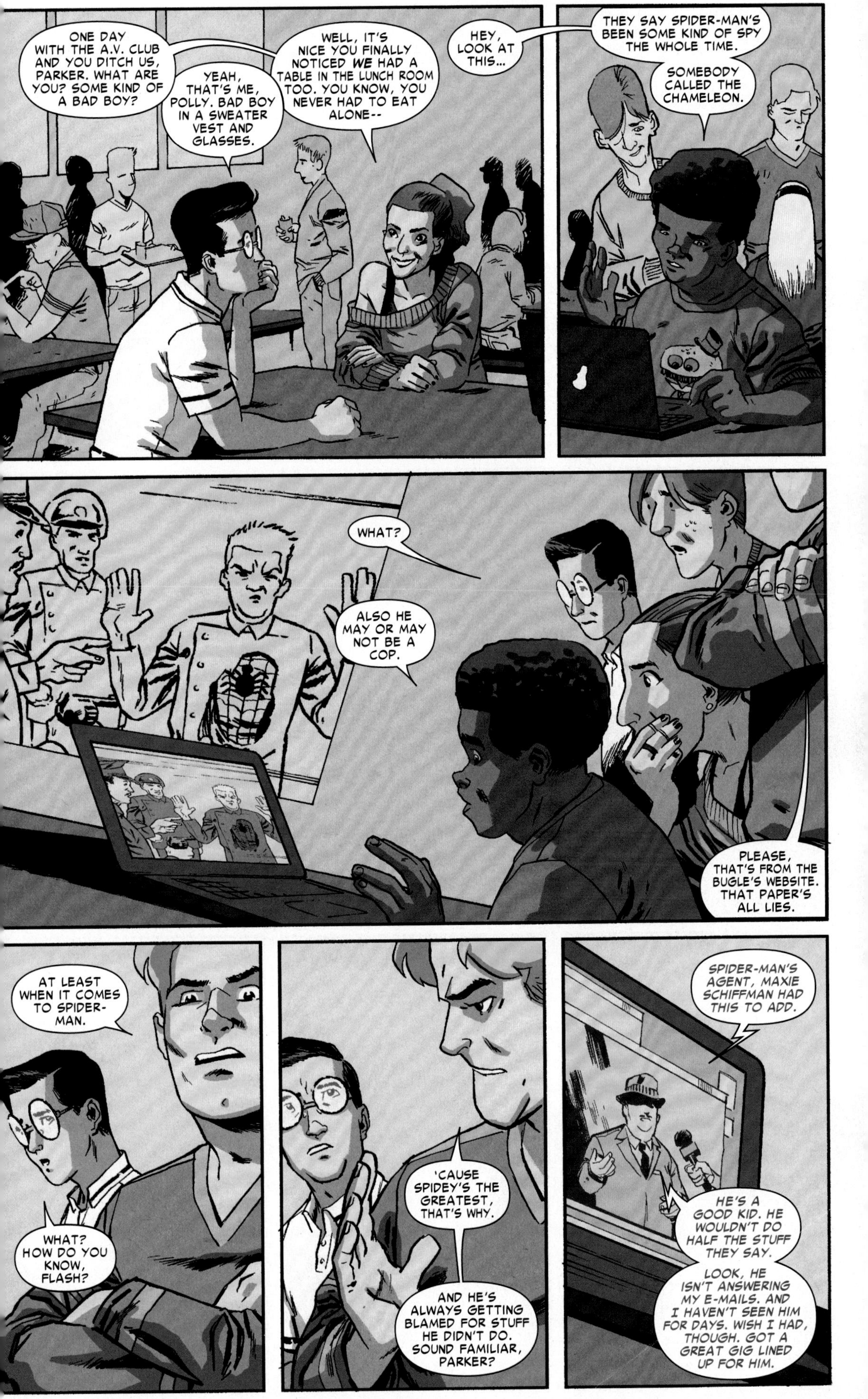
ONE DAY WITH THE A.V. CLUB AND YOU DITCH US, PARKER. WHAT ARE YOU? SOME KIND OF A BAD BOY?
YEAH, THAT'S ME, POLLY. BAD BOY IN A SWEATER VEST AND GLASSES.
WELL, IT'S NICE YOU FINALLY NOTICED WE HAD A TABLE IN THE LUNCH ROOM TOO. YOU KNOW, YOU NEVER HAD TO EAT ALONE--
HEY, LOOK AT THIS...
THEY SAY SPIDER-MAN'S BEEN SOME KIND OF SPY THE WHOLE TIME.
SOMEBODY CALLED THE CHAMELEON.
WHAT?
ALSO HE MAY OR MAY NOT BE A COP.
PLEASE, THAT'S FROM THE BUGLE'S WEBSITE. THAT PAPER'S ALL LIES.
AT LEAST WHEN IT COMES TO SPIDER-MAN.
WHAT? HOW DO YOU KNOW, FLASH?
'CAUSE SPIDEY'S THE GREATEST, THAT'S WHY.
AND HE'S ALWAYS GETTING BLAMED FOR STUFF HE DIDN'T DO. SOUND FAMILIAR, PARKER?
SPIDER-MAN'S AGENT, MAXIE SCHIFFMAN HAD THIS TO ADD.
HE'S A GOOD KID. HE WOULDN'T DO HALF THE STUFF THEY SAY.
LOOK, HE ISN'T ANSWERING MY E-MAILS. AND I HAVEN'T SEEN HIM FOR DAYS. WISH I HAD, THOUGH. GOT A GREAT GIG LINED UP FOR HIM.

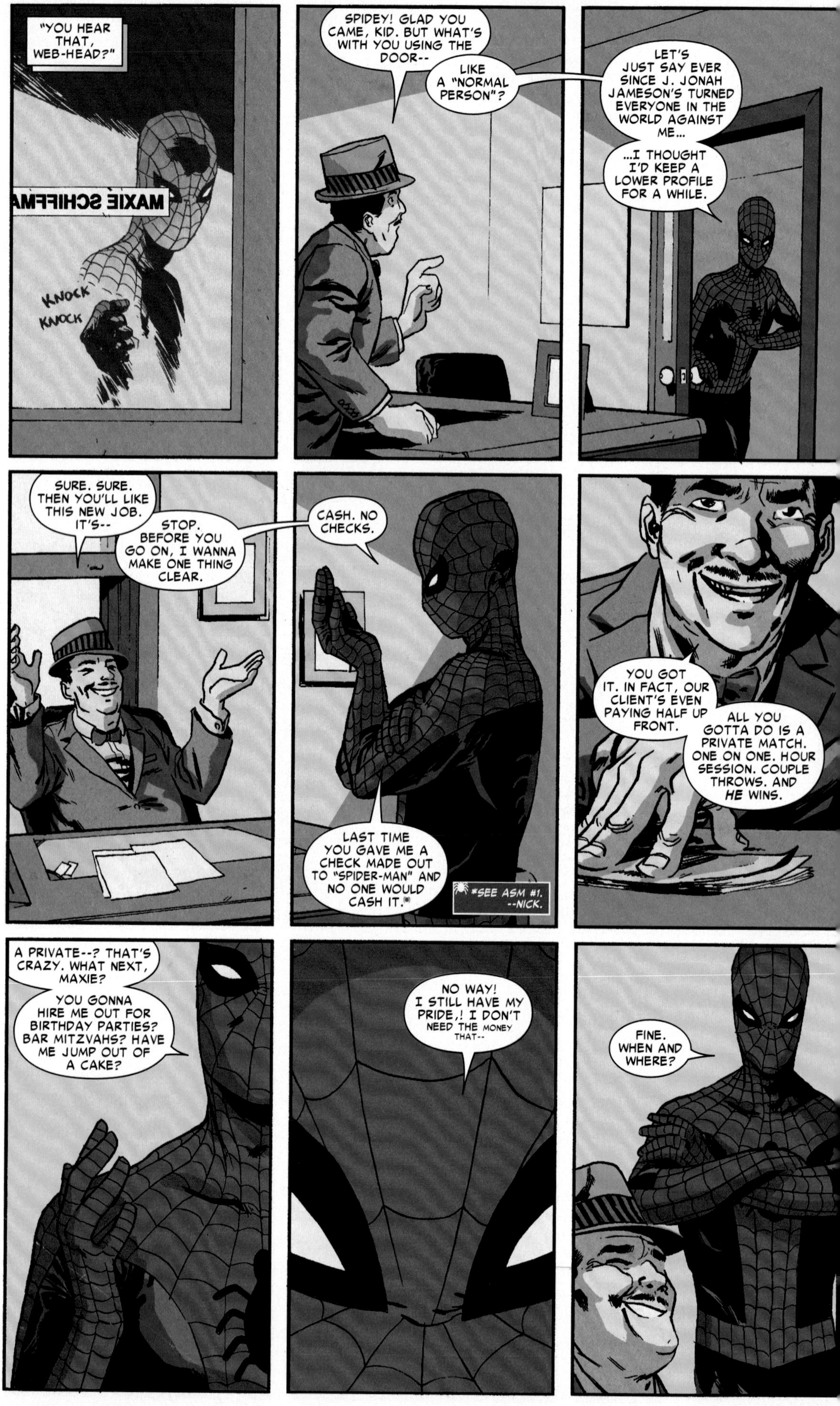
"YOU HEAR THAT, WEB-HEAD?"
MAXIE SCHIFFMA
KNOCK KNOCK
SPIDEY! GLAD YOU CAME, KID. BUT WHAT'S WITH YOU USING THE DOOR--
LIKE A "NORMAL PERSON"?
LET'S JUST SAY EVER SINCE J. JONAH JAMESON'S TURNED EVERYONE IN THE WORLD AGAINST ME...
...I THOUGHT I'D KEEP A LOWER PROFILE FOR A WHILE.
SURE. SURE. THEN YOU'LL LIKE THIS NEW JOB. IT'S--
STOP. BEFORE YOU GO ON, I WANNA MAKE ONE THING CLEAR.
CASH. NO CHECKS.
LAST TIME YOU GAVE ME A CHECK MADE OUT TO "SPIDER-MAN" AND NO ONE WOULD CASH IT.*
*SEE ASM #1. --NICK.
YOU GOT IT. IN FACT, OUR CLIENT'S EVEN PAYING HALF UP FRONT.
ALL YOU GOTTA DO IS A PRIVATE MATCH. ONE ON ONE. HOUR SESSION. COUPLE THROWS. AND HE WINS.
A PRIVATE--? THAT'S CRAZY. WHAT NEXT, MAXIE?
YOU GONNA HIRE ME OUT FOR BIRTHDAY PARTIES? BAR MITZVAHS? HAVE ME JUMP OUT OF A CAKE?
NO WAY! I STILL HAVE MY PRIDE,! I DON'T NEED THE MONEY THAT--
FINE. WHEN AND WHERE?

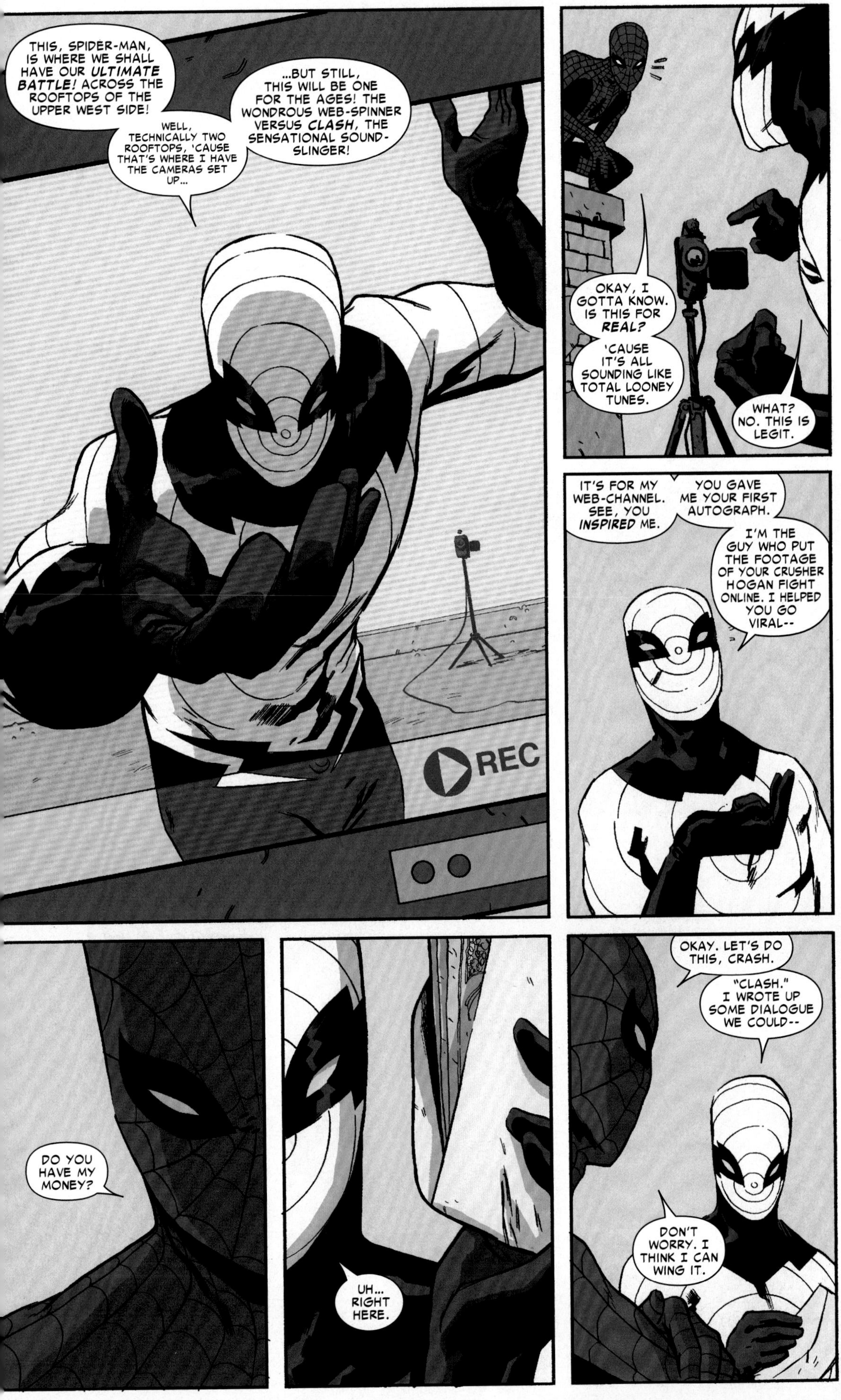
THIS, SPIDER-MAN, IS WHERE WE SHALL HAVE OUR ULTIMATE BATTLE! ACROSS THE ROOFTOPS OF THE UPPER WEST SIDE!
WELL, TECHNICALLY TWO ROOFTOPS, 'CAUSE THAT'S WHERE I HAVE THE CAMERAS SET UP...
...BUT STILL, THIS WILL BE ONE FOR THE AGES! THE WONDROUS WEB-SPINNER VERSUS CLASH, THE SENSATIONAL SOUND-SLINGER!
REC
OKAY, I GOTTA KNOW. IS THIS FOR REAL?
'CAUSE IT'S ALL SOUNDING LIKE TOTAL LOONEY TUNES.
WHAT? NO. THIS IS LEGIT.
IT'S FOR MY WEB-CHANNEL. SEE, YOU INSPIRED ME.
YOU GAVE ME YOUR FIRST AUTOGRAPH.
I'M THE GUY WHO PUT THE FOOTAGE OF YOUR CRUSHER HOGAN FIGHT ONLINE. I HELPED YOU GO VIRAL--
DO YOU HAVE MY MONEY?
UH... RIGHT HERE.
OKAY. LET'S DO THIS, CRASH.
"CLASH." I WROTE UP SOME DIALOGUE WE COULD--
DON'T WORRY. I THINK I CAN WING IT.

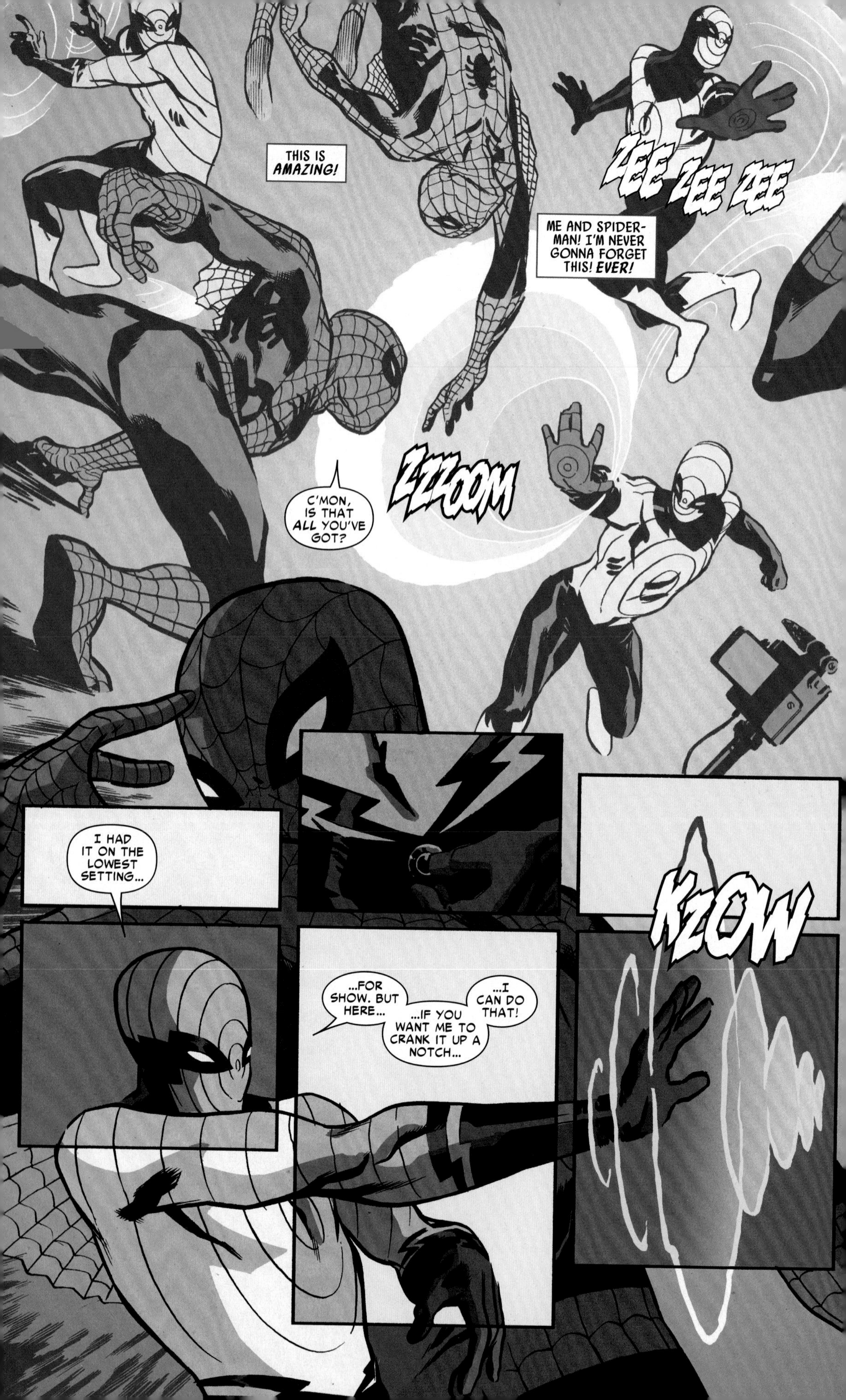

THIS IS AMAZING!
ZEE ZEE ZEE
ME AND SPIDER-MAN! I'M NEVER GONNA FORGET THIS! EVER!
C'MON, IS THAT ALL YOU'VE GOT?
ZZZOOM
I HAD IT ON THE LOWEST SETTING...
...FOR SHOW. BUT HERE...
...IF YOU WANT ME TO CRANK IT UP A NOTCH...
...I CAN DO THAT!
KZOW

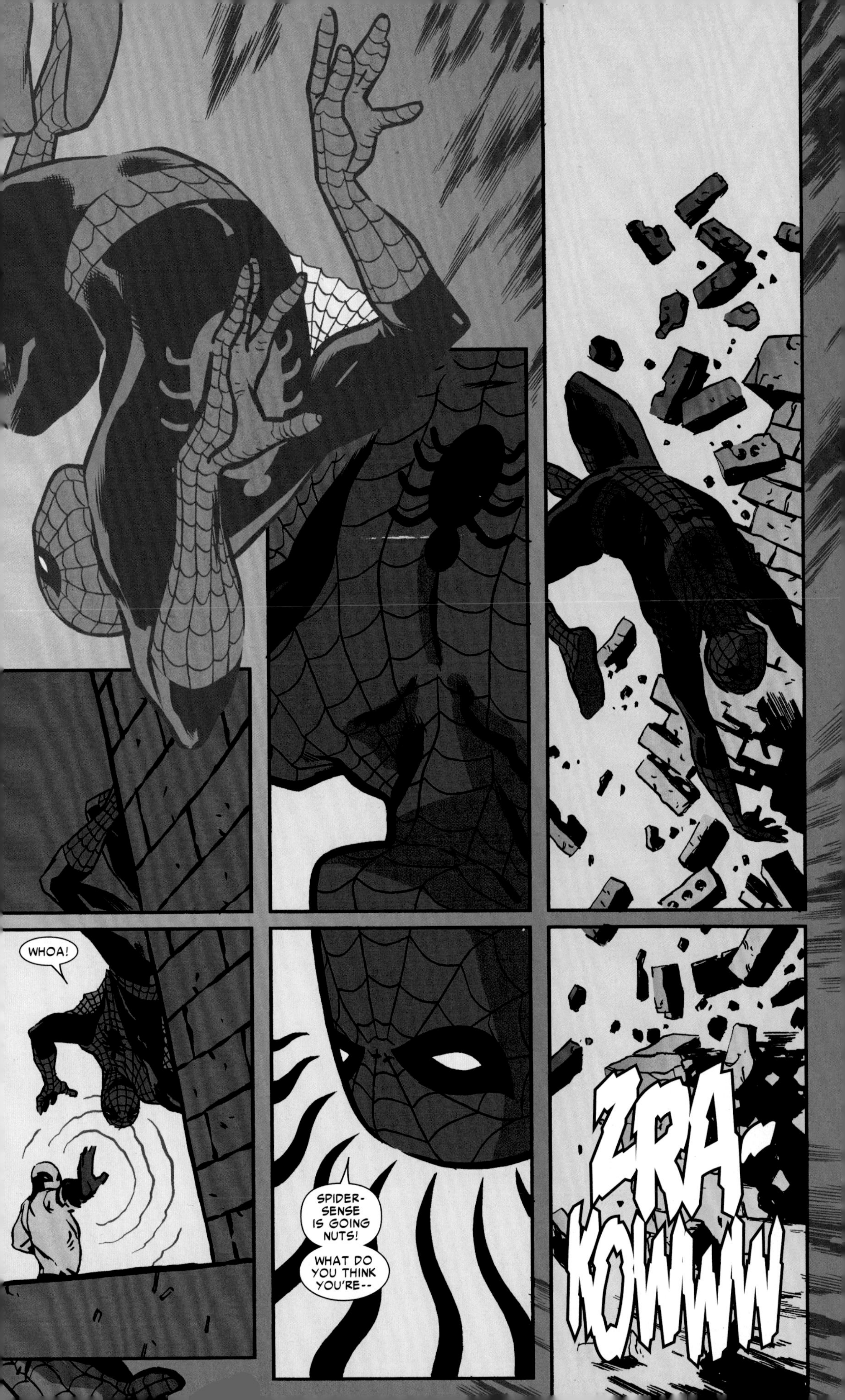
WHOA!
SPIDER-SENSE IS GOING NUTS!
WHAT DO YOU THINK YOU'RE--
ZRA-KOWWW

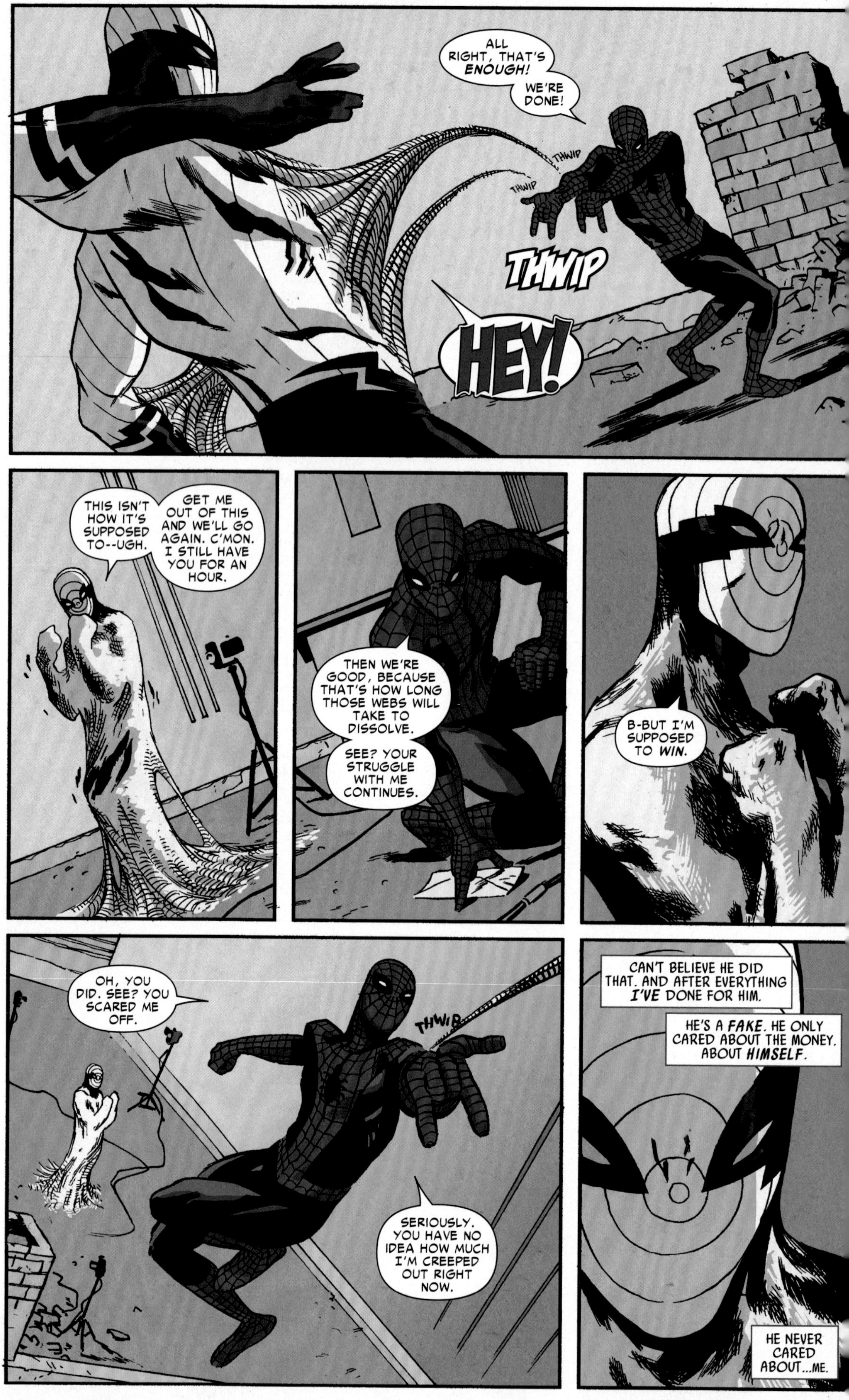

ALL RIGHT, THAT'S ENOUGH!
WE'RE DONE!
THWIP
THWIP
THWIP
HEY!
THIS ISN'T HOW IT'S SUPPOSED TO--UGH.
GET ME OUT OF THIS AND WE'LL GO AGAIN. C'MON. I STILL HAVE YOU FOR AN HOUR.
THEN WE'RE GOOD, BECAUSE THAT'S HOW LONG THOSE WEBS WILL TAKE TO DISSOLVE.
SEE? YOUR STRUGGLE WITH ME CONTINUES.
B-BUT I'M SUPPOSED TO WIN.
OH, YOU DID. SEE? YOU SCARED ME OFF.
THWIP
SERIOUSLY. YOU HAVE NO IDEA HOW MUCH I'M CREEPED OUT RIGHT NOW.
CAN'T BELIEVE HE DID THAT. AND AFTER EVERYTHING I'VE DONE FOR HIM.
HE'S A FAKE. HE ONLY CARED ABOUT THE MONEY. ABOUT HIMSELF.
HE NEVER CARED ABOUT...ME.

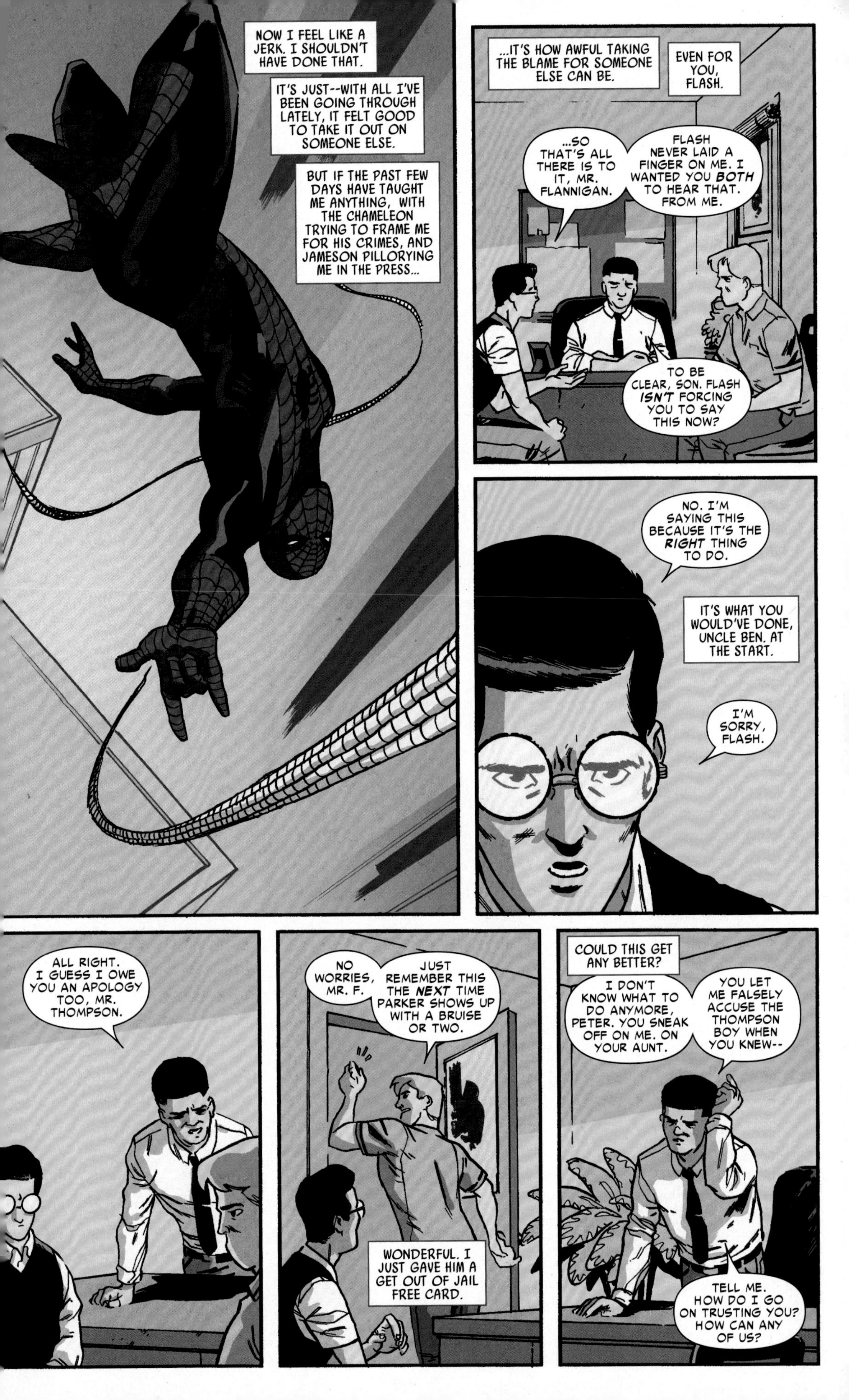
NOW I FEEL LIKE A JERK. I SHOULDN'T HAVE DONE THAT.
IT'S JUST--WITH ALL I'VE BEEN GOING THROUGH LATELY, IT FELT GOOD TO TAKE IT OUT ON SOMEONE ELSE.
BUT IF THE PAST FEW DAYS HAVE TAUGHT ME ANYTHING, WITH THE CHAMELEON TRYING TO FRAME ME FOR HIS CRIMES, AND JAMESON PILLORYING ME IN THE PRESS...
...IT'S HOW AWFUL TAKING THE BLAME FOR SOMEONE ELSE CAN BE.
EVEN FOR YOU, FLASH.
...SO THAT'S ALL THERE IS TO IT, MR. FLANNIGAN.
FLASH NEVER LAID A FINGER ON ME. I WANTED YOU BOTH TO HEAR THAT. FROM ME.
TO BE CLEAR, SON. FLASH ISN'T FORCING YOU TO SAY THIS NOW?
NO. I'M SAYING THIS BECAUSE IT'S THE RIGHT THING TO DO.
IT'S WHAT YOU WOULD'VE DONE, UNCLE BEN. AT THE START.
I'M SORRY, FLASH.
ALL RIGHT. I GUESS I OWE YOU AN APOLOGY TOO, MR. THOMPSON.
NO WORRIES, MR. F.
JUST REMEMBER THIS THE NEXT TIME PARKER SHOWS UP WITH A BRUISE OR TWO.
WONDERFUL. I JUST GAVE HIM A GET OUT OF JAIL FREE CARD.
COULD THIS GET ANY BETTER?
I DON'T KNOW WHAT TO DO ANYMORE, PETER. YOU SNEAK OFF ON ME. ON YOUR AUNT.
YOU LET ME FALSELY ACCUSE THE THOMPSON BOY WHEN YOU KNEW--
TELL ME. HOW DO I GO ON TRUSTING YOU? HOW CAN ANY OF US?

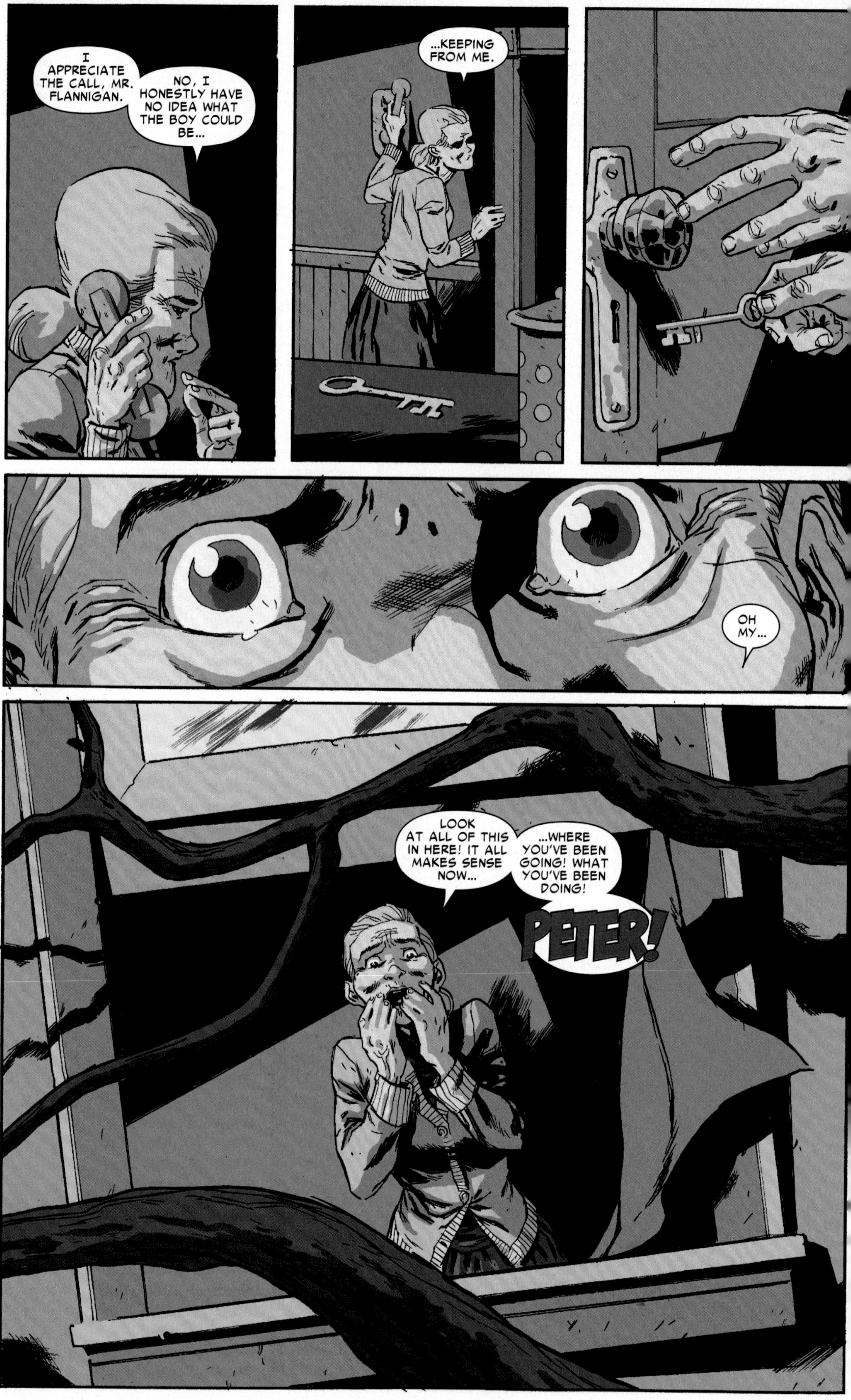
I APPRECIATE THE CALL, MR. FLANNIGAN.
NO, I HONESTLY HAVE NO IDEA WHAT THE BOY COULD BE...
...KEEPING FROM ME.
OH MY...
LOOK AT ALL OF THIS IN HERE! IT ALL MAKES SENSE NOW...
...WHERE YOU'VE BEEN GOING! WHAT YOU'VE BEEN DOING!
PETER!

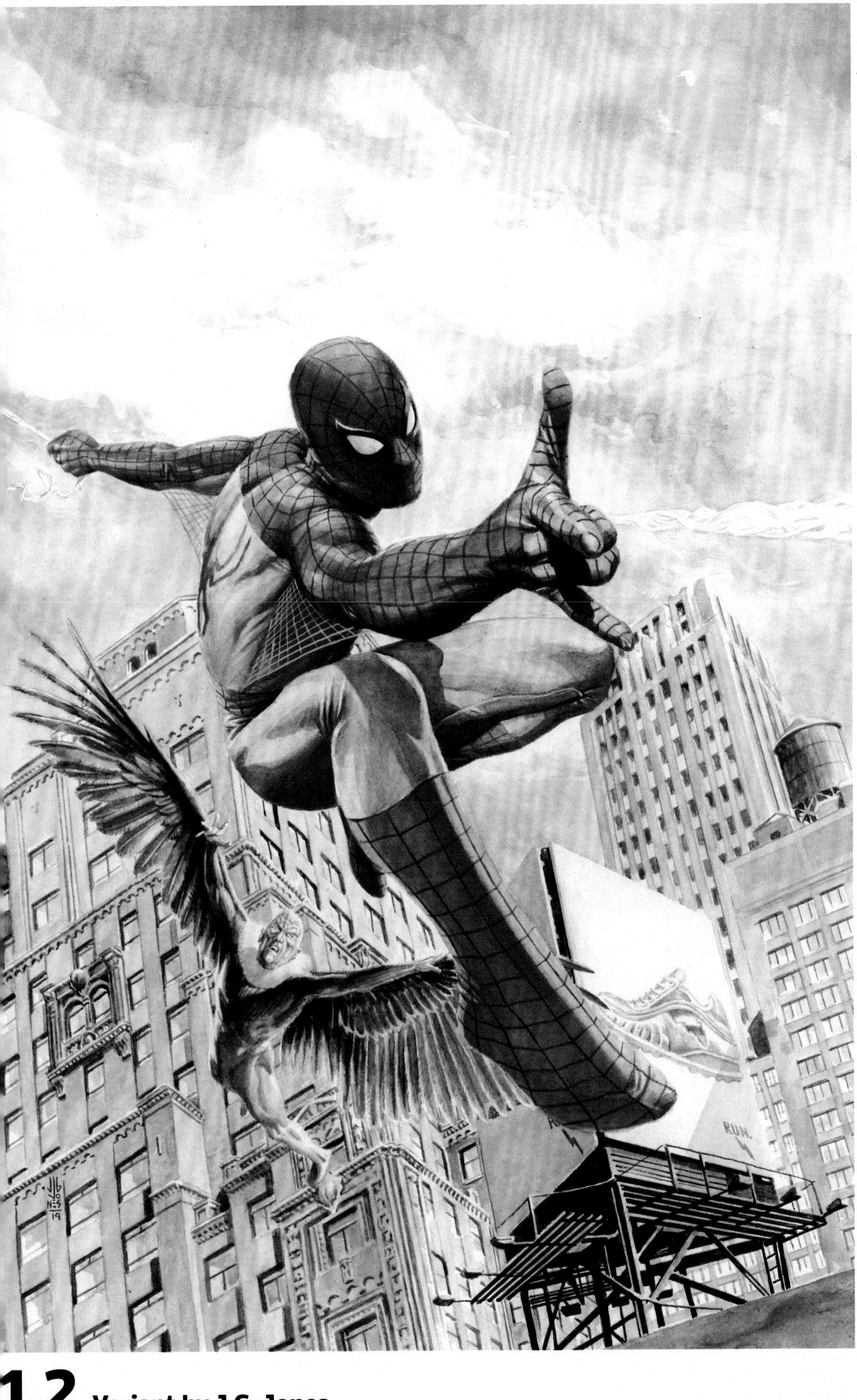
RUN.

1.2 **Variant by J.G. Jones**

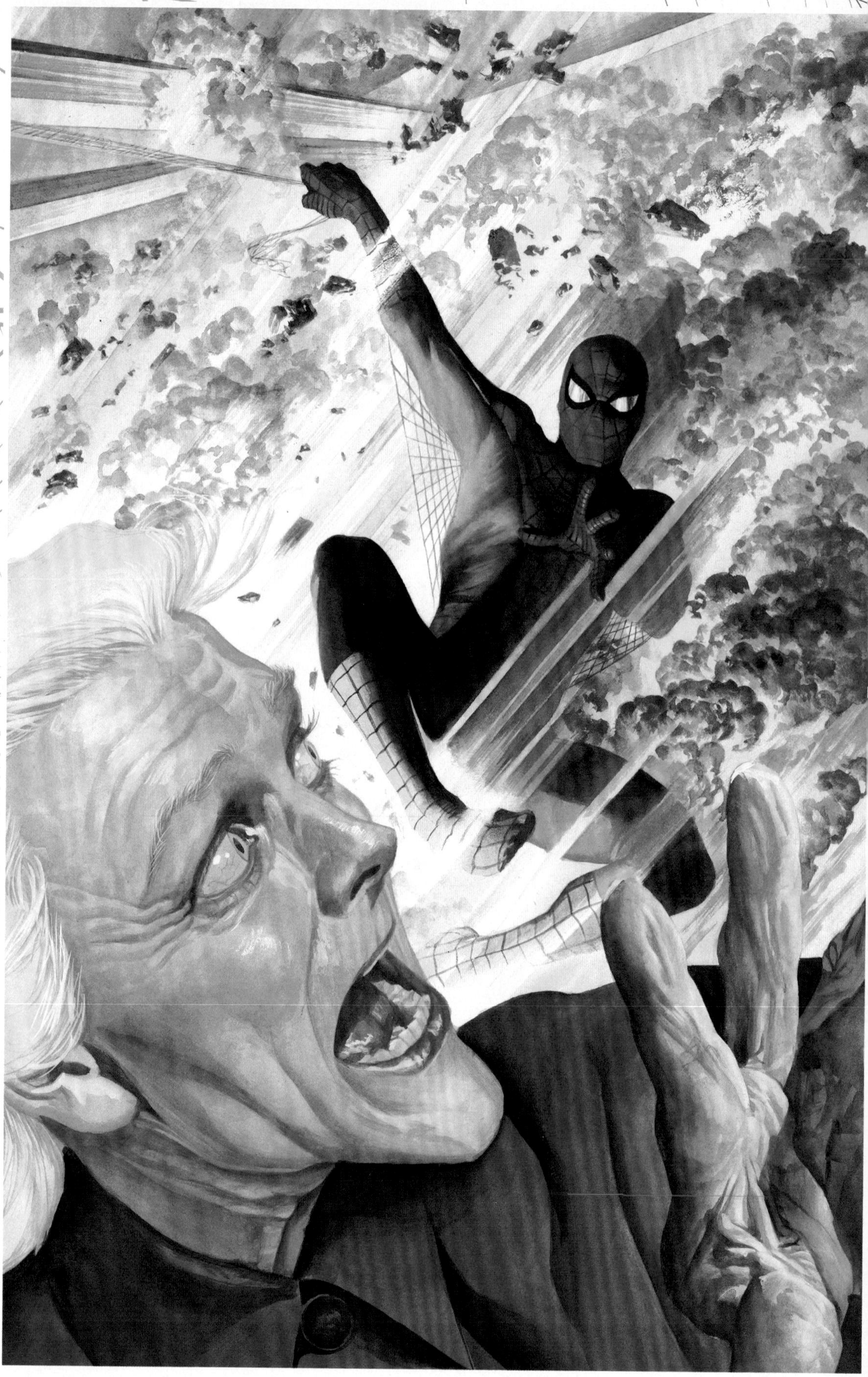

1.3

YOU'RE NOBODY TILL PEOPLE NOTICE YOU. SEE YOU. HEAR YOU.

I *MADE* SPIDER-MAN.

I'M THE GUY WHO SHOT THE VIDEO OF HIS CRUSHER HOGAN FIGHT. I PUT IT ONLINE. I MADE IT GO VIRAL.

IF I COULD DO IT FOR HIM, I CAN DO IT FOR *ME*.

WHEN PEOPLE SEE OUR FIGHT...

WHEN THEY HEAR ME SCORE IT...

...*EVERYONE'S* GONNA KNOW *ME*.

MY MUSIC.

THEY'LL ALL CHEER FOR CLASH!

I'LL BE THE BIGGEST DAMN--

IDIOT! HE MAKES ME LOOK LIKE IDIOT. I CAN'T USE ANY OF THIS.

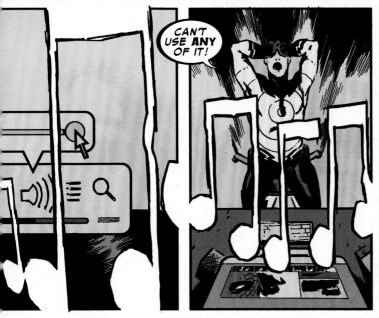

CAN'T USE *ANY* OF IT!

CLAYTON? YOU NEED TO KEEP IT DOWN, HONEY.

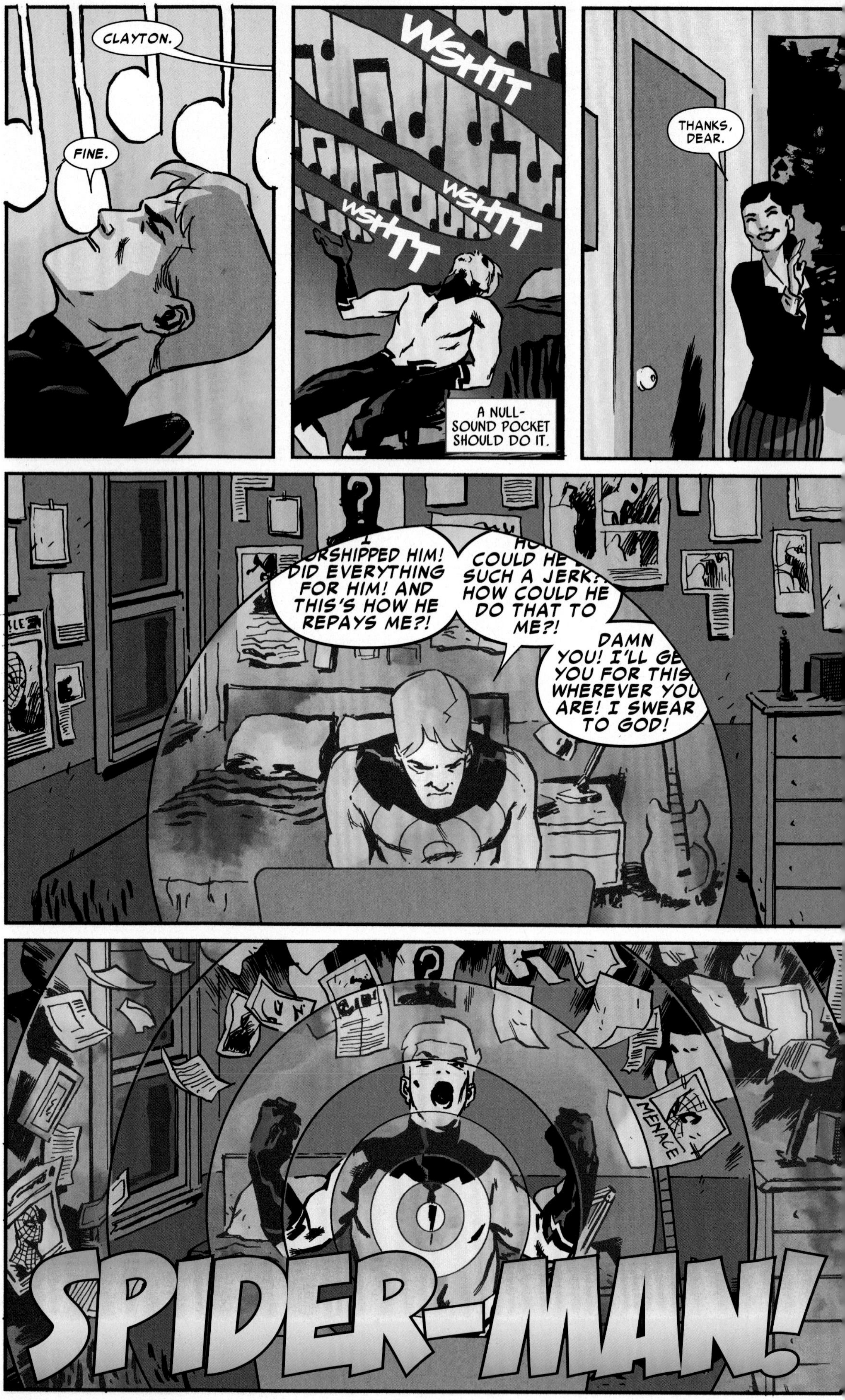
CLAYTON.
FINE.
WSHTT
WSHTT
WSHTT
A NULL-SOUND POCKET SHOULD DO IT.
THANKS, DEAR.
ORSHIPPED HIM! DID EVERYTHING FOR HIM! AND THIS'S HOW HE REPAYS ME?!
HO COULD HE SUCH A JERK? HOW COULD HE DO THAT TO ME?!
DAMN YOU! I'LL GE YOU FOR THIS WHEREVER YOU ARE! I SWEAR TO GOD!
MENACE
SPIDER-MAN!

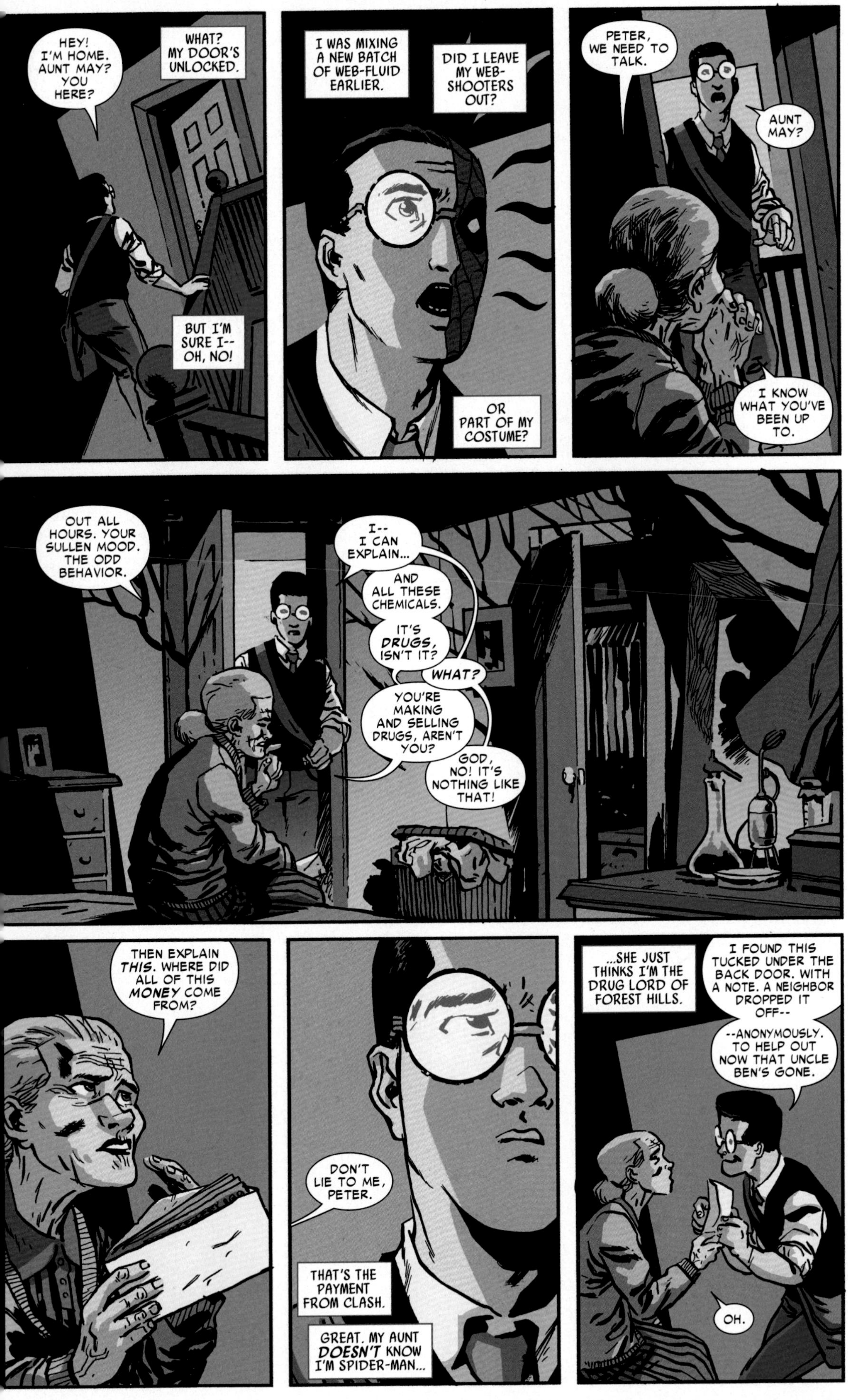
HEY! I'M HOME. AUNT MAY? YOU HERE?
WHAT? MY DOOR'S UNLOCKED.
BUT I'M SURE I-- OH, NO!
I WAS MIXING A NEW BATCH OF WEB-FLUID EARLIER.
DID I LEAVE MY WEB-SHOOTERS OUT?
OR PART OF MY COSTUME?
PETER, WE NEED TO TALK.
AUNT MAY?
I KNOW WHAT YOU'VE BEEN UP TO.
OUT ALL HOURS. YOUR SULLEN MOOD. THE ODD BEHAVIOR.
I-- I CAN EXPLAIN...
AND ALL THESE CHEMICALS.
IT'S DRUGS, ISN'T IT?
WHAT?
YOU'RE MAKING AND SELLING DRUGS, AREN'T YOU?
GOD, NO! IT'S NOTHING LIKE THAT!
THEN EXPLAIN THIS. WHERE DID ALL OF THIS MONEY COME FROM?
DON'T LIE TO ME, PETER.
THAT'S THE PAYMENT FROM CLASH.
GREAT. MY AUNT DOESN'T KNOW I'M SPIDER-MAN...
...SHE JUST THINKS I'M THE DRUG LORD OF FOREST HILLS.
I FOUND THIS TUCKED UNDER THE BACK DOOR. WITH A NOTE. A NEIGHBOR DROPPED IT OFF--
--ANONYMOUSLY. TO HELP OUT NOW THAT UNCLE BEN'S GONE.
OH.

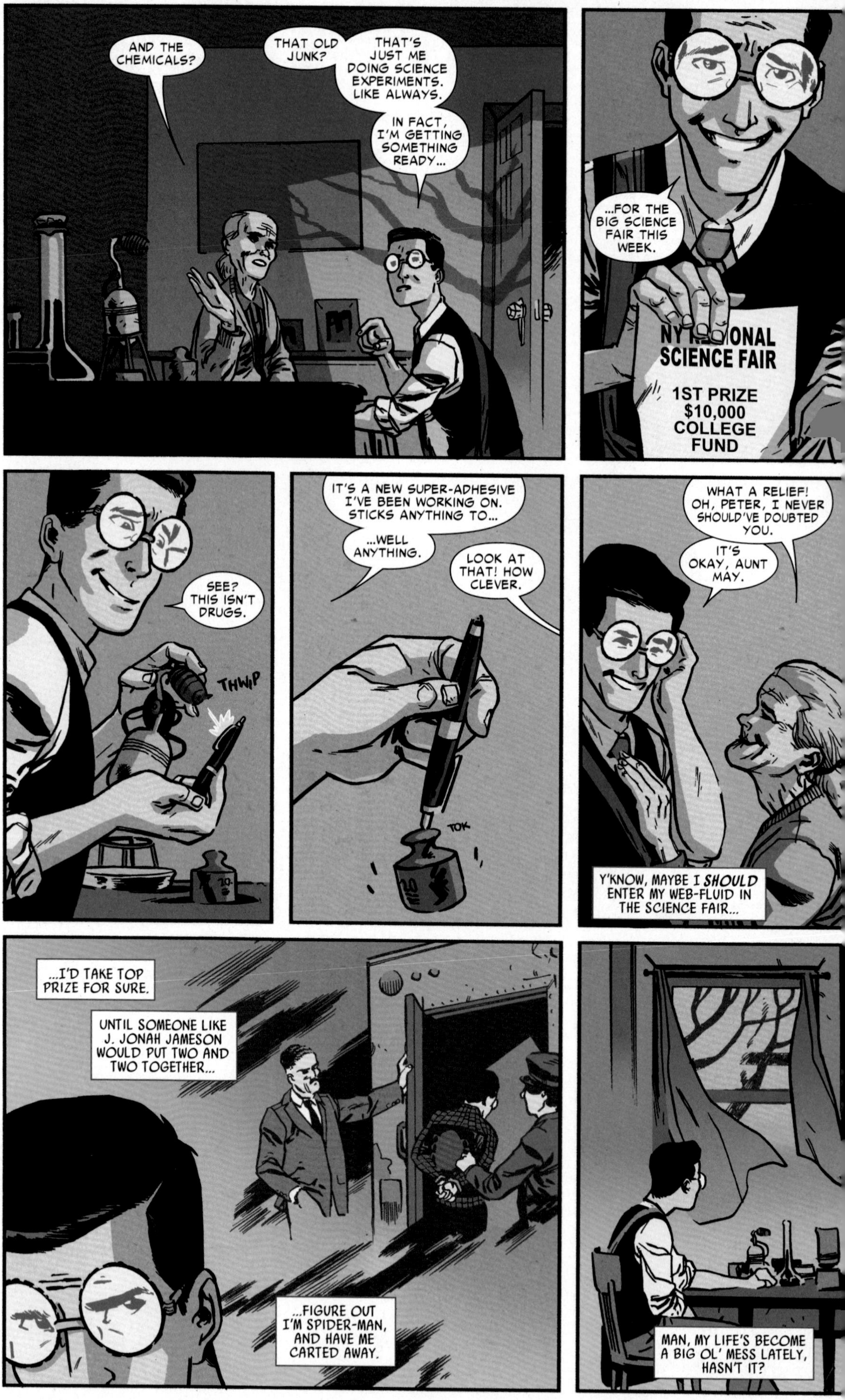
AND THE CHEMICALS?
THAT OLD JUNK?
THAT'S JUST ME DOING SCIENCE EXPERIMENTS. LIKE ALWAYS.
IN FACT, I'M GETTING SOMETHING READY...
...FOR THE BIG SCIENCE FAIR THIS WEEK.
SCIENCE FAIR
1ST PRIZE $10,000 COLLEGE FUND
SEE? THIS ISN'T DRUGS.
THWIP
IT'S A NEW SUPER-ADHESIVE I'VE BEEN WORKING ON. STICKS ANYTHING TO...
...WELL ANYTHING.
LOOK AT THAT! HOW CLEVER.
TOK
WHAT A RELIEF! OH, PETER, I NEVER SHOULD'VE DOUBTED YOU.
IT'S OKAY, AUNT MAY.
Y'KNOW, MAYBE I SHOULD ENTER MY WEB-FLUID IN THE SCIENCE FAIR...
...I'D TAKE TOP PRIZE FOR SURE.
UNTIL SOMEONE LIKE J. JONAH JAMESON WOULD PUT TWO AND TWO TOGETHER...
...FIGURE OUT I'M SPIDER-MAN, AND HAVE ME CARTED AWAY.
MAN, MY LIFE'S BECOME A BIG OL' MESS LATELY, HASN'T IT?

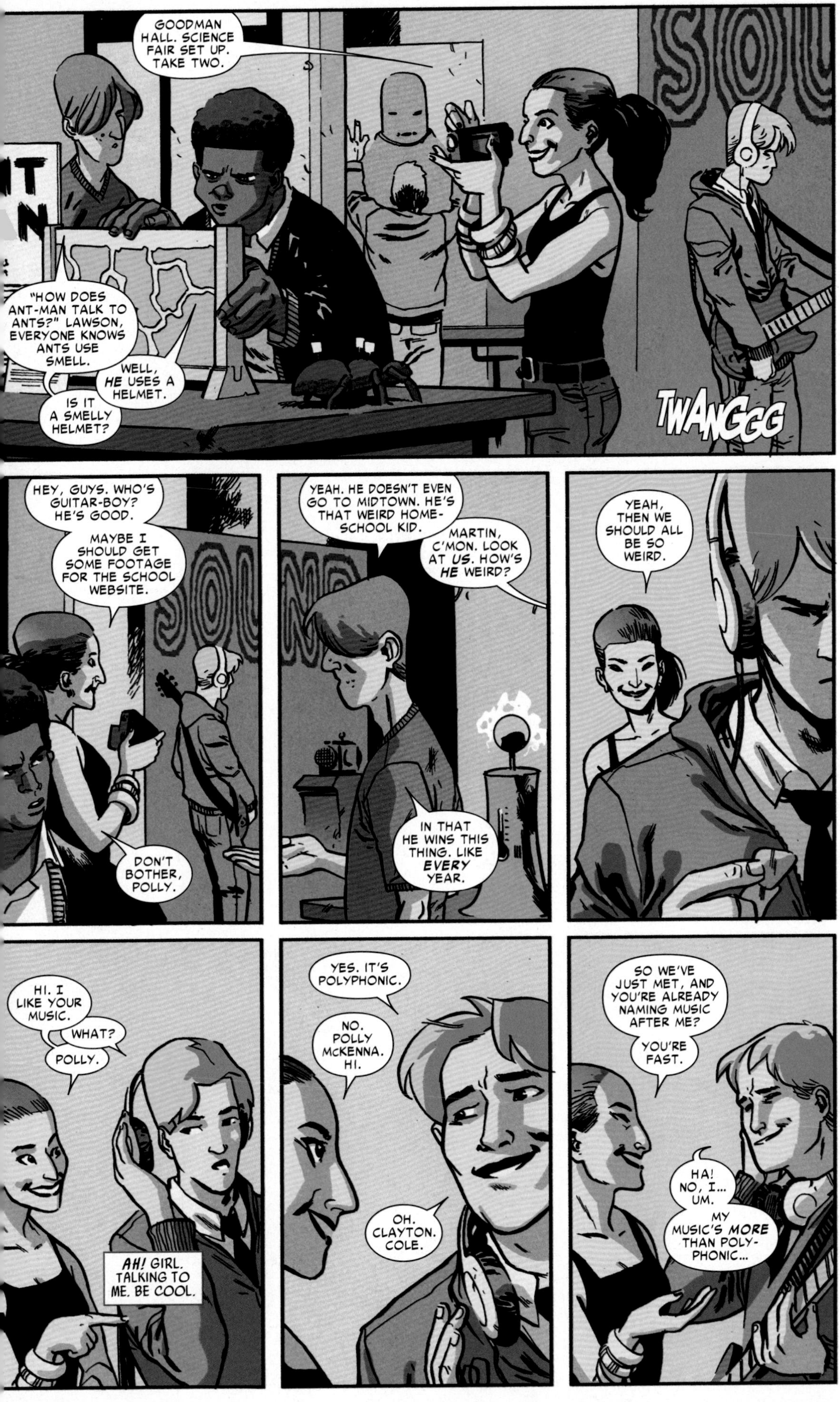
GOODMAN HALL. SCIENCE FAIR SET UP. TAKE TWO.
"HOW DOES ANT-MAN TALK TO ANTS?" LAWSON, EVERYONE KNOWS ANTS USE SMELL.
WELL, HE USES A HELMET.
IS IT A SMELLY HELMET?
TWANGGG
HEY, GUYS. WHO'S GUITAR-BOY? HE'S GOOD.
MAYBE I SHOULD GET SOME FOOTAGE FOR THE SCHOOL WEBSITE.
DON'T BOTHER, POLLY.
YEAH. HE DOESN'T EVEN GO TO MIDTOWN. HE'S THAT WEIRD HOME-SCHOOL KID.
MARTIN, C'MON. LOOK AT US. HOW'S HE WEIRD?
IN THAT HE WINS THIS THING. LIKE EVERY YEAR.
YEAH, THEN WE SHOULD ALL BE SO WEIRD.
HI. I LIKE YOUR MUSIC.
WHAT?
POLLY.
AH! GIRL. TALKING TO ME. BE COOL.
YES. IT'S POLYPHONIC.
NO. POLLY McKENNA. HI.
OH. CLAYTON. COLE.
SO WE'VE JUST MET, AND YOU'RE ALREADY NAMING MUSIC AFTER ME?
YOU'RE FAST.
HA! NO, I... UM.
MY MUSIC'S MORE THAN POLY-PHONIC...

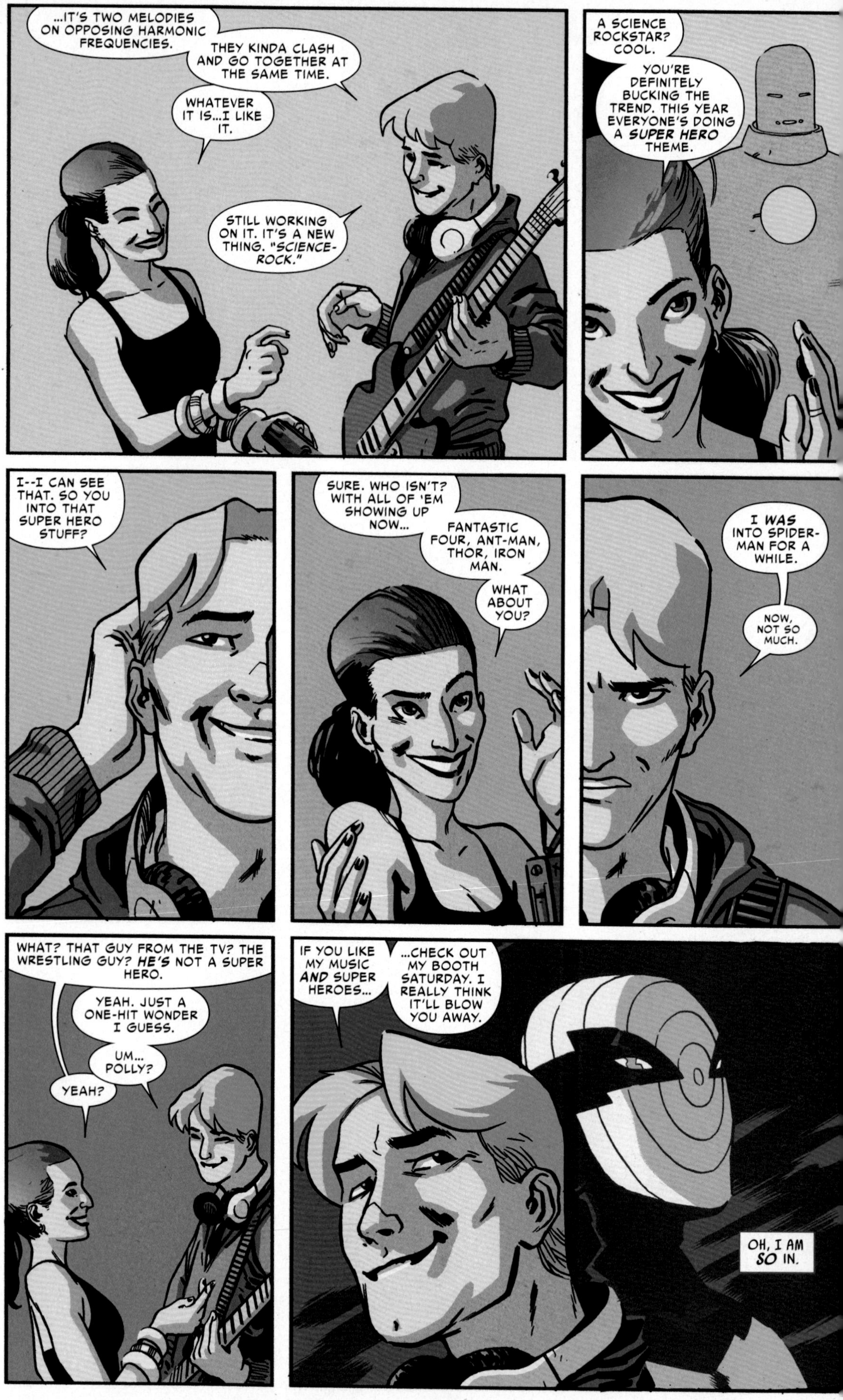
...IT'S TWO MELODIES ON OPPOSING HARMONIC FREQUENCIES.
THEY KINDA CLASH AND GO TOGETHER AT THE SAME TIME.
WHATEVER IT IS...I LIKE IT.
STILL WORKING ON IT. IT'S A NEW THING. "SCIENCE-ROCK."
A SCIENCE ROCKSTAR? COOL.
YOU'RE DEFINITELY BUCKING THE TREND. THIS YEAR EVERYONE'S DOING A SUPER HERO THEME.
I--I CAN SEE THAT. SO YOU INTO THAT SUPER HERO STUFF?
SURE. WHO ISN'T? WITH ALL OF 'EM SHOWING UP NOW...
FANTASTIC FOUR, ANT-MAN, THOR, IRON MAN.
WHAT ABOUT YOU?
I WAS INTO SPIDER-MAN FOR A WHILE.
NOW, NOT SO MUCH.
WHAT? THAT GUY FROM THE TV? THE WRESTLING GUY? HE'S NOT A SUPER HERO.
YEAH. JUST A ONE-HIT WONDER I GUESS.
UM... POLLY?
YEAH?
IF YOU LIKE MY MUSIC AND SUPER HEROES...
...CHECK OUT MY BOOTH SATURDAY. I REALLY THINK IT'LL BLOW YOU AWAY.
OH, I AM SO IN.

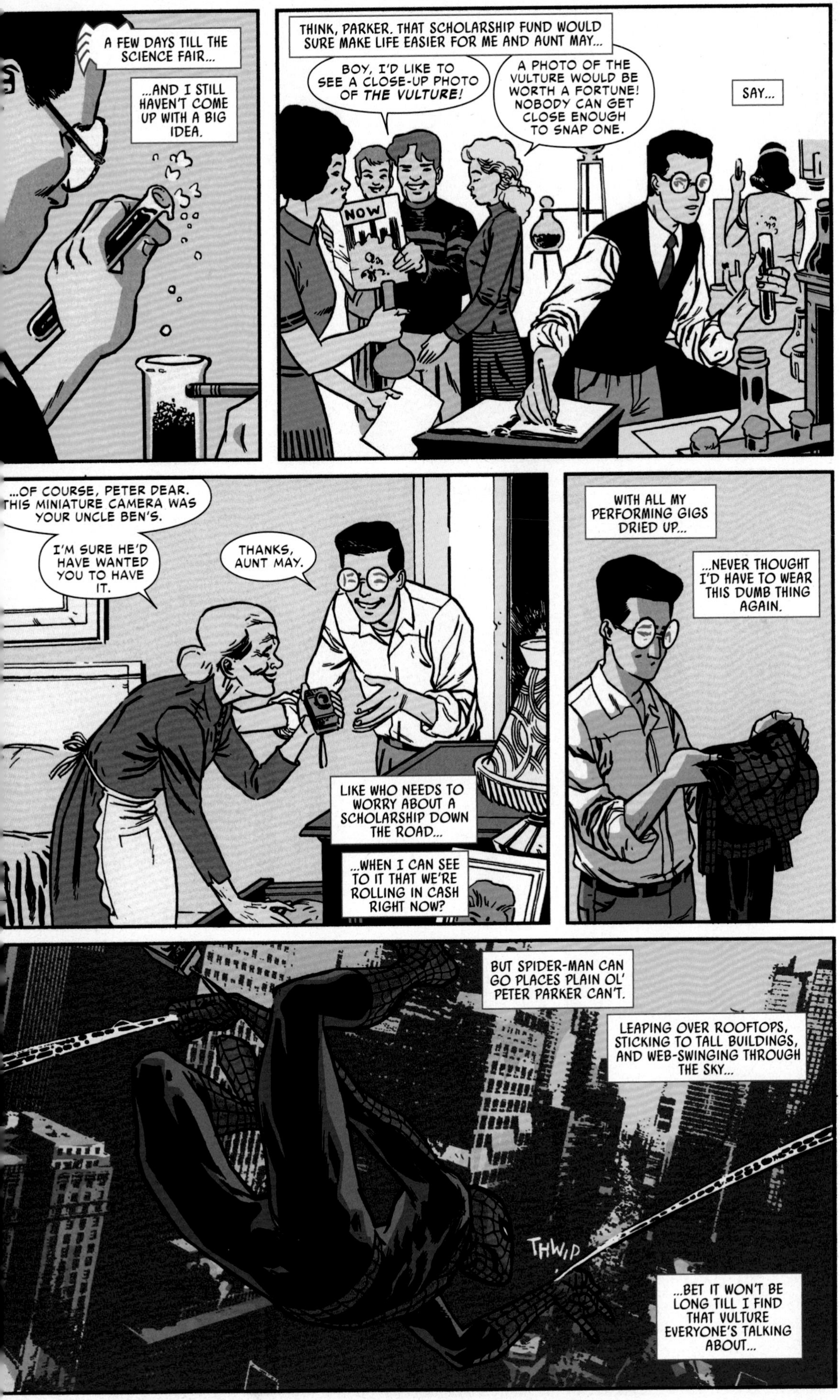
A FEW DAYS TILL THE SCIENCE FAIR...
...AND I STILL HAVEN'T COME UP WITH A BIG IDEA.
THINK, PARKER. THAT SCHOLARSHIP FUND WOULD SURE MAKE LIFE EASIER FOR ME AND AUNT MAY...
BOY, I'D LIKE TO SEE A CLOSE-UP PHOTO OF *THE VULTURE!*
A PHOTO OF THE VULTURE WOULD BE WORTH A FORTUNE! NOBODY CAN GET CLOSE ENOUGH TO SNAP ONE.
SAY...
NOW
...OF COURSE, PETER DEAR. THIS MINIATURE CAMERA WAS YOUR UNCLE BEN'S.
I'M SURE HE'D HAVE WANTED YOU TO HAVE IT.
THANKS, AUNT MAY.
LIKE WHO NEEDS TO WORRY ABOUT A SCHOLARSHIP DOWN THE ROAD...
...WHEN I CAN SEE TO IT THAT WE'RE ROLLING IN CASH RIGHT NOW?
WITH ALL MY PERFORMING GIGS DRIED UP...
...NEVER THOUGHT I'D HAVE TO WEAR THIS DUMB THING AGAIN.
BUT SPIDER-MAN CAN GO PLACES PLAIN OL' PETER PARKER CAN'T.
LEAPING OVER ROOFTOPS, STICKING TO TALL BUILDINGS, AND WEB-SWINGING THROUGH THE SKY...
THWIP
...BET IT WON'T BE LONG TILL I FIND THAT VULTURE EVERYONE'S TALKING ABOUT...

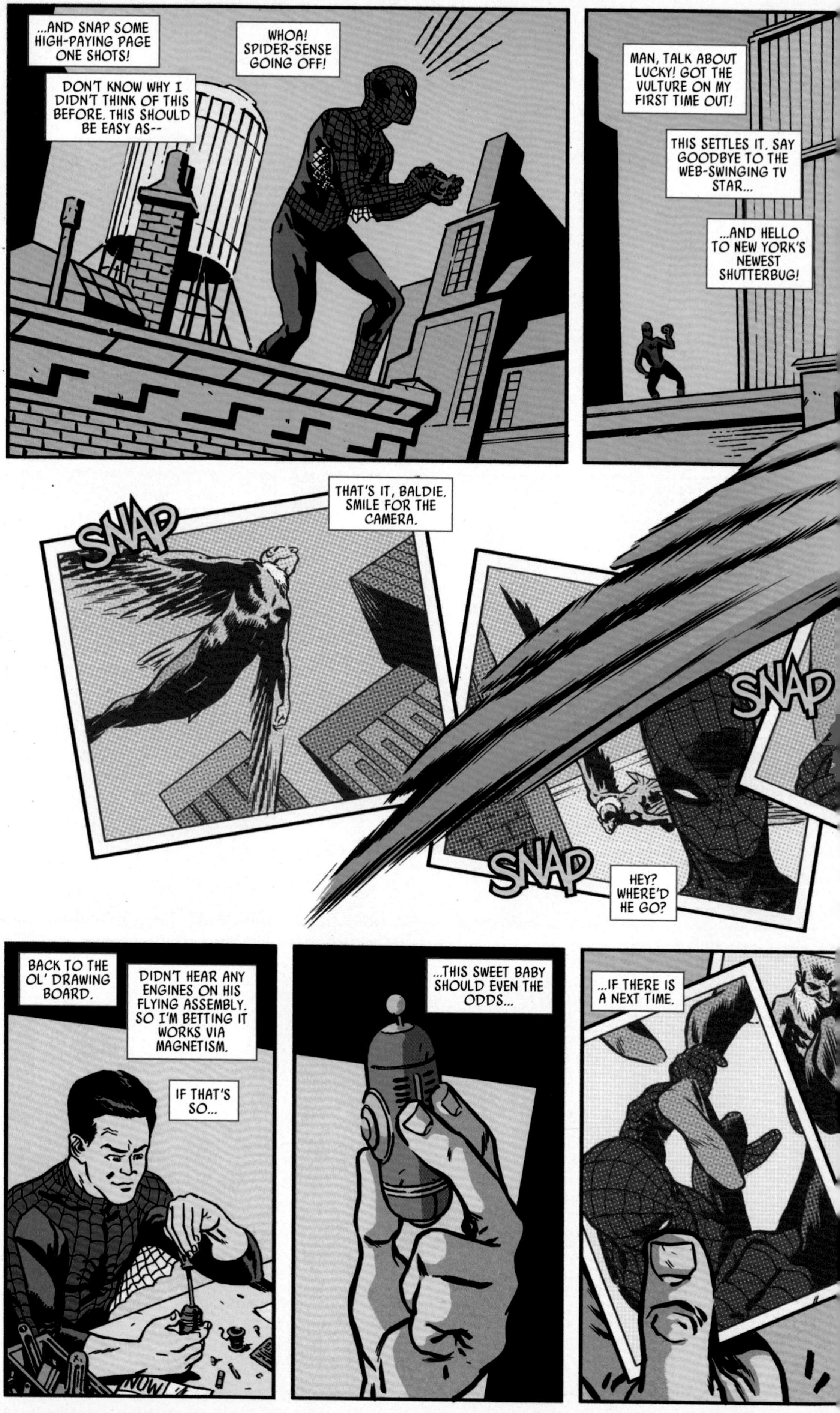
...AND SNAP SOME HIGH-PAYING PAGE ONE SHOTS!
DON'T KNOW WHY I DIDN'T THINK OF THIS BEFORE. THIS SHOULD BE EASY AS--
WHOA! SPIDER-SENSE GOING OFF!
MAN, TALK ABOUT LUCKY! GOT THE VULTURE ON MY FIRST TIME OUT!
THIS SETTLES IT. SAY GOODBYE TO THE WEB-SWINGING TV STAR...
...AND HELLO TO NEW YORK'S NEWEST SHUTTERBUG!
THAT'S IT, BALDIE. SMILE FOR THE CAMERA.
SNAP
SNAP
SNAP
HEY? WHERE'D HE GO?
BACK TO THE OL' DRAWING BOARD.
DIDN'T HEAR ANY ENGINES ON HIS FLYING ASSEMBLY, SO I'M BETTING IT WORKS VIA MAGNETISM.
IF THAT'S SO...
...THIS SWEET BABY SHOULD EVEN THE ODDS...
...IF THERE IS A NEXT TIME.

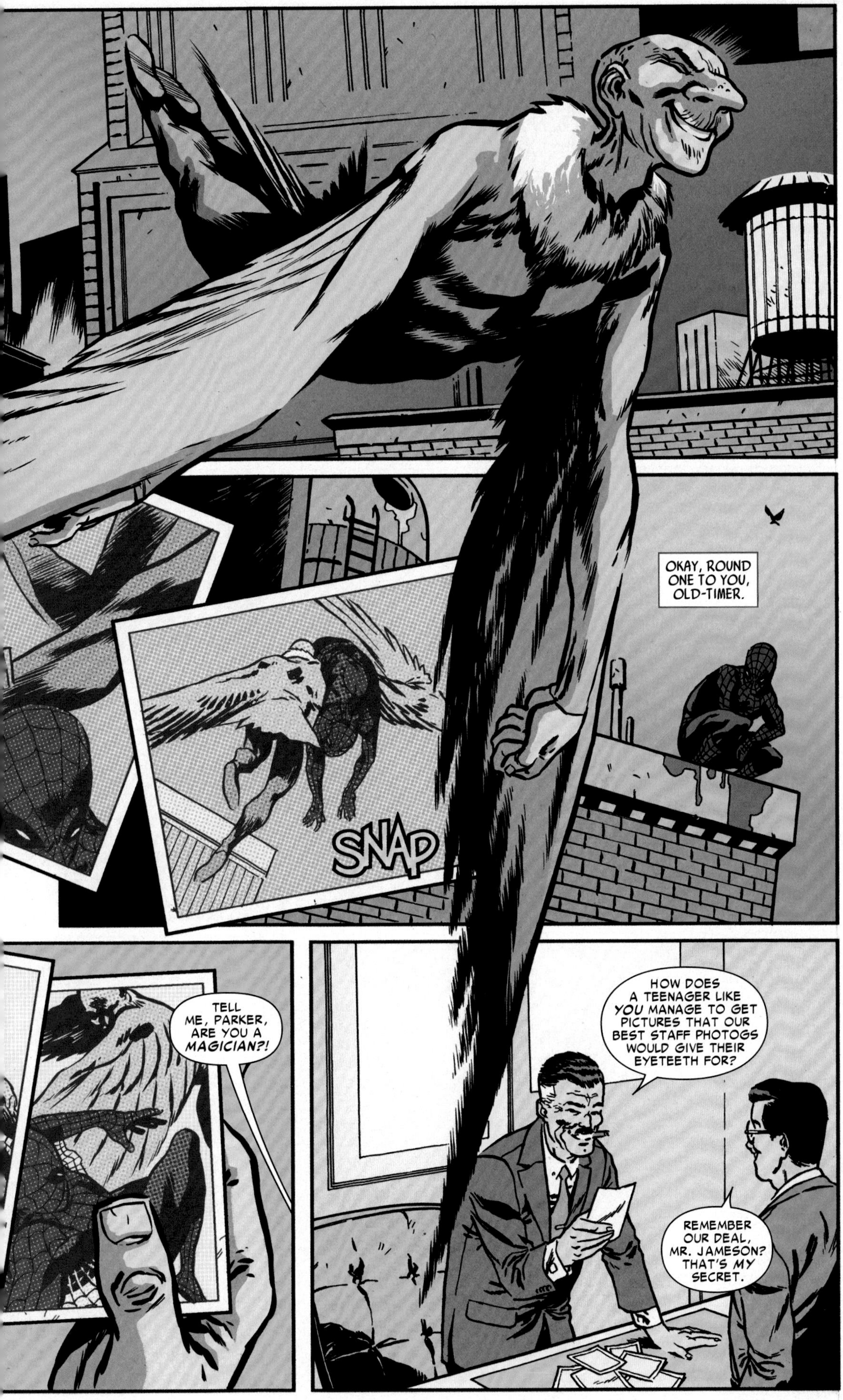
OKAY, ROUND ONE TO YOU, OLD-TIMER.
SNAP
TELL ME, PARKER, ARE YOU A *MAGICIAN?!*
HOW DOES A TEENAGER LIKE *YOU* MANAGE TO GET PICTURES THAT OUR BEST STAFF PHOTOGS WOULD GIVE THEIR EYETEETH FOR?
REMEMBER OUR DEAL, MR. JAMESON? THAT'S *MY* SECRET.

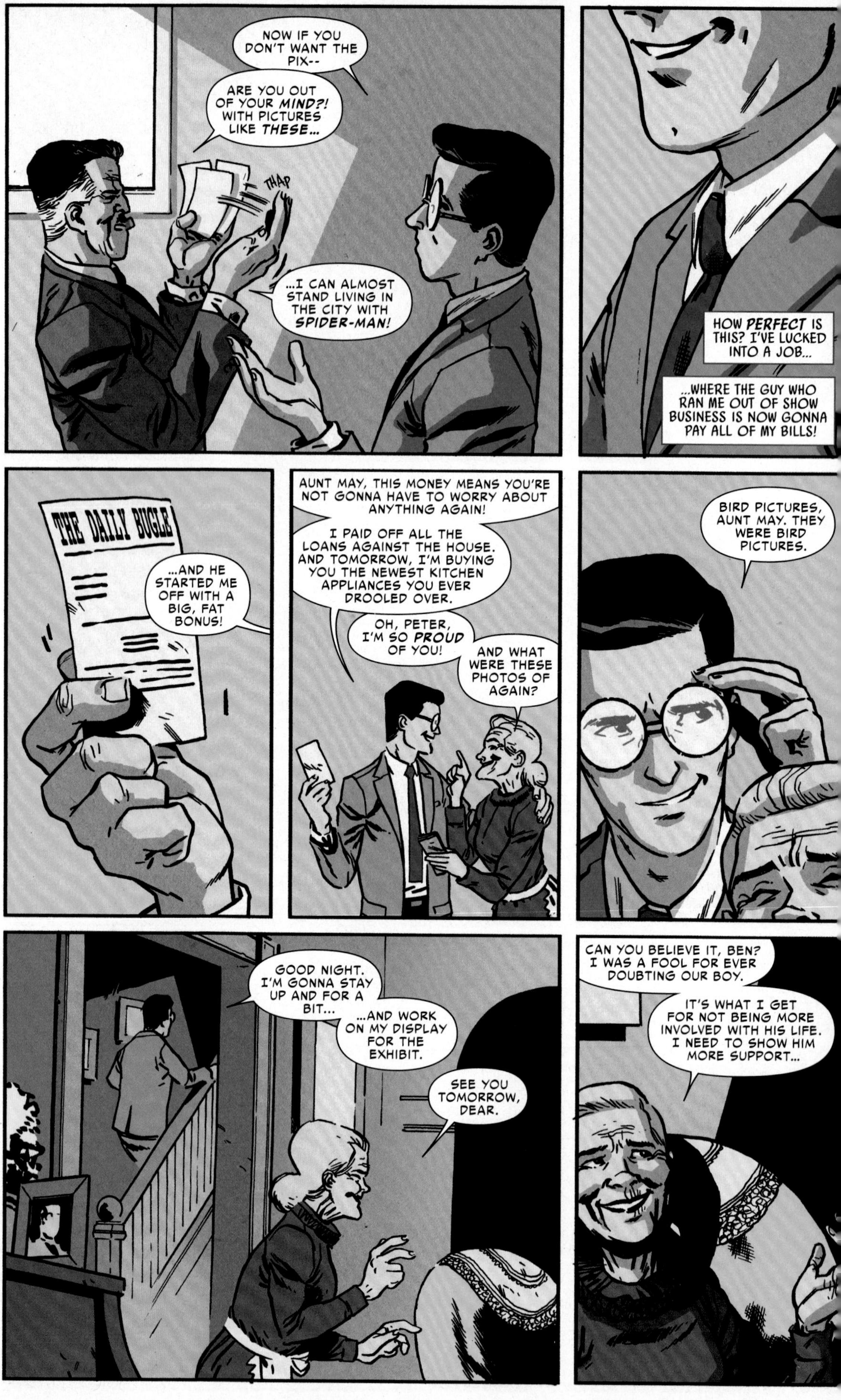
NOW IF YOU DON'T WANT THE PIX--
ARE YOU OUT OF YOUR *MIND?!* WITH PICTURES LIKE *THESE*...
THAP
...I CAN ALMOST STAND LIVING IN THE CITY WITH *SPIDER-MAN!*
HOW *PERFECT* IS THIS? I'VE LUCKED INTO A JOB...
...WHERE THE GUY WHO RAN ME OUT OF SHOW BUSINESS IS NOW GONNA PAY ALL OF MY BILLS!
THE DAILY BUGLE
...AND HE STARTED ME OFF WITH A BIG, FAT BONUS!
AUNT MAY, THIS MONEY MEANS YOU'RE NOT GONNA HAVE TO WORRY ABOUT ANYTHING AGAIN!
I PAID OFF ALL THE LOANS AGAINST THE HOUSE. AND TOMORROW, I'M BUYING YOU THE NEWEST KITCHEN APPLIANCES YOU EVER DROOLED OVER.
OH, PETER, I'M SO *PROUD* OF YOU!
AND WHAT WERE THESE PHOTOS OF AGAIN?
BIRD PICTURES, AUNT MAY. THEY WERE BIRD PICTURES.
GOOD NIGHT. I'M GONNA STAY UP AND FOR A BIT...
...AND WORK ON MY DISPLAY FOR THE EXHIBIT.
SEE YOU TOMORROW, DEAR.
CAN YOU BELIEVE IT, BEN? I WAS A FOOL FOR EVER DOUBTING OUR BOY.
IT'S WHAT I GET FOR NOT BEING MORE INVOLVED WITH HIS LIFE. I NEED TO SHOW HIM MORE SUPPORT...

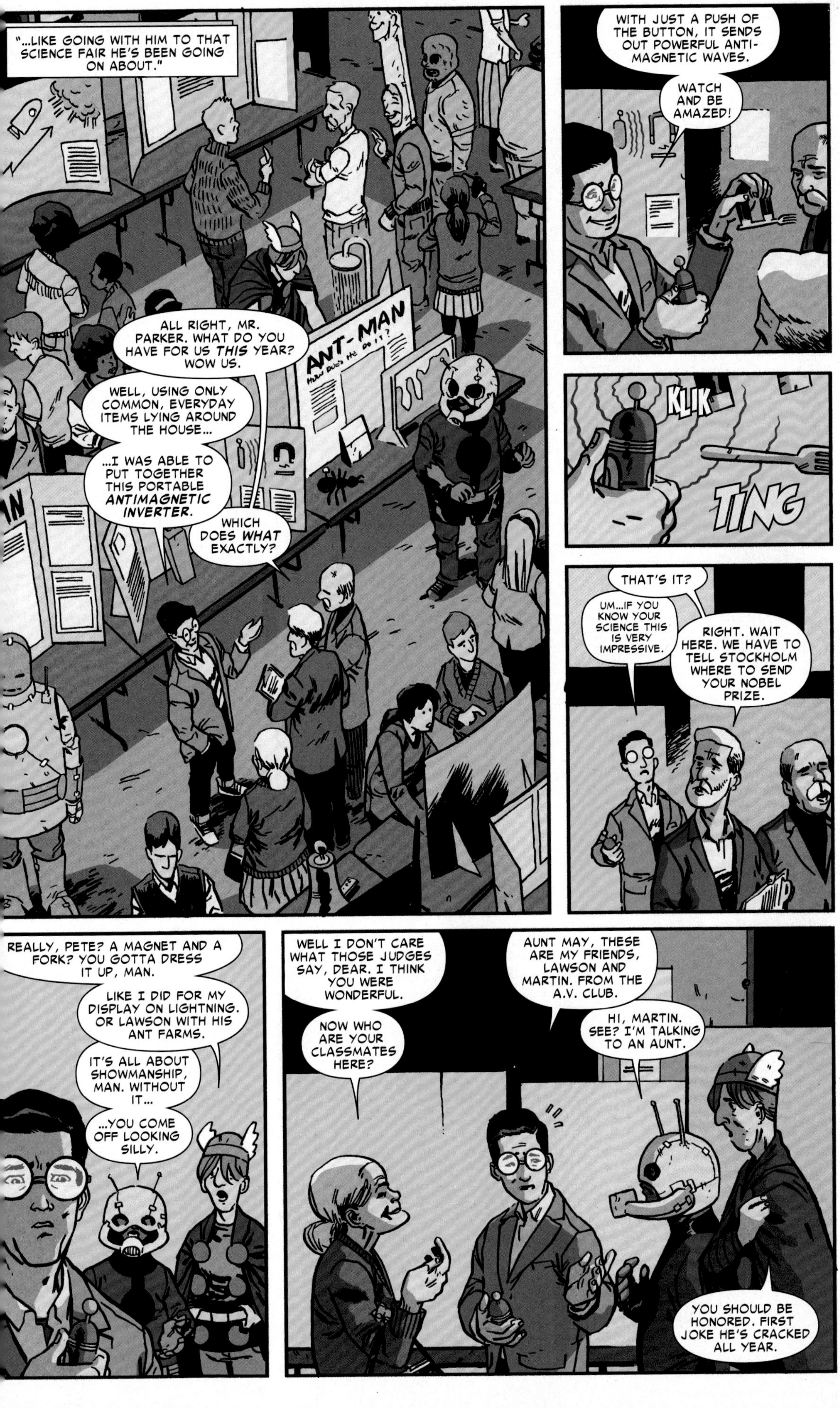
"...LIKE GOING WITH HIM TO THAT SCIENCE FAIR HE'S BEEN GOING ON ABOUT."
ANT-MAN
ALL RIGHT, MR. PARKER. WHAT DO YOU HAVE FOR US THIS YEAR? WOW US.
WELL, USING ONLY COMMON, EVERYDAY ITEMS LYING AROUND THE HOUSE...
...I WAS ABLE TO PUT TOGETHER THIS PORTABLE ANTIMAGNETIC INVERTER.
WHICH DOES WHAT EXACTLY?
WITH JUST A PUSH OF THE BUTTON, IT SENDS OUT POWERFUL ANTI-MAGNETIC WAVES.
WATCH AND BE AMAZED!
KLIK
TING
THAT'S IT?
UM...IF YOU KNOW YOUR SCIENCE THIS IS VERY IMPRESSIVE.
RIGHT. WAIT HERE. WE HAVE TO TELL STOCKHOLM WHERE TO SEND YOUR NOBEL PRIZE.
REALLY, PETE? A MAGNET AND A FORK? YOU GOTTA DRESS IT UP, MAN.
LIKE I DID FOR MY DISPLAY ON LIGHTNING. OR LAWSON WITH HIS ANT FARMS.
IT'S ALL ABOUT SHOWMANSHIP, MAN. WITHOUT IT...
...YOU COME OFF LOOKING SILLY.
WELL I DON'T CARE WHAT THOSE JUDGES SAY, DEAR. I THINK YOU WERE WONDERFUL.
NOW WHO ARE YOUR CLASSMATES HERE?
AUNT MAY, THESE ARE MY FRIENDS, LAWSON AND MARTIN. FROM THE A.V. CLUB.
HI, MARTIN. SEE? I'M TALKING TO AN AUNT.
YOU SHOULD BE HONORED. FIRST JOKE HE'S CRACKED ALL YEAR.

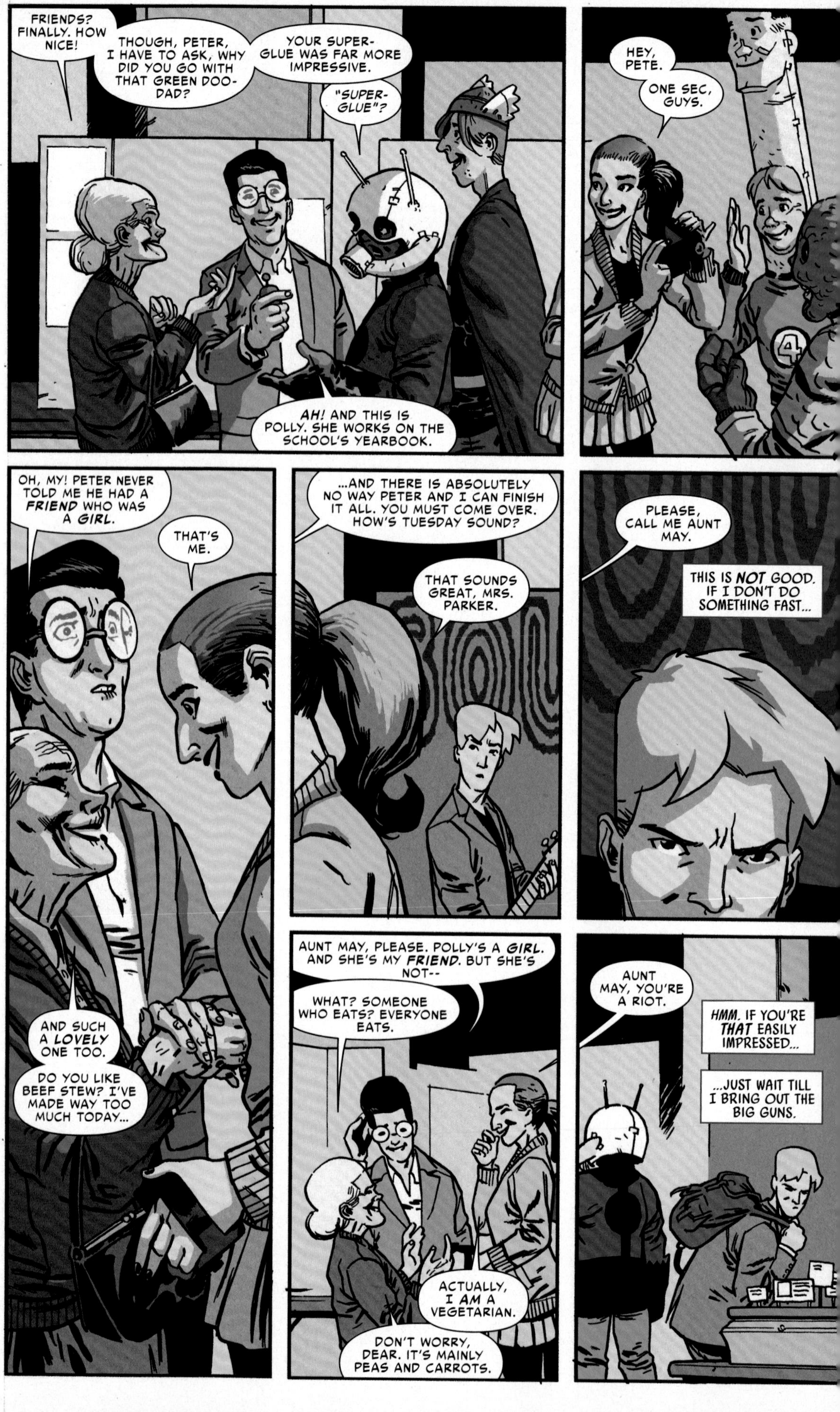
FRIENDS? FINALLY. HOW NICE!
THOUGH, PETER, I HAVE TO ASK, WHY DID YOU GO WITH THAT GREEN DOO-DAD?
YOUR SUPER-GLUE WAS FAR MORE IMPRESSIVE.
"SUPER-GLUE"?
AH! AND THIS IS POLLY. SHE WORKS ON THE SCHOOL'S YEARBOOK.
HEY, PETE.
ONE SEC, GUYS.
OH, MY! PETER NEVER TOLD ME HE HAD A FRIEND WHO WAS A GIRL.
THAT'S ME.
AND SUCH A LOVELY ONE TOO.
DO YOU LIKE BEEF STEW? I'VE MADE WAY TOO MUCH TODAY...
...AND THERE IS ABSOLUTELY NO WAY PETER AND I CAN FINISH IT ALL. YOU MUST COME OVER. HOW'S TUESDAY SOUND?
THAT SOUNDS GREAT, MRS. PARKER.
PLEASE, CALL ME AUNT MAY.
THIS IS NOT GOOD. IF I DON'T DO SOMETHING FAST...
AUNT MAY, PLEASE. POLLY'S A GIRL. AND SHE'S MY FRIEND. BUT SHE'S NOT--
WHAT? SOMEONE WHO EATS? EVERYONE EATS.
ACTUALLY, I AM A VEGETARIAN.
DON'T WORRY, DEAR. IT'S MAINLY PEAS AND CARROTS.
AUNT MAY, YOU'RE A RIOT.
HMM. IF YOU'RE THAT EASILY IMPRESSED...
...JUST WAIT TILL I BRING OUT THE BIG GUNS.

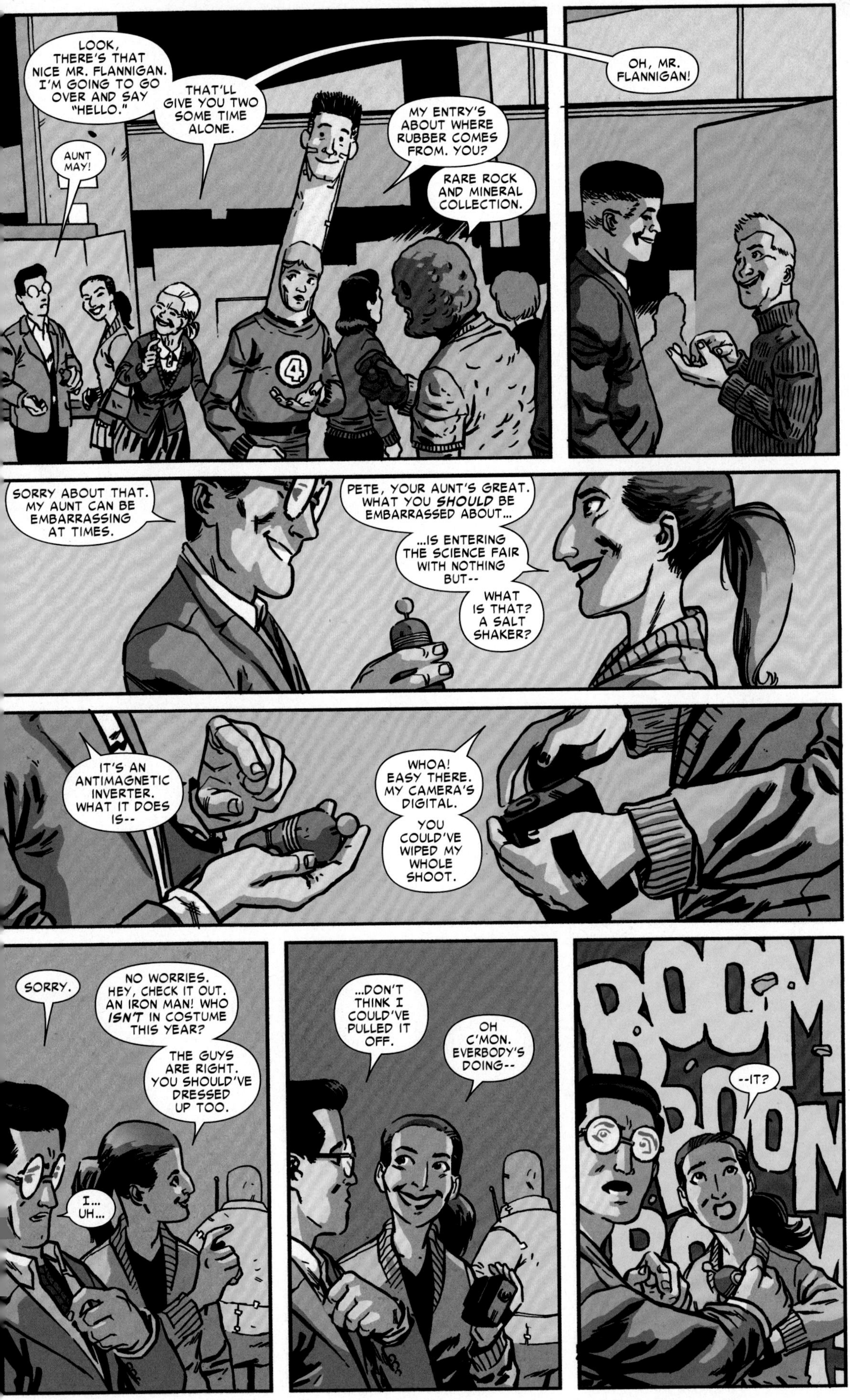
LOOK, THERE'S THAT NICE MR. FLANNIGAN. I'M GOING TO GO OVER AND SAY "HELLO."
THAT'LL GIVE YOU TWO SOME TIME ALONE.
AUNT MAY!
MY ENTRY'S ABOUT WHERE RUBBER COMES FROM. YOU?
RARE ROCK AND MINERAL COLLECTION.
OH, MR. FLANNIGAN!
SORRY ABOUT THAT. MY AUNT CAN BE EMBARRASSING AT TIMES.
PETE, YOUR AUNT'S GREAT. WHAT YOU SHOULD BE EMBARRASSED ABOUT...
...IS ENTERING THE SCIENCE FAIR WITH NOTHING BUT--
WHAT IS THAT? A SALT SHAKER?
IT'S AN ANTIMAGNETIC INVERTER. WHAT IT DOES IS--
WHOA! EASY THERE. MY CAMERA'S DIGITAL.
YOU COULD'VE WIPED MY WHOLE SHOOT.
SORRY.
NO WORRIES. HEY, CHECK IT OUT. AN IRON MAN! WHO ISN'T IN COSTUME THIS YEAR?
THE GUYS ARE RIGHT. YOU SHOULD'VE DRESSED UP TOO.
I... UH...
...DON'T THINK I COULD'VE PULLED IT OFF.
OH C'MON. EVERBODY'S DOING--
BOOM
BOOM
--IT?

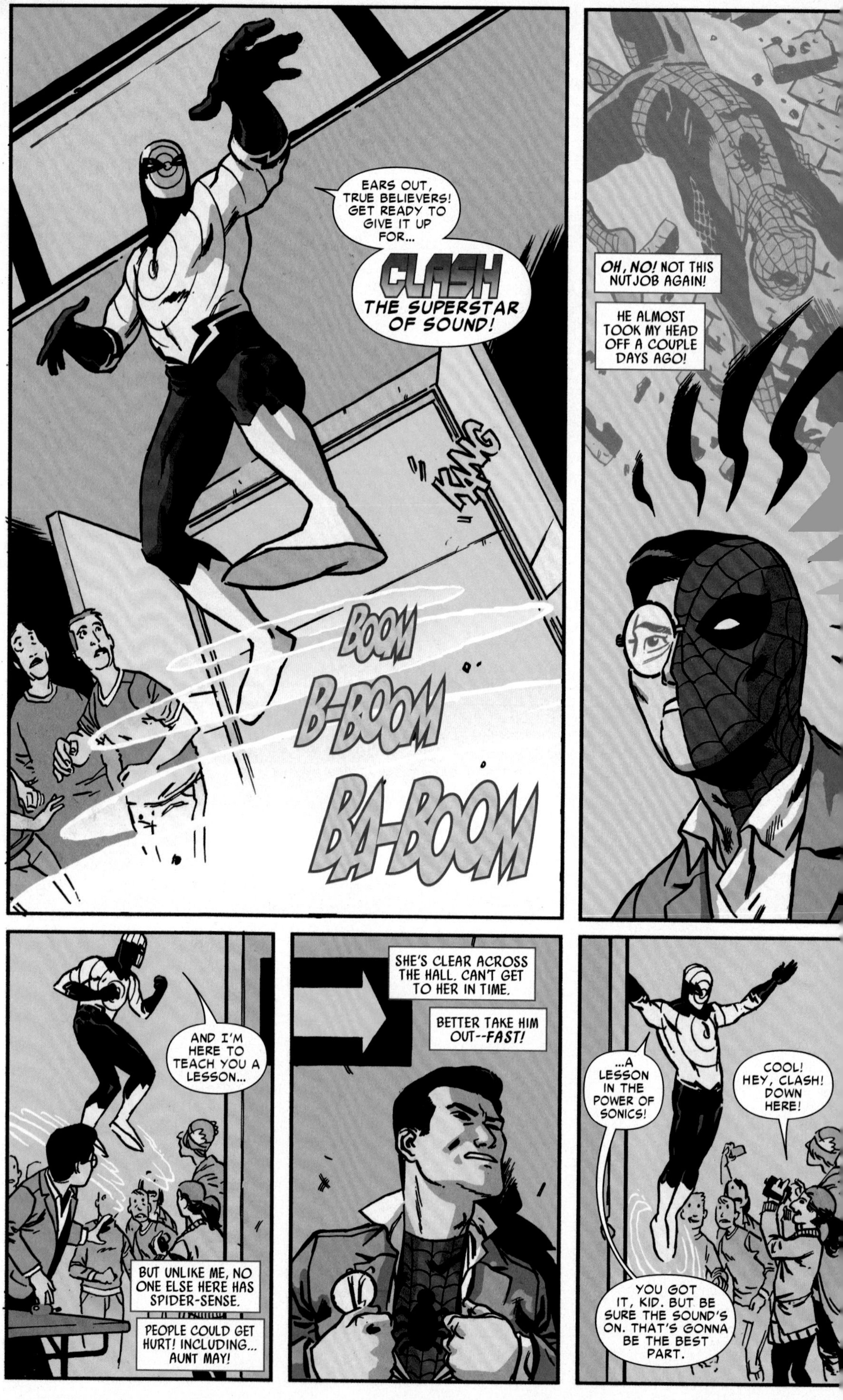
EARS OUT, TRUE BELIEVERS! GET READY TO GIVE IT UP FOR...
CLASH THE SUPERSTAR OF SOUND!
KLANG
BOOM
B-BOOM
BA-BOOM
OH, NO! NOT THIS NUTJOB AGAIN!
HE ALMOST TOOK MY HEAD OFF A COUPLE DAYS AGO!
AND I'M HERE TO TEACH YOU A LESSON...
BUT UNLIKE ME, NO ONE ELSE HERE HAS SPIDER-SENSE.
PEOPLE COULD GET HURT! INCLUDING... AUNT MAY!
SHE'S CLEAR ACROSS THE HALL. CAN'T GET TO HER IN TIME.
BETTER TAKE HIM OUT--FAST!
...A LESSON IN THE POWER OF SONICS!
COOL! HEY, CLASH! DOWN HERE!
YOU GOT IT, KID. BUT BE SURE THE SOUND'S ON. THAT'S GONNA BE THE BEST PART.

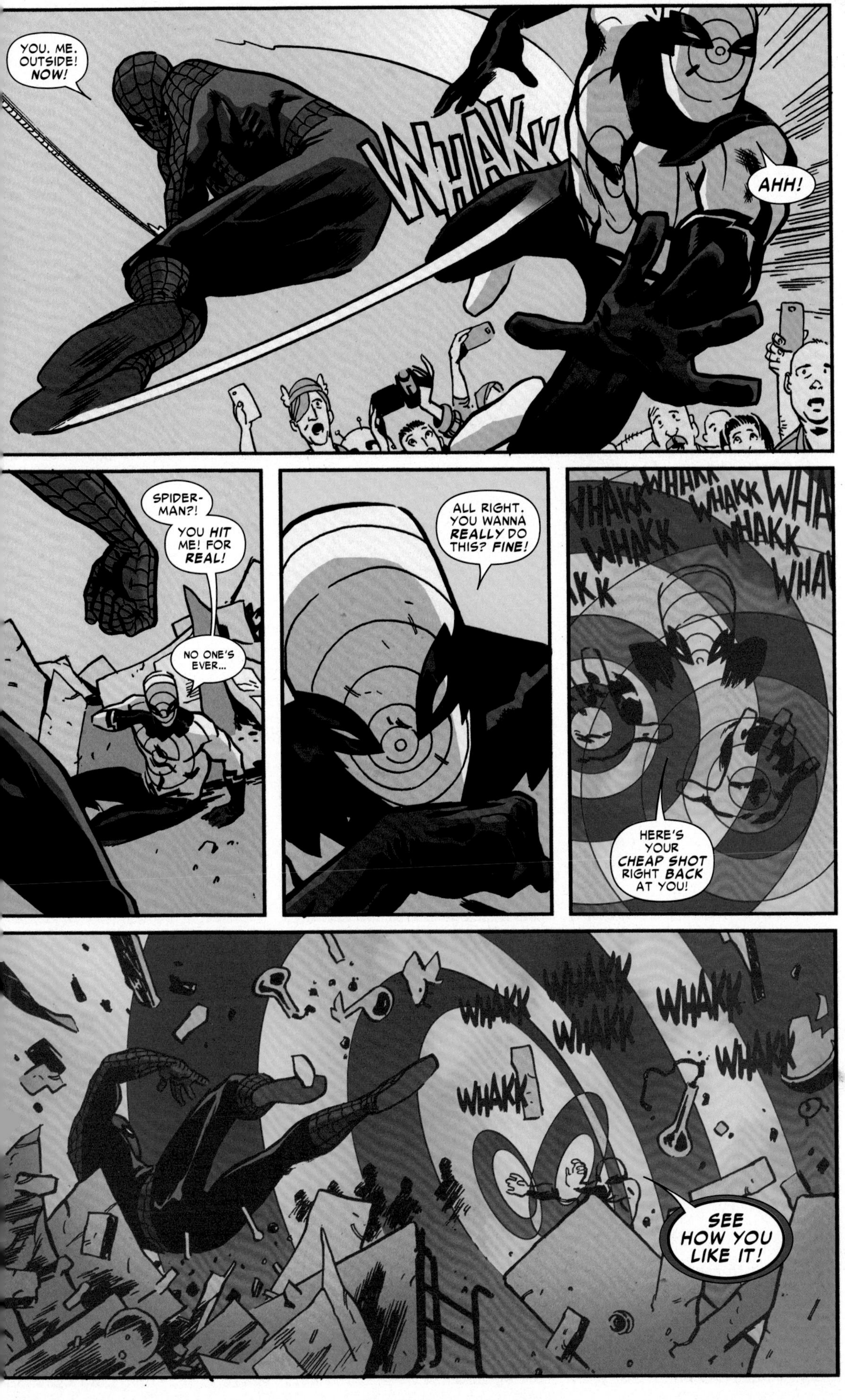
YOU. ME. OUTSIDE! NOW!
WHAKK
AHH!
SPIDER-MAN?!
YOU HIT ME! FOR REAL!
NO ONE'S EVER...
ALL RIGHT. YOU WANNA REALLY DO THIS? FINE!
WHAKK WHAKK WHAKK WHAKK
HERE'S YOUR CHEAP SHOT RIGHT BACK AT YOU!
WHAKK WHAKK WHAKK WHAKK WHAKK WHAKK
SEE HOW YOU LIKE IT!

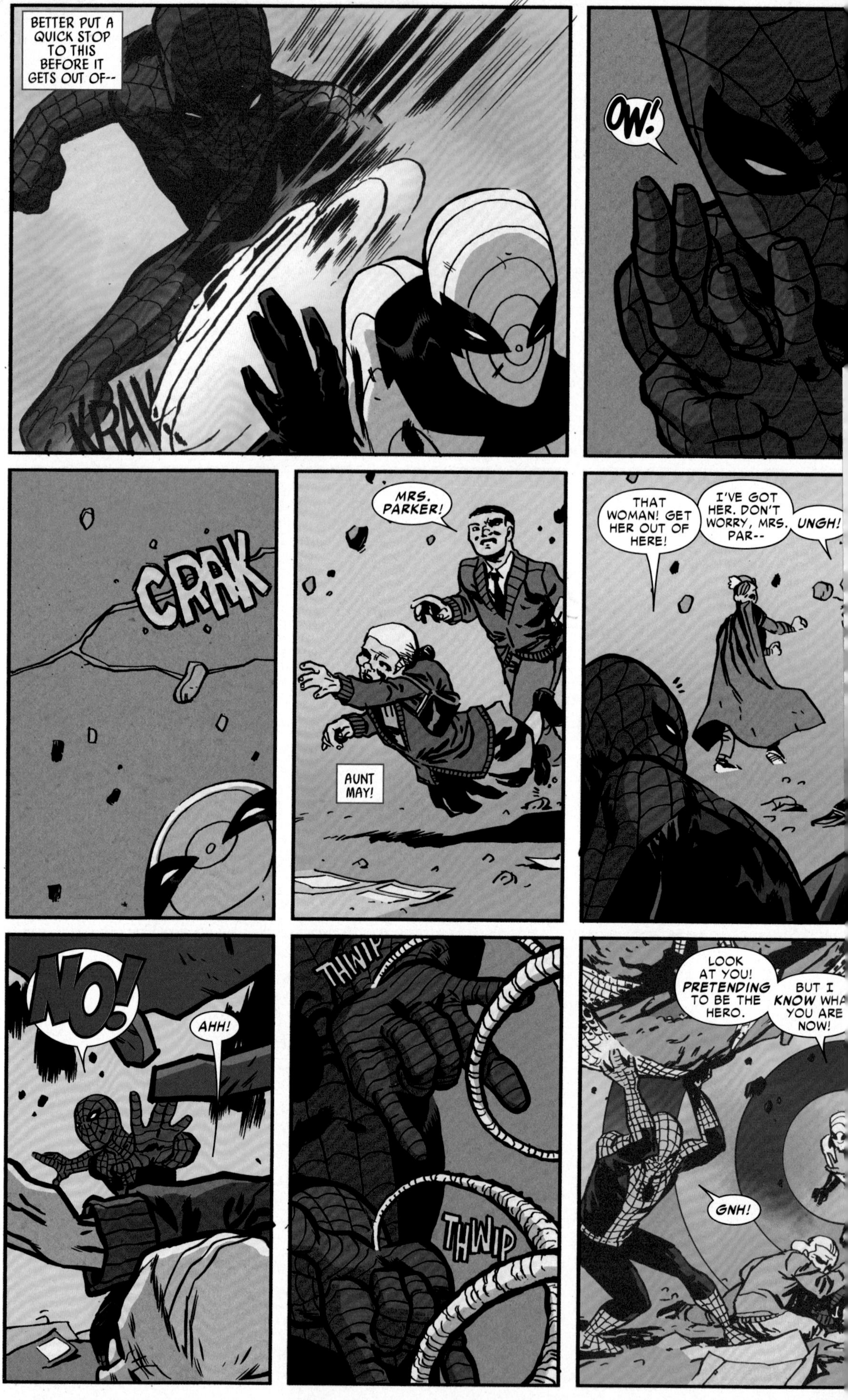
BETTER PUT A QUICK STOP TO THIS BEFORE IT GETS OUT OF--
KRAK
OW!
CRAK
MRS. PARKER!
AUNT MAY!
THAT WOMAN! GET HER OUT OF HERE!
I'VE GOT HER. DON'T WORRY, MRS. PAR--
UNGH!
NO!
AHH!
THWIP
THWIP
LOOK AT YOU! PRETENDING TO BE THE HERO.
GNH!

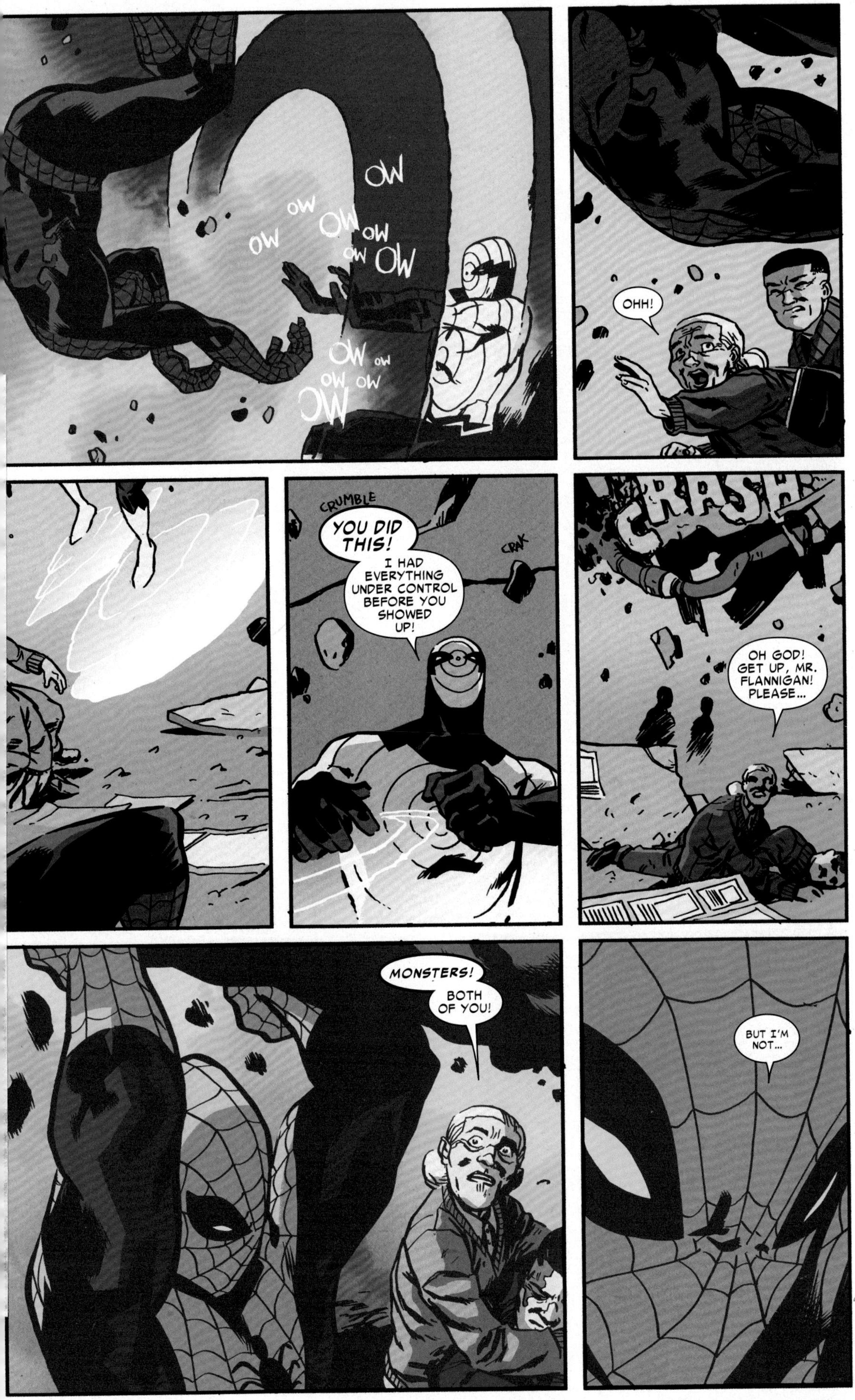
OW
OW
OW
OW
OW
OW
OW
OW
OW
OW
OW
OW
OHH!
CRUMBLE
YOU DID THIS!
I HAD EVERYTHING UNDER CONTROL BEFORE YOU SHOWED UP!
CRAK
CRASH
OH GOD! GET UP, MR. FLANNIGAN! PLEASE...
MONSTERS!
BOTH OF YOU!
BUT I'M NOT...

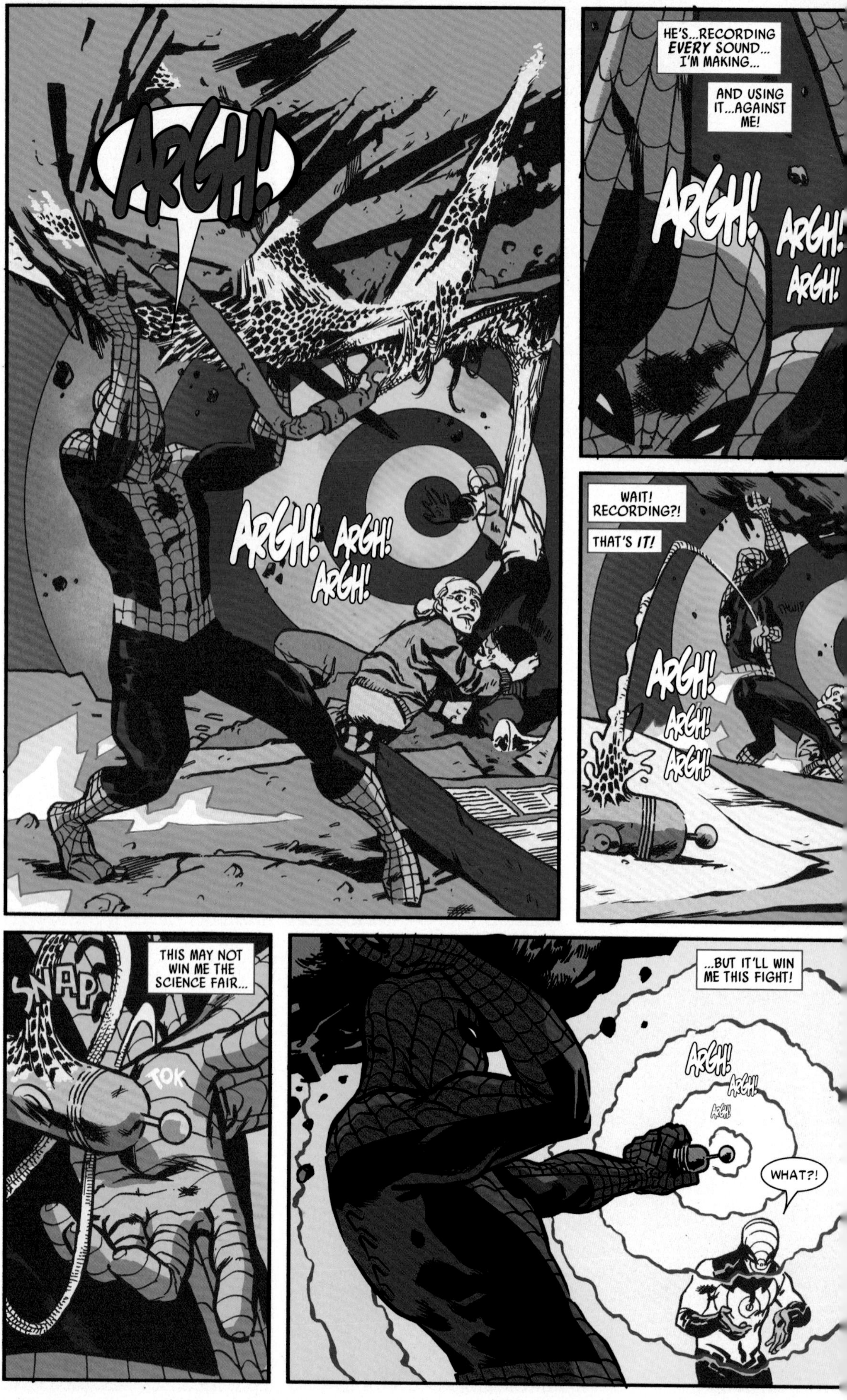
ARGH!
ARGH! ARGH! ARGH!
HE'S...RECORDING EVERY SOUND... I'M MAKING...
AND USING IT...AGAINST ME!
ARGH! ARGH! ARGH!
WAIT! RECORDING?!
THAT'S IT!
THWIP
ARGH! ARGH! ARGH!
THIS MAY NOT WIN ME THE SCIENCE FAIR...
SNAP
TOK
...BUT IT'LL WIN ME THIS FIGHT!
ARGH! ARGH! ARGH!
WHAT?!

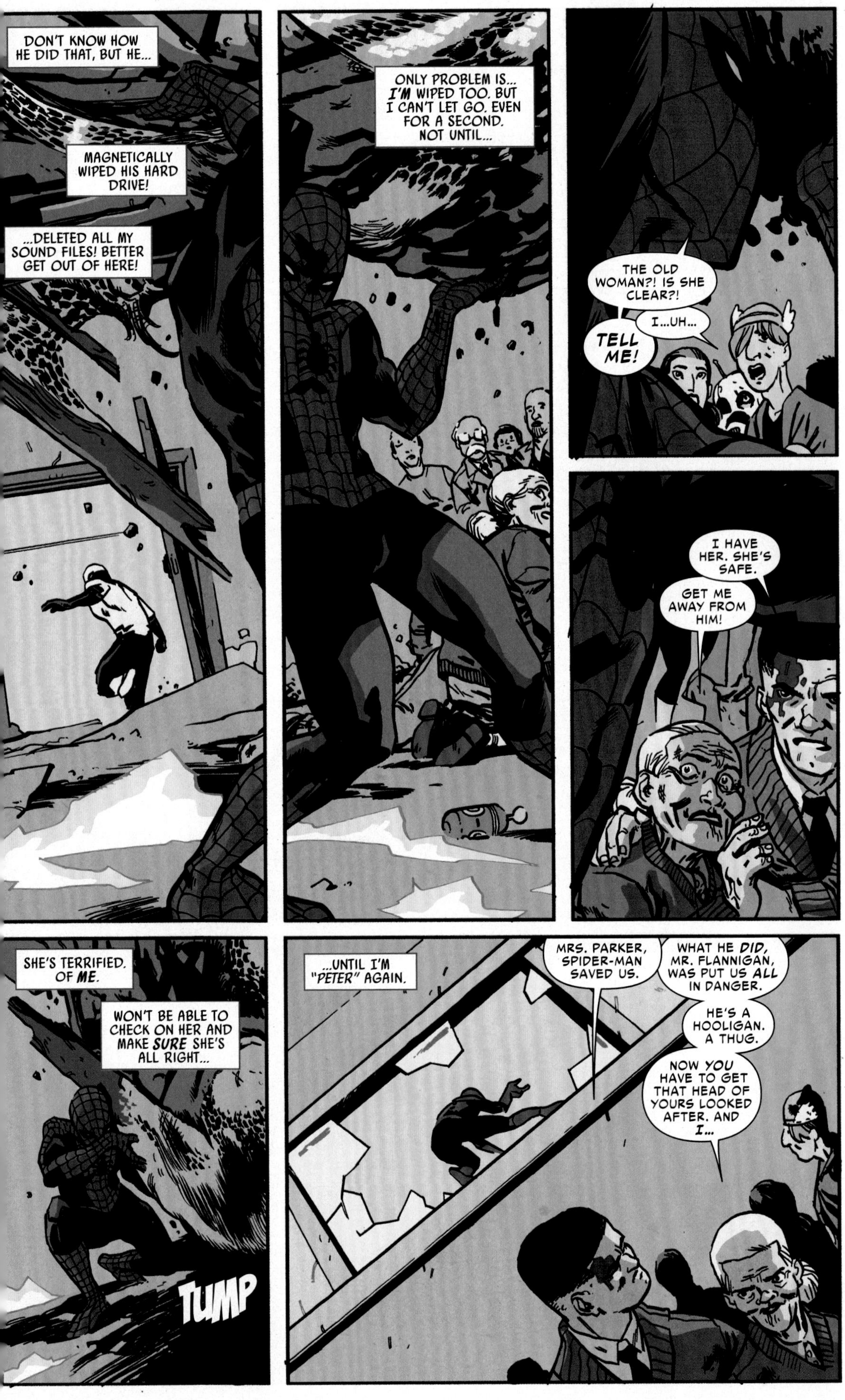

DON'T KNOW HOW HE DID THAT, BUT HE...
MAGNETICALLY WIPED HIS HARD DRIVE!
...DELETED ALL MY SOUND FILES! BETTER GET OUT OF HERE!
ONLY PROBLEM IS... *I'M* WIPED TOO. BUT I CAN'T LET GO. EVEN FOR A SECOND. NOT UNTIL...
THE OLD WOMAN?! IS SHE CLEAR?!
I...UH...
TELL ME!
I HAVE HER. SHE'S SAFE.
GET ME AWAY FROM HIM!
SHE'S TERRIFIED. OF *ME*.
WON'T BE ABLE TO CHECK ON HER AND MAKE *SURE* SHE'S ALL RIGHT...
TUMP
...UNTIL I'M "*PETER*" AGAIN.
MRS. PARKER, SPIDER-MAN SAVED US.
WHAT HE *DID*, MR. FLANNIGAN, WAS PUT US *ALL* IN DANGER.
HE'S A HOOLIGAN. A THUG.
NOW *YOU* HAVE TO GET THAT HEAD OF YOURS LOOKED AFTER. AND *I*...

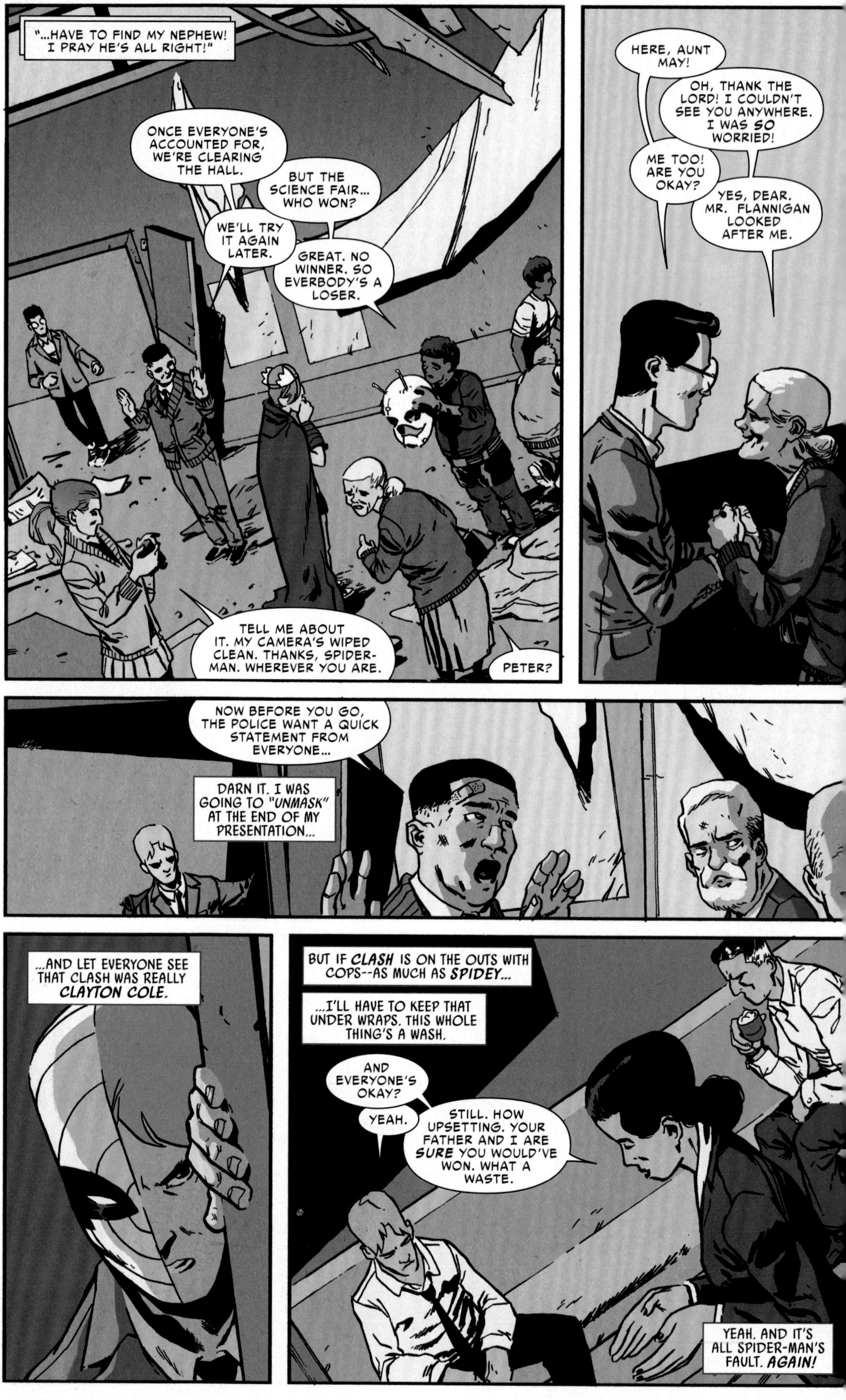
"...HAVE TO FIND MY NEPHEW! I PRAY HE'S ALL RIGHT!"
ONCE EVERYONE'S ACCOUNTED FOR, WE'RE CLEARING THE HALL.
BUT THE SCIENCE FAIR... WHO WON?
WE'LL TRY IT AGAIN LATER.
GREAT. NO WINNER. SO EVERBODY'S A LOSER.
TELL ME ABOUT IT. MY CAMERA'S WIPED CLEAN. THANKS, SPIDER-MAN. WHEREVER YOU ARE.
PETER?
HERE, AUNT MAY!
OH, THANK THE LORD! I COULDN'T SEE YOU ANYWHERE. I WAS SO WORRIED!
ME TOO! ARE YOU OKAY?
YES, DEAR. MR. FLANNIGAN LOOKED AFTER ME.
NOW BEFORE YOU GO, THE POLICE WANT A QUICK STATEMENT FROM EVERYONE...
DARN IT. I WAS GOING TO "UNMASK" AT THE END OF MY PRESENTATION...
...AND LET EVERYONE SEE THAT CLASH WAS REALLY CLAYTON COLE.
BUT IF CLASH IS ON THE OUTS WITH COPS--AS MUCH AS SPIDEY...
...I'LL HAVE TO KEEP THAT UNDER WRAPS. THIS WHOLE THING'S A WASH.
AND EVERYONE'S OKAY?
YEAH.
STILL. HOW UPSETTING. YOUR FATHER AND I ARE SURE YOU WOULD'VE WON. WHAT A WASTE.
YEAH. AND IT'S ALL SPIDER-MAN'S FAULT. AGAIN!

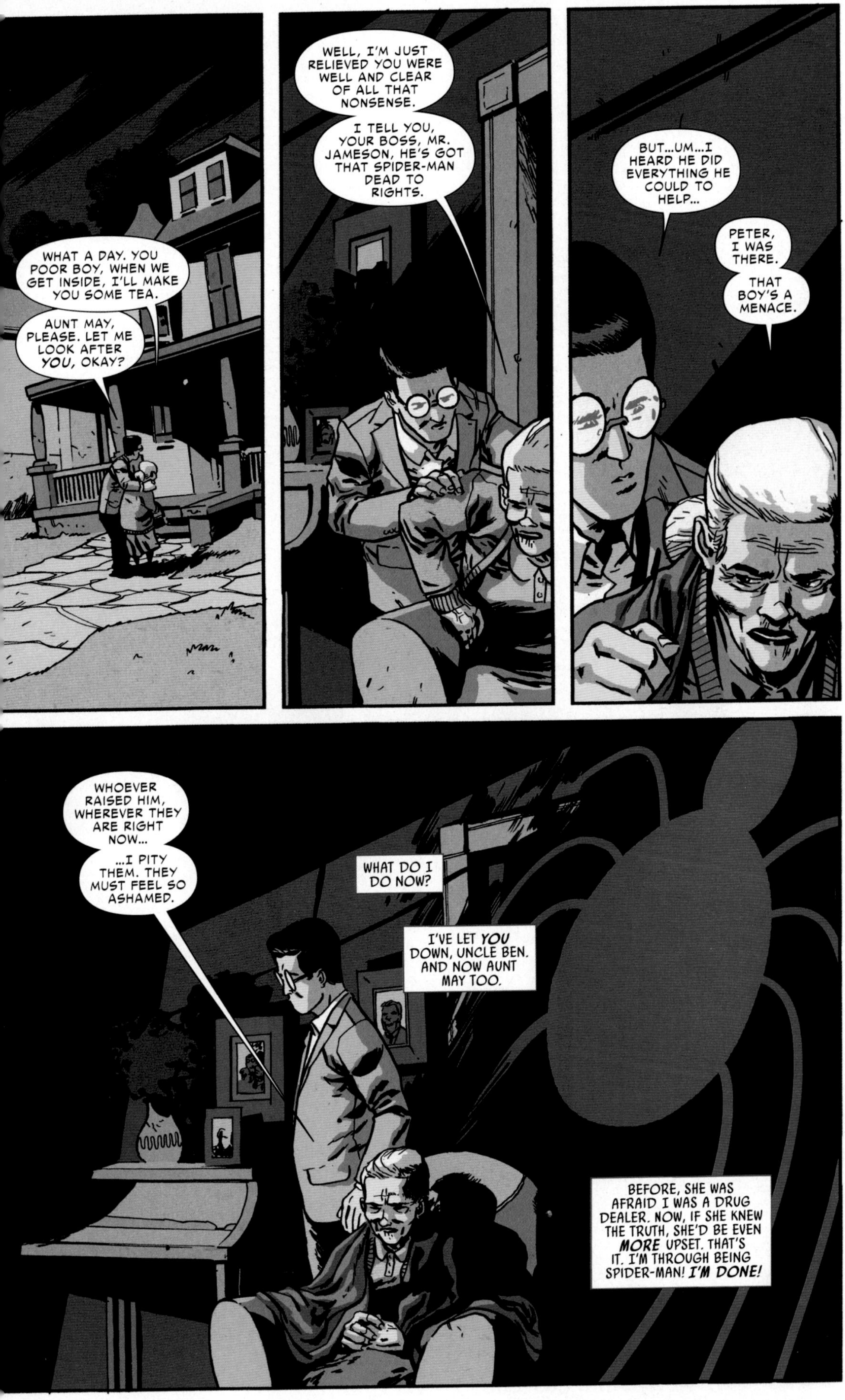

WHAT A DAY. YOU POOR BOY, WHEN WE GET INSIDE, I'LL MAKE YOU SOME TEA.
AUNT MAY, PLEASE. LET ME LOOK AFTER *YOU*, OKAY?
WELL, I'M JUST RELIEVED YOU WERE WELL AND CLEAR OF ALL THAT NONSENSE.
I TELL YOU, YOUR BOSS, MR. JAMESON, HE'S GOT THAT SPIDER-MAN DEAD TO RIGHTS.
BUT...UM...I HEARD HE DID EVERYTHING HE COULD TO HELP...
PETER, I WAS THERE.
THAT BOY'S A MENACE.
WHOEVER RAISED HIM, WHEREVER THEY ARE RIGHT NOW...
...I PITY THEM. THEY MUST FEEL SO ASHAMED.
WHAT DO I DO NOW?
I'VE LET *YOU* DOWN, UNCLE BEN. AND NOW AUNT MAY TOO.
BEFORE, SHE WAS AFRAID I WAS A DRUG DEALER. NOW, IF SHE KNEW THE TRUTH, SHE'D BE EVEN *MORE* UPSET. THAT'S IT. I'M THROUGH BEING SPIDER-MAN! *I'M DONE!*

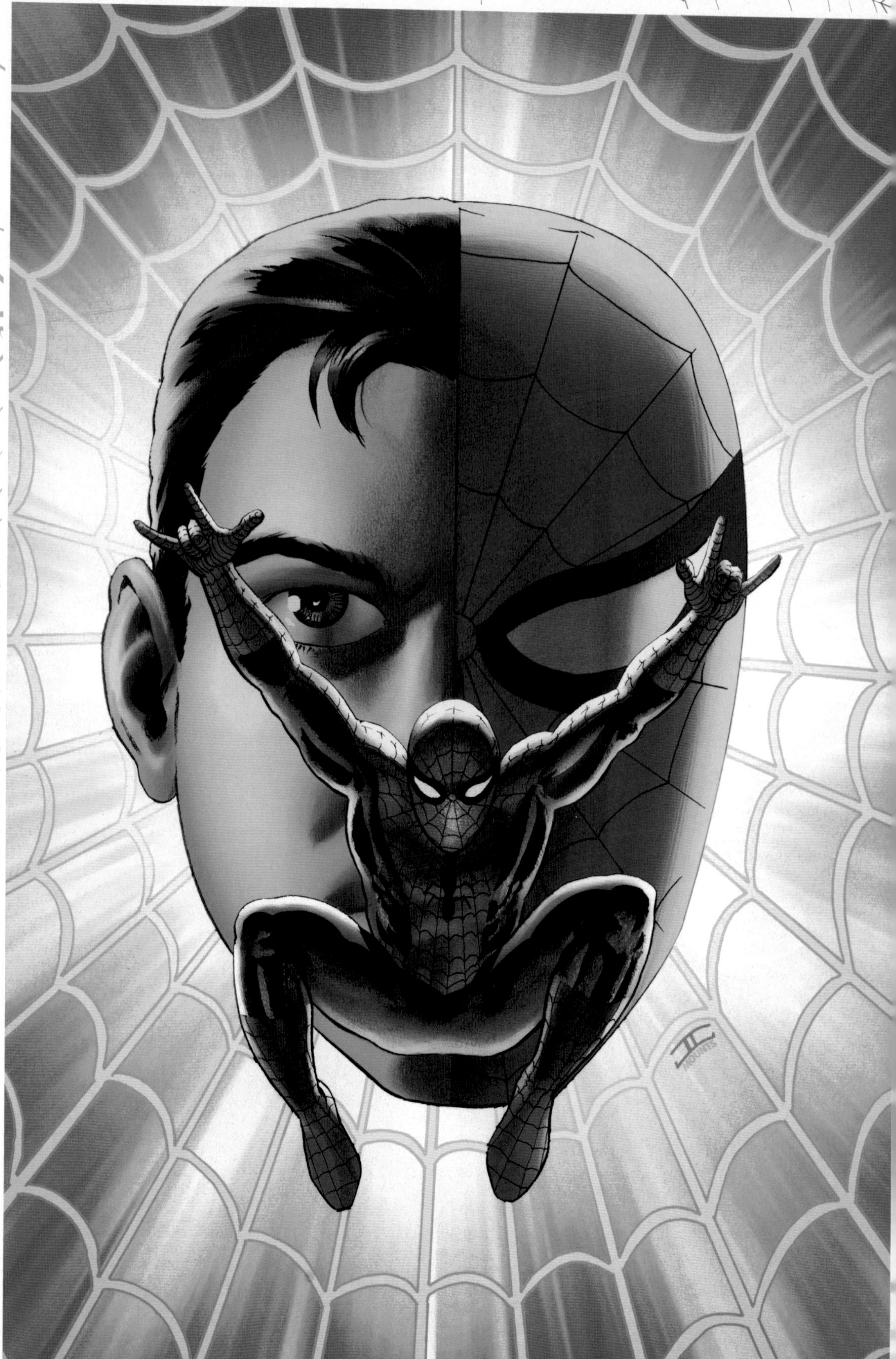

1.3 Variant by John Cassaday & Paul Mounts

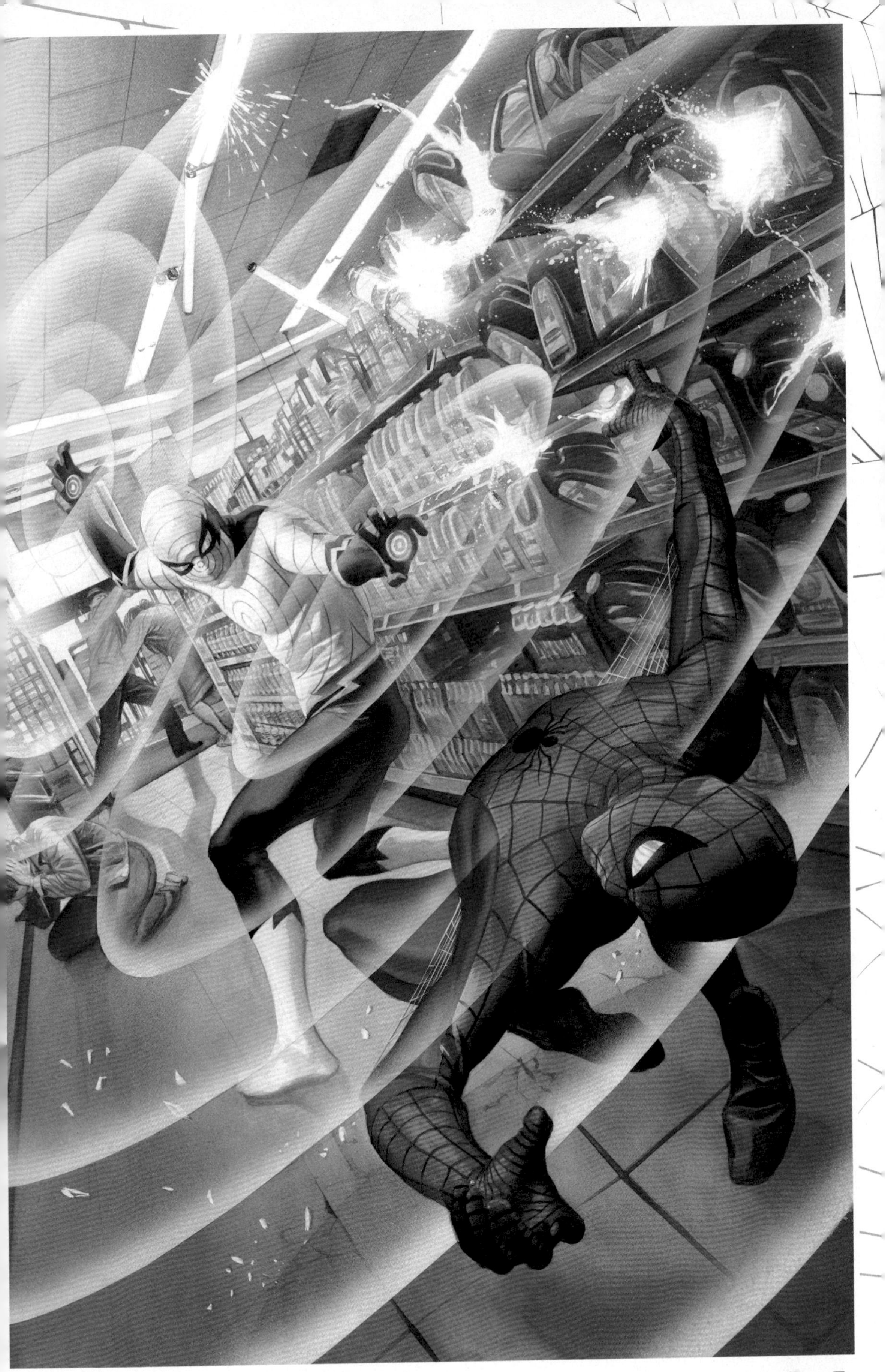

1.4

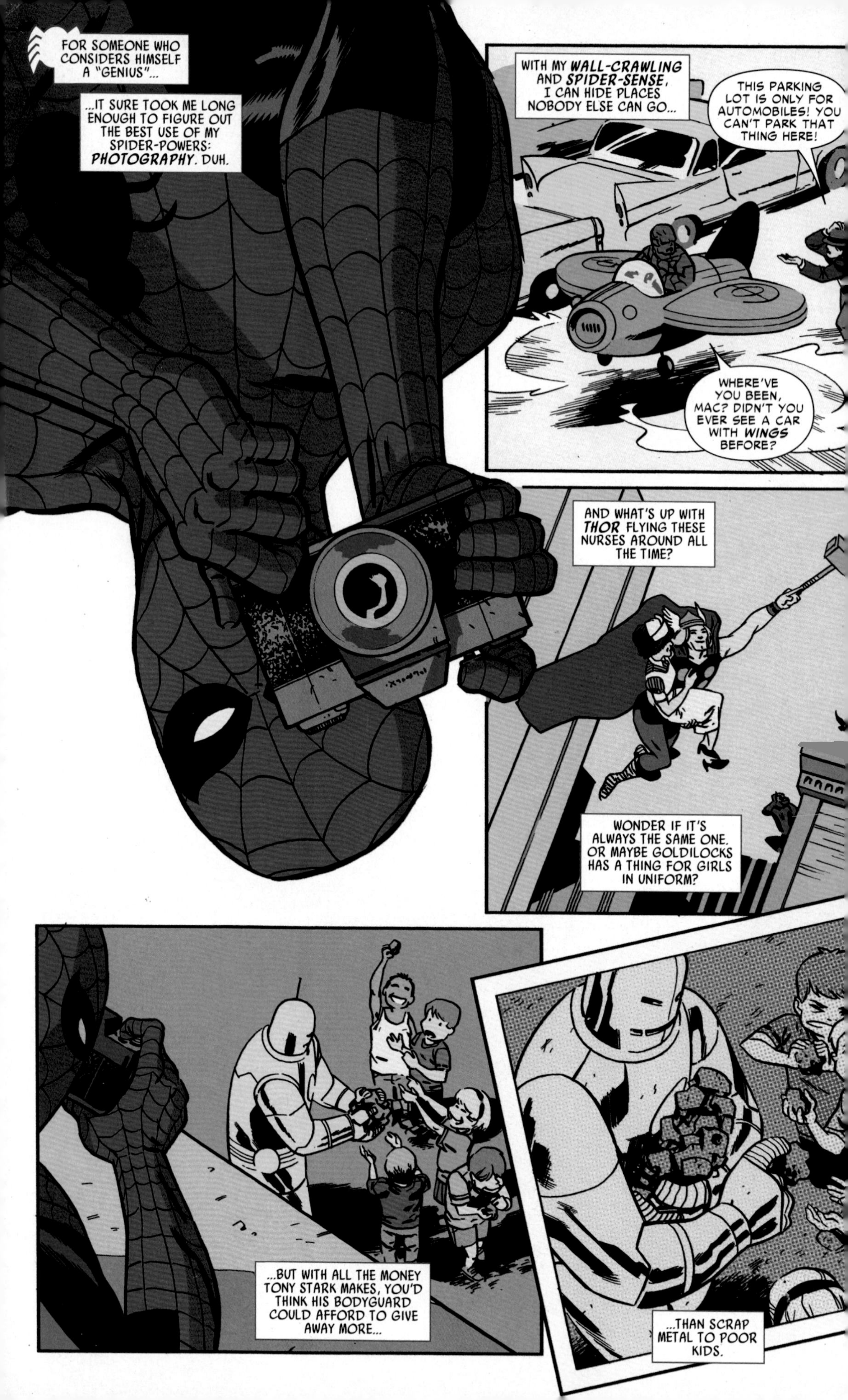

FOR SOMEONE WHO CONSIDERS HIMSELF A "GENIUS"...
...IT SURE TOOK ME LONG ENOUGH TO FIGURE OUT THE BEST USE OF MY SPIDER-POWERS: PHOTOGRAPHY. DUH.
WITH MY WALL-CRAWLING AND SPIDER-SENSE, I CAN HIDE PLACES NOBODY ELSE CAN GO...
THIS PARKING LOT IS ONLY FOR AUTOMOBILES! YOU CAN'T PARK THAT THING HERE!
WHERE'VE YOU BEEN, MAC? DIDN'T YOU EVER SEE A CAR WITH WINGS BEFORE?
AND WHAT'S UP WITH THOR FLYING THESE NURSES AROUND ALL THE TIME?
WONDER IF IT'S ALWAYS THE SAME ONE. OR MAYBE GOLDILOCKS HAS A THING FOR GIRLS IN UNIFORM?
...BUT WITH ALL THE MONEY TONY STARK MAKES, YOU'D THINK HIS BODYGUARD COULD AFFORD TO GIVE AWAY MORE...
...THAN SCRAP METAL TO POOR KIDS.

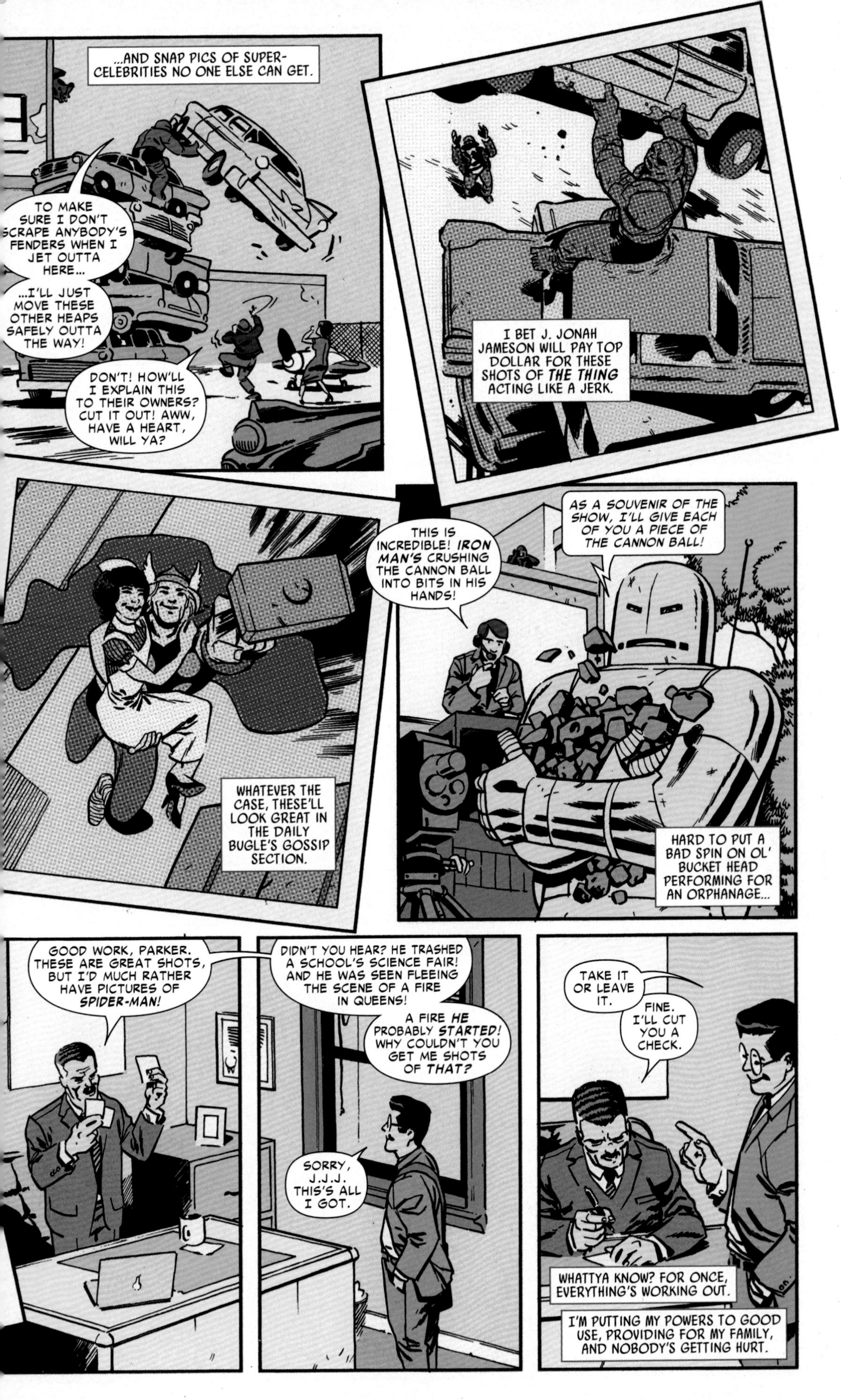
...AND SNAP PICS OF SUPER-CELEBRITIES NO ONE ELSE CAN GET.
TO MAKE SURE I DON'T SCRAPE ANYBODY'S FENDERS WHEN I JET OUTTA HERE...
...I'LL JUST MOVE THESE OTHER HEAPS SAFELY OUTTA THE WAY!
DON'T! HOW'LL I EXPLAIN THIS TO THEIR OWNERS? CUT IT OUT! AWW, HAVE A HEART, WILL YA?
I BET J. JONAH JAMESON WILL PAY TOP DOLLAR FOR THESE SHOTS OF ***THE THING*** ACTING LIKE A JERK.
WHATEVER THE CASE, THESE'LL LOOK GREAT IN THE DAILY BUGLE'S GOSSIP SECTION.
THIS IS INCREDIBLE! ***IRON MAN'S*** CRUSHING THE CANNON BALL INTO BITS IN HIS HANDS!
AS A SOUVENIR OF THE SHOW, I'LL GIVE EACH OF YOU A PIECE OF THE CANNON BALL!
HARD TO PUT A BAD SPIN ON OL' BUCKET HEAD PERFORMING FOR AN ORPHANAGE...
GOOD WORK, PARKER. THESE ARE GREAT SHOTS, BUT I'D MUCH RATHER HAVE PICTURES OF ***SPIDER-MAN!***
DIDN'T YOU HEAR? HE TRASHED A SCHOOL'S SCIENCE FAIR! AND HE WAS SEEN FLEEING THE SCENE OF A FIRE IN QUEENS!
A FIRE ***HE*** PROBABLY ***STARTED!*** WHY COULDN'T YOU GET ME SHOTS OF ***THAT?***
SORRY, J.J.J. THIS'S ALL I GOT.
TAKE IT OR LEAVE IT.
FINE. I'LL CUT YOU A CHECK.
WHATTYA KNOW? FOR ONCE, EVERYTHING'S WORKING OUT.
I'M PUTTING MY POWERS TO GOOD USE, PROVIDING FOR MY FAMILY, AND NOBODY'S GETTING HURT.

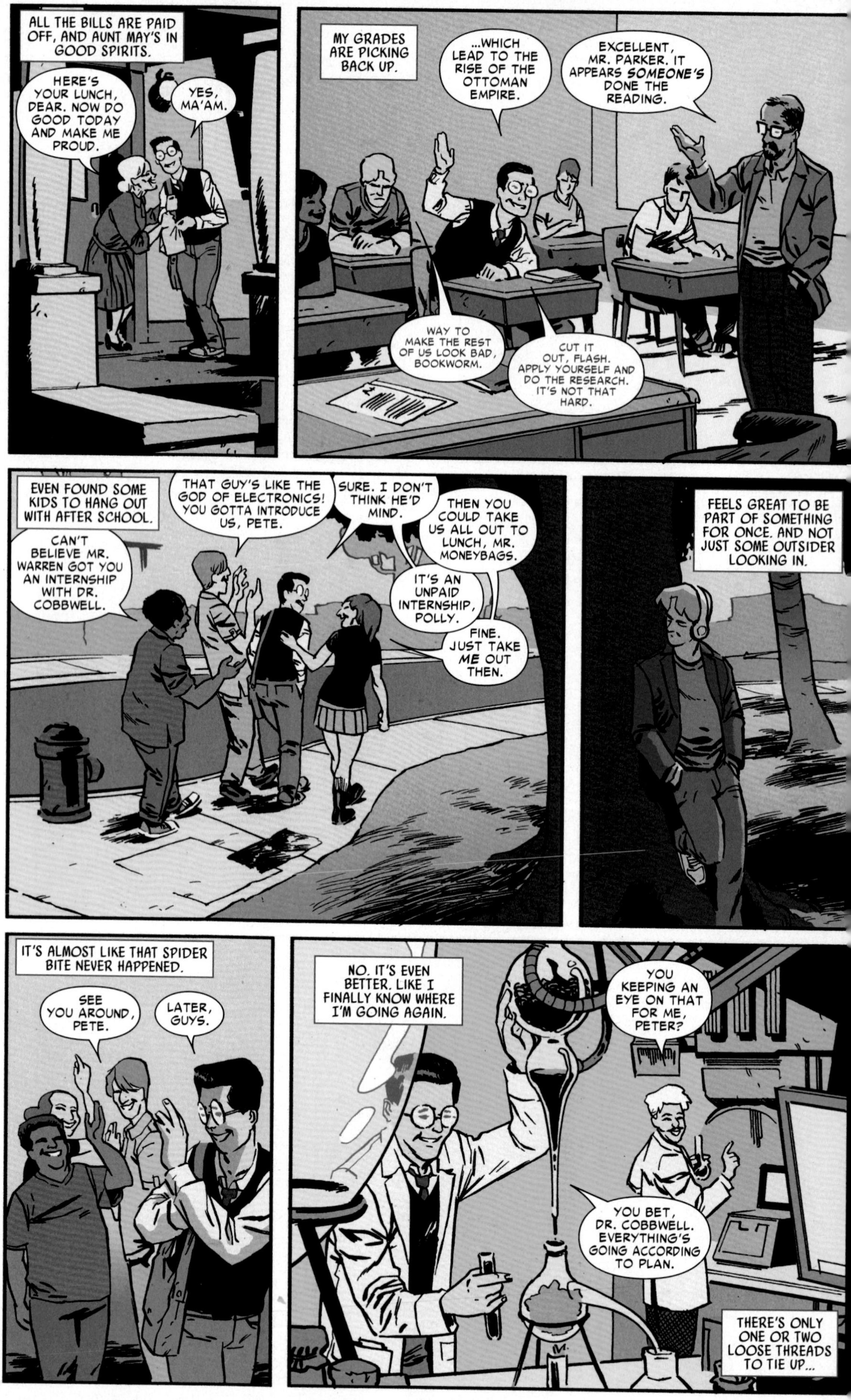
ALL THE BILLS ARE PAID OFF, AND AUNT MAY'S IN GOOD SPIRITS.
HERE'S YOUR LUNCH, DEAR. NOW DO GOOD TODAY AND MAKE ME PROUD.
YES, MA'AM.
MY GRADES ARE PICKING BACK UP.
...WHICH LEAD TO THE RISE OF THE OTTOMAN EMPIRE.
EXCELLENT, MR. PARKER. IT APPEARS SOMEONE'S DONE THE READING.
WAY TO MAKE THE REST OF US LOOK BAD, BOOKWORM.
CUT IT OUT, FLASH. APPLY YOURSELF AND DO THE RESEARCH. IT'S NOT THAT HARD.
EVEN FOUND SOME KIDS TO HANG OUT WITH AFTER SCHOOL.
CAN'T BELIEVE MR. WARREN GOT YOU AN INTERNSHIP WITH DR. COBBWELL.
THAT GUY'S LIKE THE GOD OF ELECTRONICS! YOU GOTTA INTRODUCE US, PETE.
SURE. I DON'T THINK HE'D MIND.
THEN YOU COULD TAKE US ALL OUT TO LUNCH, MR. MONEYBAGS.
IT'S AN UNPAID INTERNSHIP, POLLY.
FINE. JUST TAKE ME OUT THEN.
FEELS GREAT TO BE PART OF SOMETHING FOR ONCE. AND NOT JUST SOME OUTSIDER LOOKING IN.
IT'S ALMOST LIKE THAT SPIDER BITE NEVER HAPPENED.
SEE YOU AROUND, PETE.
LATER, GUYS.
NO. IT'S EVEN BETTER. LIKE I FINALLY KNOW WHERE I'M GOING AGAIN.
YOU KEEPING AN EYE ON THAT FOR ME, PETER?
YOU BET, DR. COBBWELL. EVERYTHING'S GOING ACCORDING TO PLAN.
THERE'S ONLY ONE OR TWO LOOSE THREADS TO TIE UP...

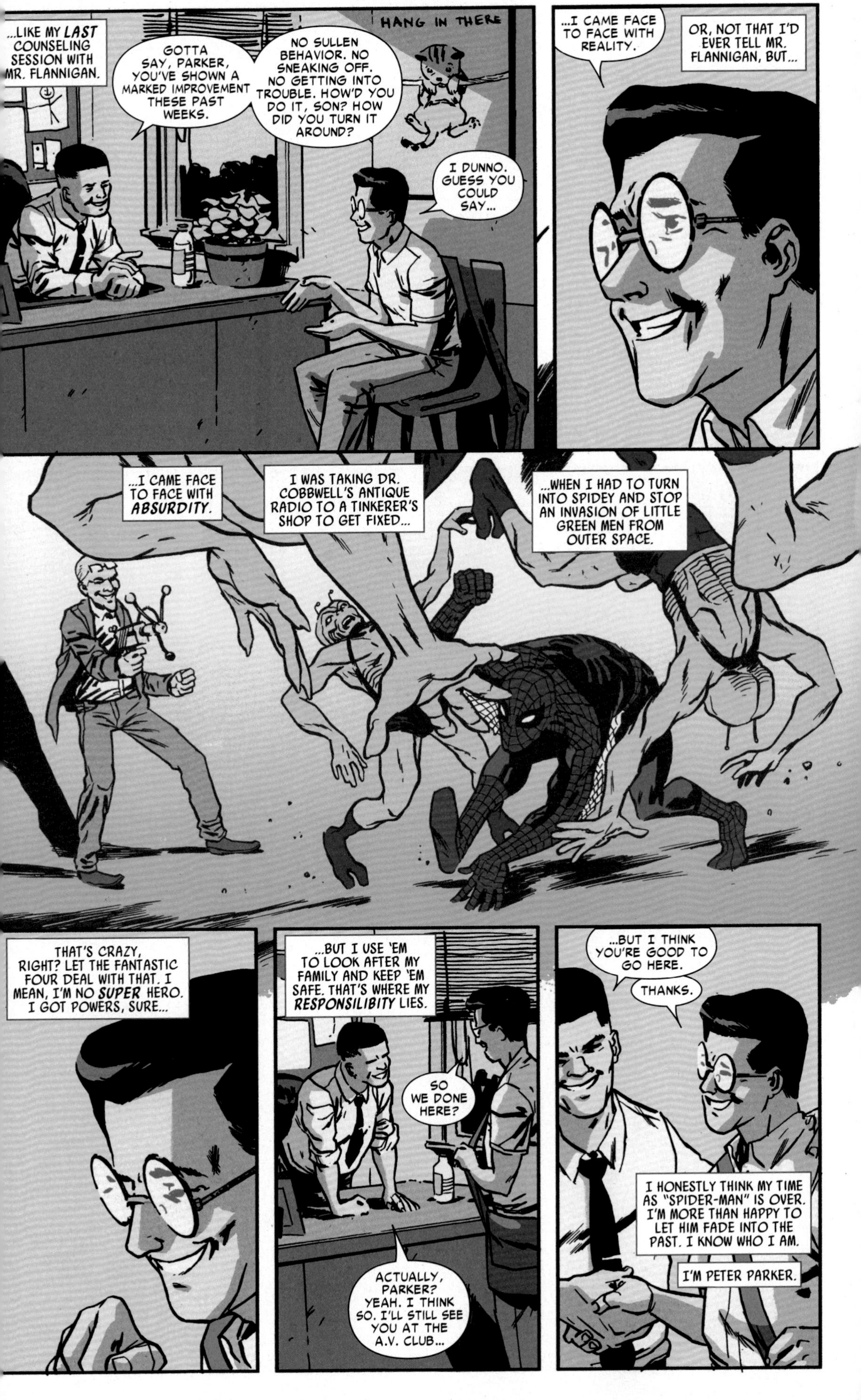
...LIKE MY LAST COUNSELING SESSION WITH MR. FLANNIGAN.
HANG IN THERE
GOTTA SAY, PARKER, YOU'VE SHOWN A MARKED IMPROVEMENT THESE PAST WEEKS.
NO SULLEN BEHAVIOR. NO SNEAKING OFF. NO GETTING INTO TROUBLE. HOW'D YOU DO IT, SON? HOW DID YOU TURN IT AROUND?
I DUNNO. GUESS YOU COULD SAY...
...I CAME FACE TO FACE WITH REALITY.
OR, NOT THAT I'D EVER TELL MR. FLANNIGAN, BUT...
...I CAME FACE TO FACE WITH ABSURDITY.
I WAS TAKING DR. COBBWELL'S ANTIQUE RADIO TO A TINKERER'S SHOP TO GET FIXED...
...WHEN I HAD TO TURN INTO SPIDEY AND STOP AN INVASION OF LITTLE GREEN MEN FROM OUTER SPACE.
THAT'S CRAZY, RIGHT? LET THE FANTASTIC FOUR DEAL WITH THAT. I MEAN, I'M NO SUPER HERO. I GOT POWERS, SURE...
...BUT I USE 'EM TO LOOK AFTER MY FAMILY AND KEEP 'EM SAFE. THAT'S WHERE MY RESPONSILIBITY LIES.
SO WE DONE HERE?
ACTUALLY, PARKER? YEAH. I THINK SO. I'LL STILL SEE YOU AT THE A.V. CLUB...
...BUT I THINK YOU'RE GOOD TO GO HERE.
THANKS.
I HONESTLY THINK MY TIME AS "SPIDER-MAN" IS OVER. I'M MORE THAN HAPPY TO LET HIM FADE INTO THE PAST. I KNOW WHO I AM.
I'M PETER PARKER.

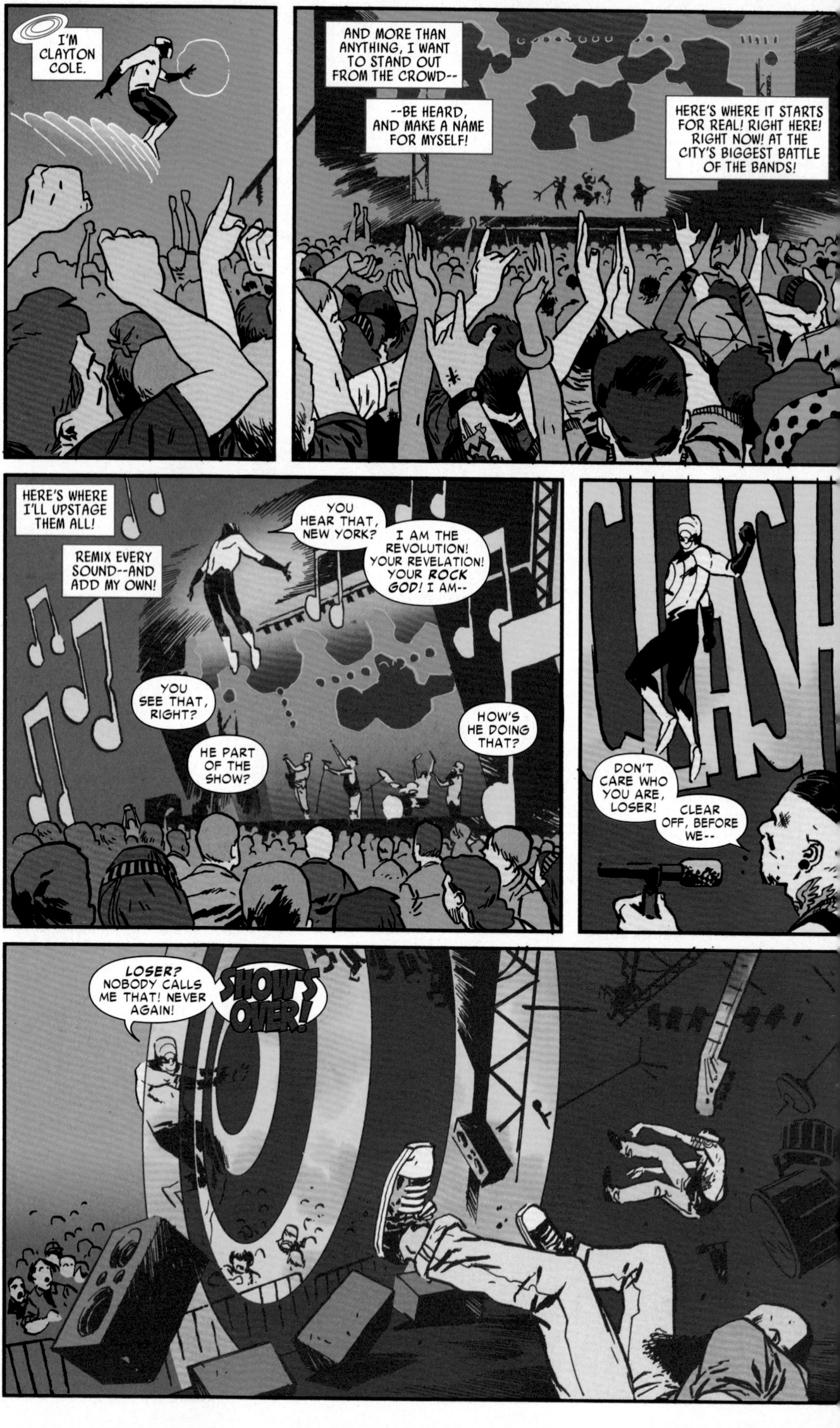

I'M CLAYTON COLE.
AND MORE THAN ANYTHING, I WANT TO STAND OUT FROM THE CROWD--
--BE HEARD, AND MAKE A NAME FOR MYSELF!
HERE'S WHERE IT STARTS FOR REAL! RIGHT HERE! RIGHT NOW! AT THE CITY'S BIGGEST BATTLE OF THE BANDS!
HERE'S WHERE I'LL UPSTAGE THEM ALL!
REMIX EVERY SOUND--AND ADD MY OWN!
YOU HEAR THAT, NEW YORK?
I AM THE REVOLUTION! YOUR REVELATION! YOUR ROCK GOD! I AM--
YOU SEE THAT, RIGHT?
HE PART OF THE SHOW?
HOW'S HE DOING THAT?
DON'T CARE WHO YOU ARE, LOSER!
CLEAR OFF, BEFORE WE--
LOSER? NOBODY CALLS ME THAT! NEVER AGAIN!
SHOW'S OVER!

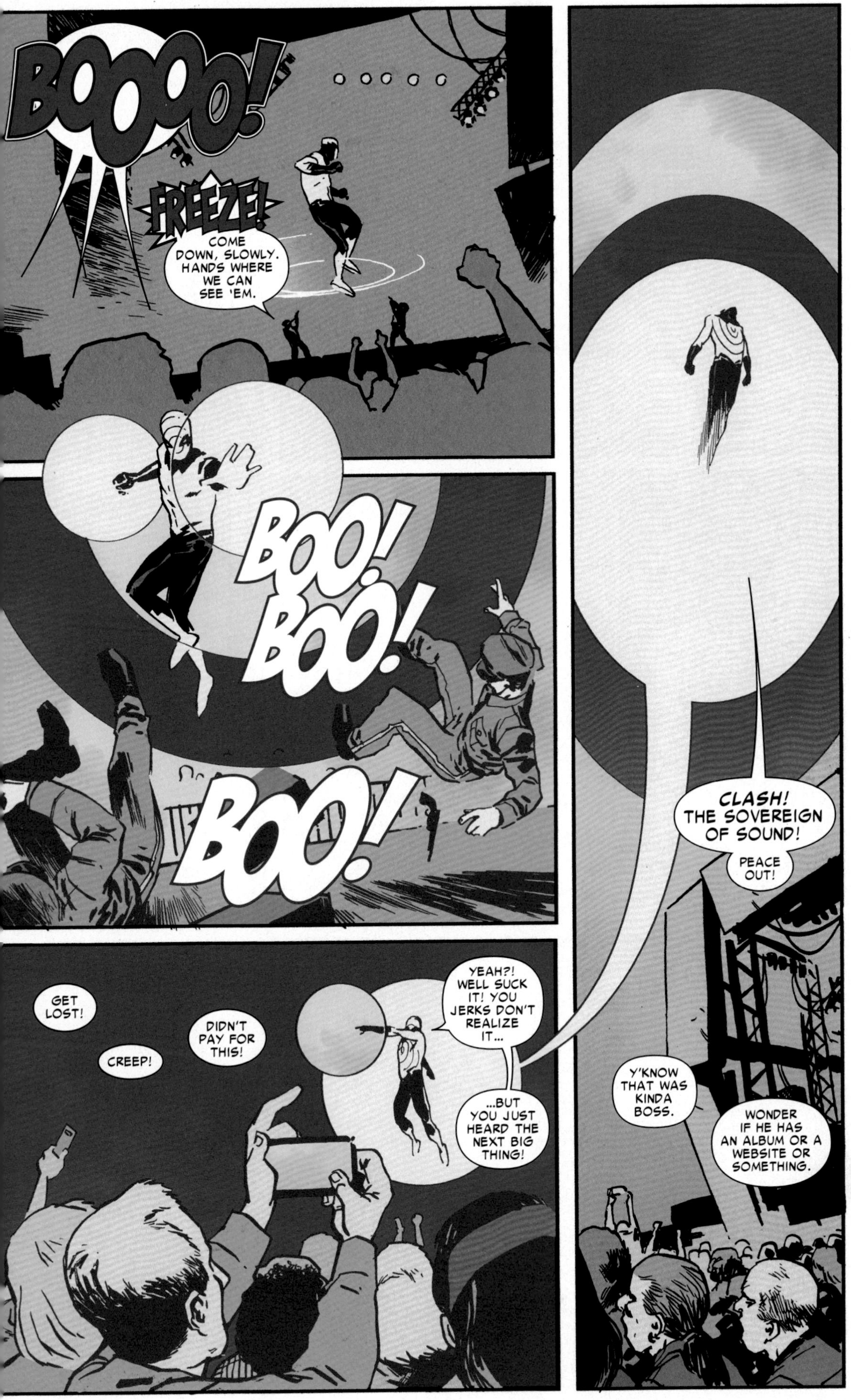
BOOOO!
FREEZE!
COME DOWN, SLOWLY. HANDS WHERE WE CAN SEE 'EM.
BOO! BOO!
BOO!
GET LOST!
CREEP!
DIDN'T PAY FOR THIS!
YEAH?! WELL SUCK IT! YOU JERKS DON'T REALIZE IT...
...BUT YOU JUST HEARD THE NEXT BIG THING!
CLASH! THE SOVEREIGN OF SOUND!
PEACE OUT!
Y'KNOW THAT WAS KINDA BOSS.
WONDER IF HE HAS AN ALBUM OR A WEBSITE OR SOMETHING.

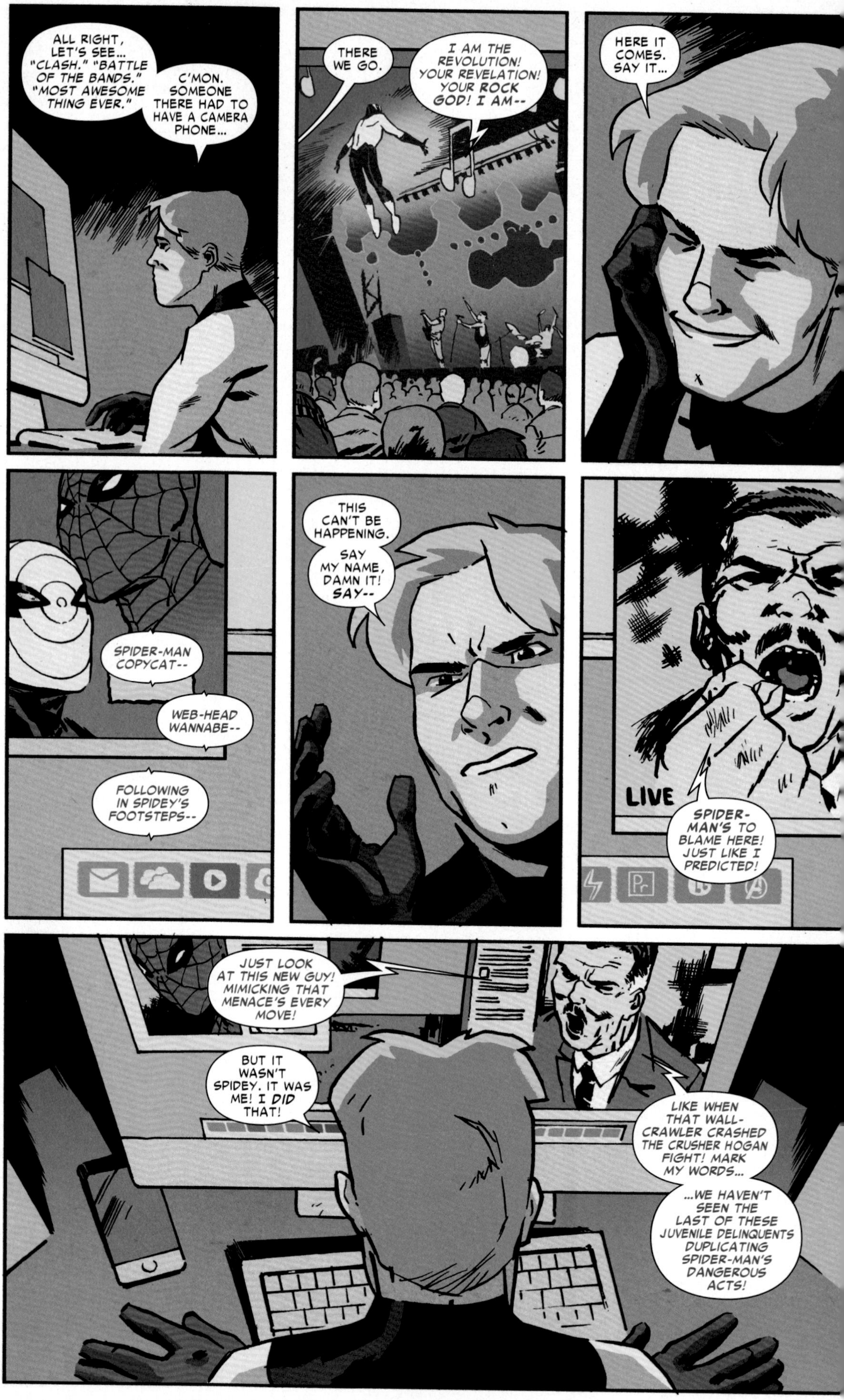
ALL RIGHT, LET'S SEE... "CLASH." "BATTLE OF THE BANDS." "MOST AWESOME THING EVER."
C'MON. SOMEONE THERE HAD TO HAVE A CAMERA PHONE...
THERE WE GO.
I AM THE REVOLUTION! YOUR REVELATION! YOUR ROCK GOD! I AM--
HERE IT COMES. SAY IT...
SPIDER-MAN COPYCAT--
WEB-HEAD WANNABE--
FOLLOWING IN SPIDEY'S FOOTSTEPS--
THIS CAN'T BE HAPPENING.
SAY MY NAME, DAMN IT! SAY--
LIVE
SPIDER-MAN'S TO BLAME HERE! JUST LIKE I PREDICTED!
JUST LOOK AT THIS NEW GUY! MIMICKING THAT MENACE'S EVERY MOVE!
BUT IT WASN'T SPIDEY. IT WAS ME! I DID THAT!
LIKE WHEN THAT WALL-CRAWLER CRASHED THE CRUSHER HOGAN FIGHT! MARK MY WORDS...
...WE HAVEN'T SEEN THE LAST OF THESE JUVENILE DELINQUENTS DUPLICATING SPIDER-MAN'S DANGEROUS ACTS!

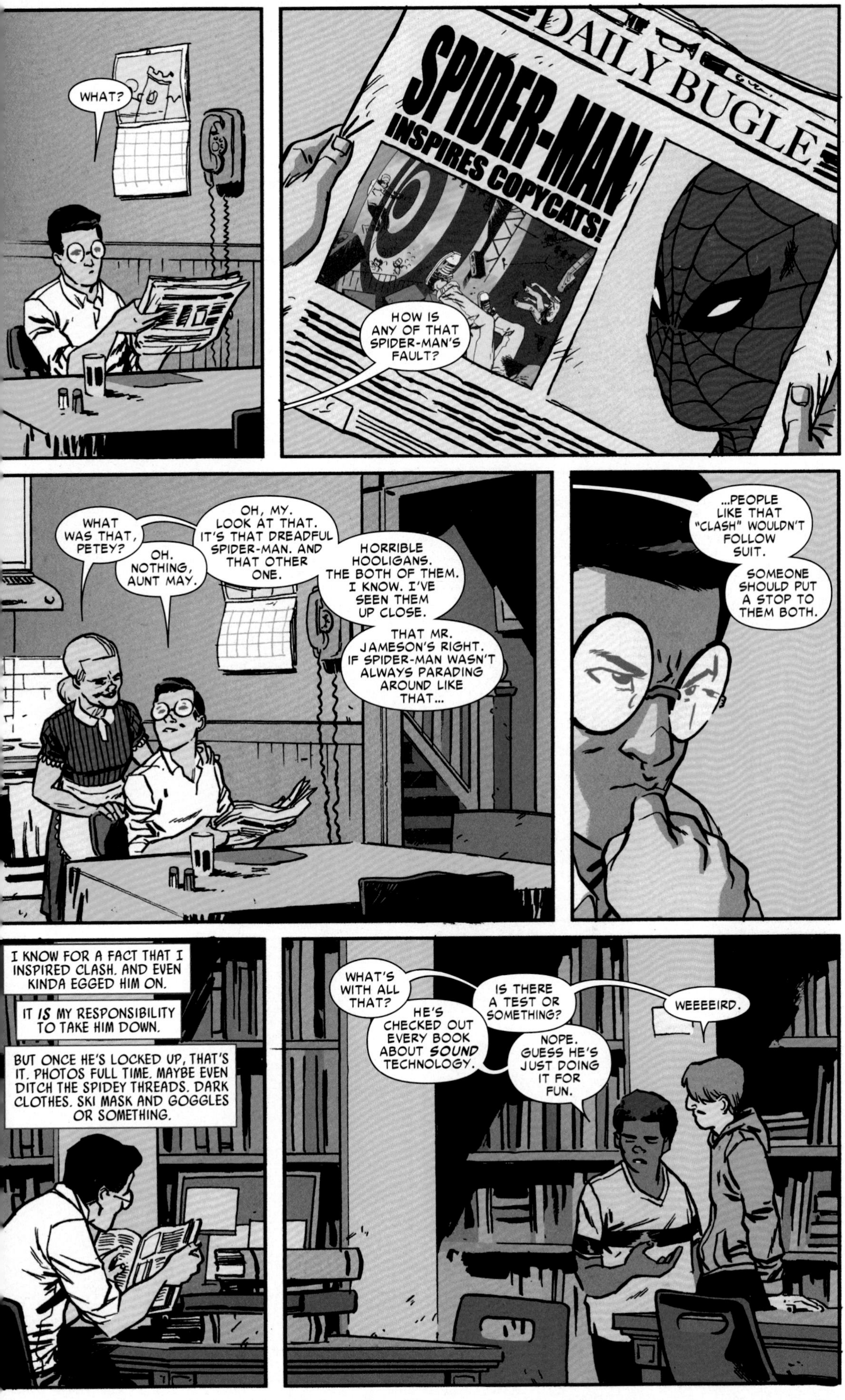
WHAT?
DAILY BUGLE
SPIDER-MAN INSPIRES COPYCATS!
HOW IS ANY OF THAT SPIDER-MAN'S FAULT?
WHAT WAS THAT, PETEY?
OH, MY. LOOK AT THAT. IT'S THAT DREADFUL SPIDER-MAN. AND THAT OTHER ONE.
OH. NOTHING, AUNT MAY.
HORRIBLE HOOLIGANS. THE BOTH OF THEM. I KNOW. I'VE SEEN THEM UP CLOSE.
THAT MR. JAMESON'S RIGHT. IF SPIDER-MAN WASN'T ALWAYS PARADING AROUND LIKE THAT...
...PEOPLE LIKE THAT "CLASH" WOULDN'T FOLLOW SUIT.
SOMEONE SHOULD PUT A STOP TO THEM BOTH.
I KNOW FOR A FACT THAT I INSPIRED CLASH. AND EVEN KINDA EGGED HIM ON.
IT IS MY RESPONSIBILITY TO TAKE HIM DOWN.
BUT ONCE HE'S LOCKED UP, THAT'S IT. PHOTOS FULL TIME. MAYBE EVEN DITCH THE SPIDEY THREADS. DARK CLOTHES. SKI MASK AND GOGGLES OR SOMETHING.
WHAT'S WITH ALL THAT?
HE'S CHECKED OUT EVERY BOOK ABOUT SOUND TECHNOLOGY.
IS THERE A TEST OR SOMETHING?
NOPE. GUESS HE'S JUST DOING IT FOR FUN.
WEEEEIRD.

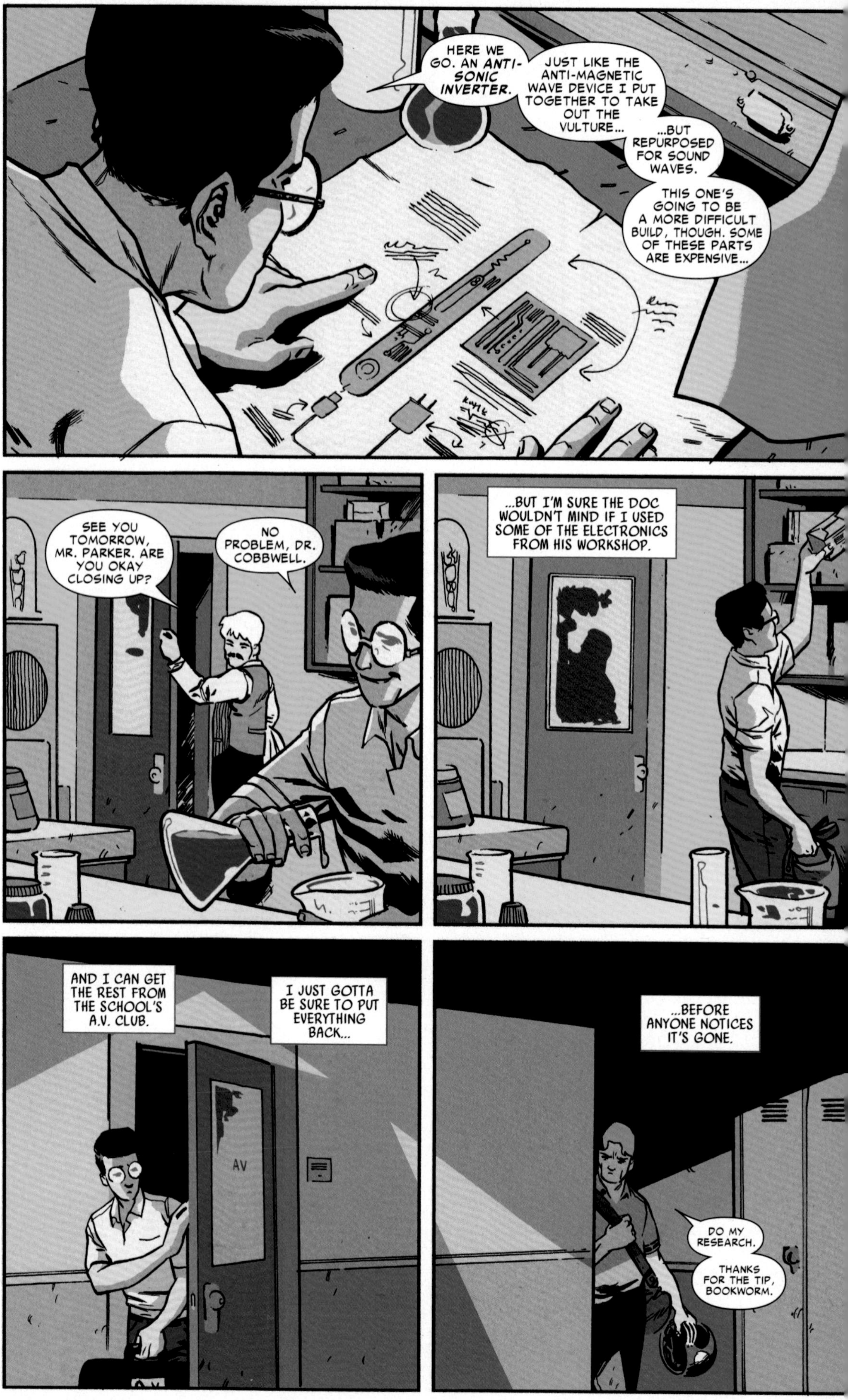
HERE WE GO. AN ANTI-SONIC INVERTER.
JUST LIKE THE ANTI-MAGNETIC WAVE DEVICE I PUT TOGETHER TO TAKE OUT THE VULTURE...
...BUT REPURPOSED FOR SOUND WAVES.
THIS ONE'S GOING TO BE A MORE DIFFICULT BUILD, THOUGH. SOME OF THESE PARTS ARE EXPENSIVE...
SEE YOU TOMORROW, MR. PARKER. ARE YOU OKAY CLOSING UP?
NO PROBLEM, DR. COBBWELL.
...BUT I'M SURE THE DOC WOULDN'T MIND IF I USED SOME OF THE ELECTRONICS FROM HIS WORKSHOP.
AND I CAN GET THE REST FROM THE SCHOOL'S A.V. CLUB.
I JUST GOTTA BE SURE TO PUT EVERYTHING BACK...
AV
...BEFORE ANYONE NOTICES IT'S GONE.
DO MY RESEARCH.
THANKS FOR THE TIP, BOOKWORM.

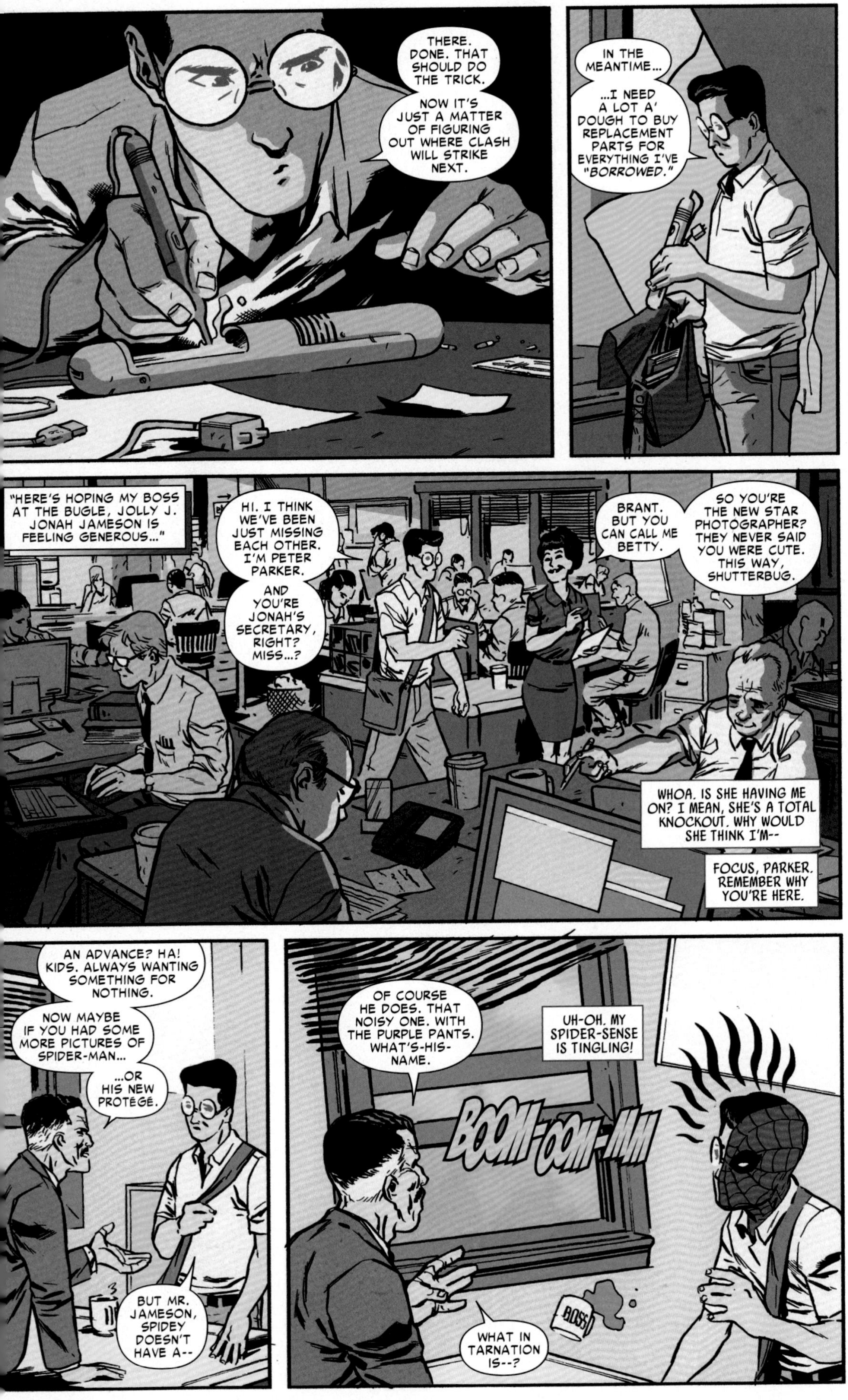
THERE. DONE. THAT SHOULD DO THE TRICK.
NOW IT'S JUST A MATTER OF FIGURING OUT WHERE CLASH WILL STRIKE NEXT.
IN THE MEANTIME...
...I NEED A LOT A' DOUGH TO BUY REPLACEMENT PARTS FOR EVERYTHING I'VE "BORROWED."
"HERE'S HOPING MY BOSS AT THE BUGLE, JOLLY J. JONAH JAMESON IS FEELING GENEROUS..."
HI. I THINK WE'VE BEEN JUST MISSING EACH OTHER. I'M PETER PARKER.
AND YOU'RE JONAH'S SECRETARY, RIGHT? MISS...?
BRANT. BUT YOU CAN CALL ME BETTY.
SO YOU'RE THE NEW STAR PHOTOGRAPHER? THEY NEVER SAID YOU WERE CUTE. THIS WAY, SHUTTERBUG.
WHOA. IS SHE HAVING ME ON? I MEAN, SHE'S A TOTAL KNOCKOUT. WHY WOULD SHE THINK I'M--
FOCUS, PARKER. REMEMBER WHY YOU'RE HERE.
AN ADVANCE? HA! KIDS. ALWAYS WANTING SOMETHING FOR NOTHING.
NOW MAYBE IF YOU HAD SOME MORE PICTURES OF SPIDER-MAN...
...OR HIS NEW PROTÉGÉ.
BUT MR. JAMESON, SPIDEY DOESN'T HAVE A--
OF COURSE HE DOES. THAT NOISY ONE. WITH THE PURPLE PANTS. WHAT'S-HIS-NAME.
UH-OH. MY SPIDER-SENSE IS TINGLING!
BOOM-OOM-MM
WHAT IN TARNATION IS--?
BOSS

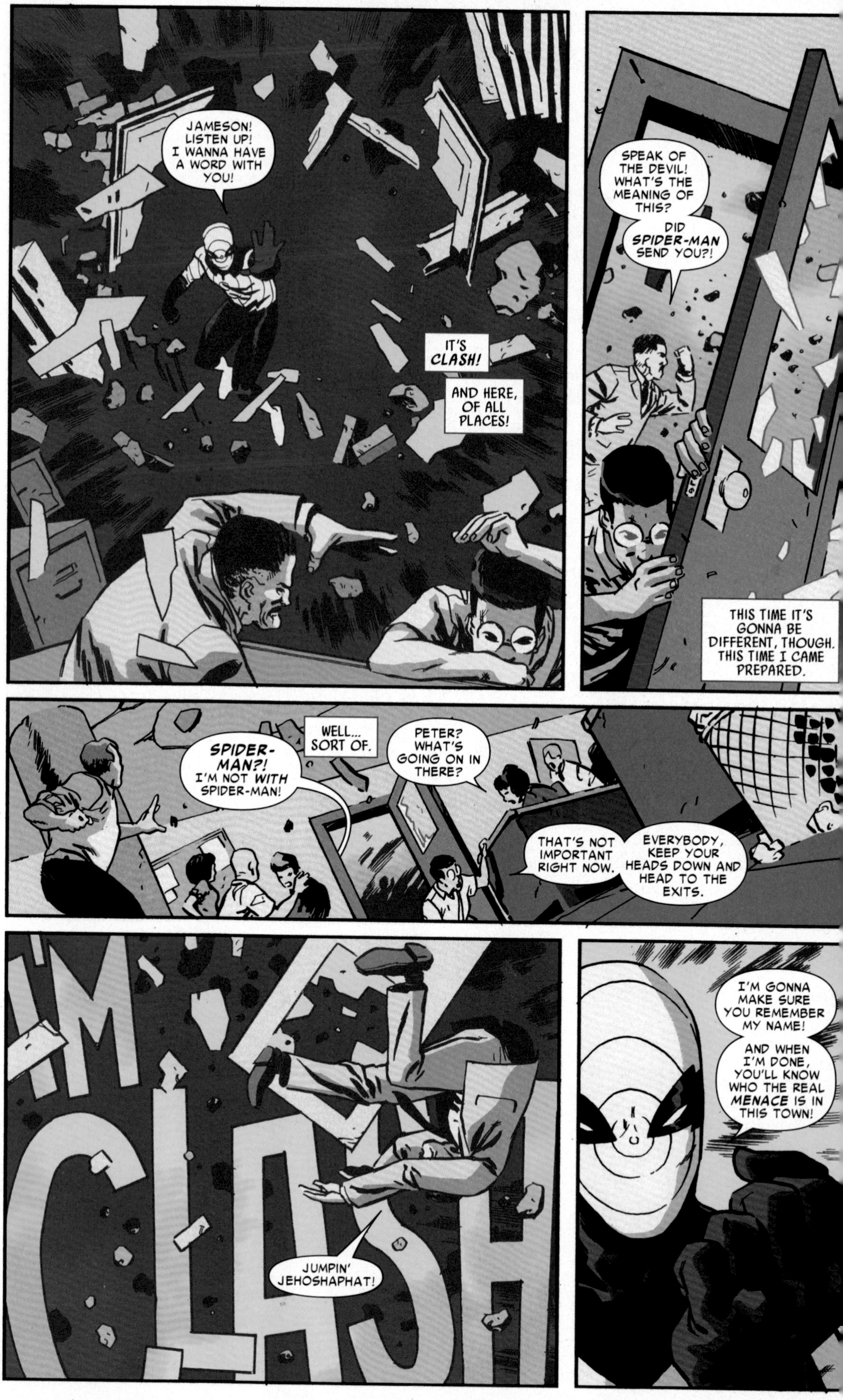
JAMESON! LISTEN UP! I WANNA HAVE A WORD WITH YOU!
IT'S CLASH!
AND HERE, OF ALL PLACES!
SPEAK OF THE DEVIL! WHAT'S THE MEANING OF THIS?
DID SPIDER-MAN SEND YOU?!
THIS TIME IT'S GONNA BE DIFFERENT, THOUGH. THIS TIME I CAME PREPARED.
SPIDER-MAN?! I'M NOT WITH SPIDER-MAN!
WELL... SORT OF.
PETER? WHAT'S GOING ON IN THERE?
THAT'S NOT IMPORTANT RIGHT NOW.
EVERYBODY, KEEP YOUR HEADS DOWN AND HEAD TO THE EXITS.
I'M CLASH!
JUMPIN' JEHOSHAPHAT!
I'M GONNA MAKE SURE YOU REMEMBER MY NAME!
AND WHEN I'M DONE, YOU'LL KNOW WHO THE REAL MENACE IS IN THIS TOWN!

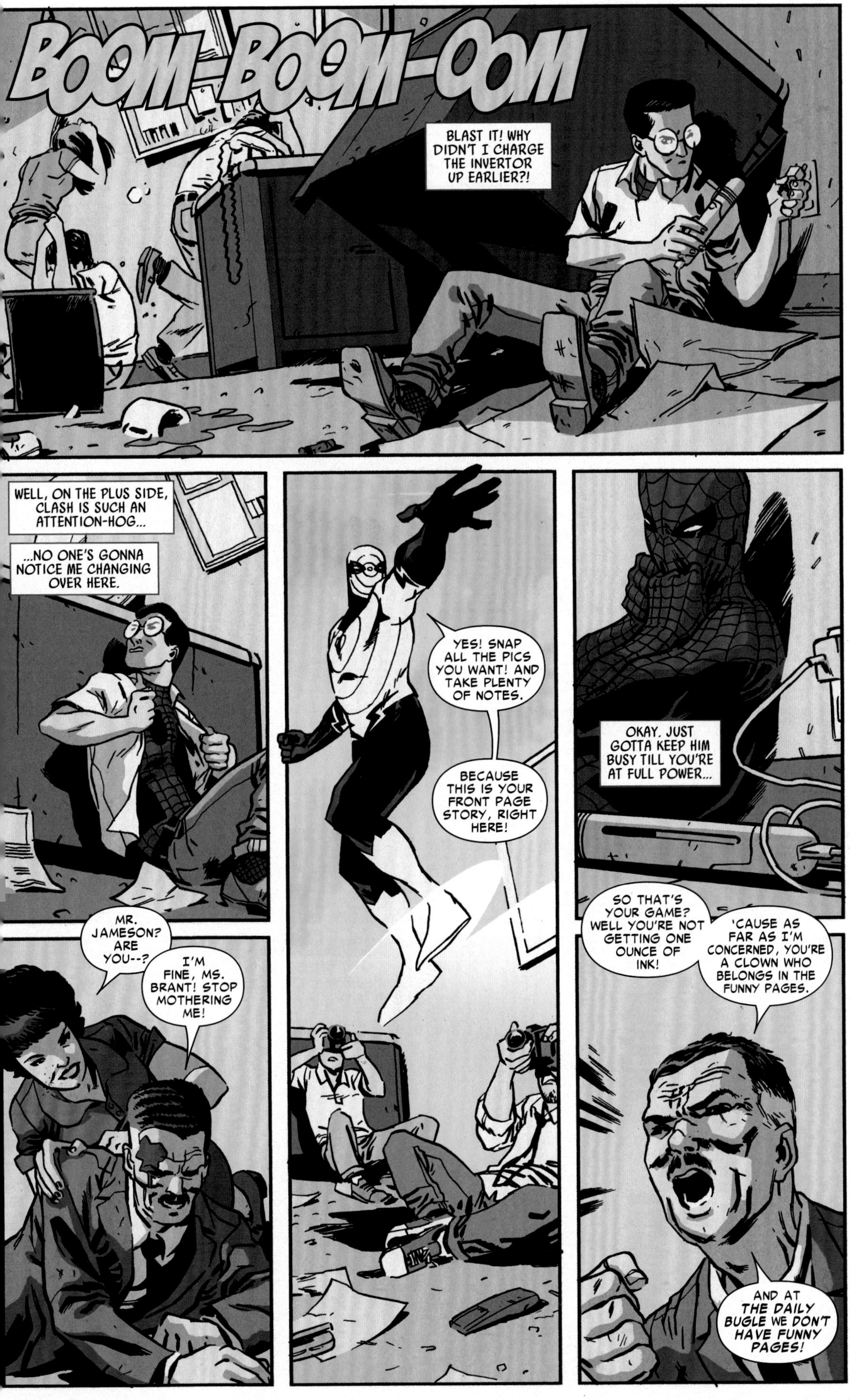
BOOM-BOOM-OOM
BLAST IT! WHY DIDN'T I CHARGE THE INVERTOR UP EARLIER?!
WELL, ON THE PLUS SIDE, CLASH IS SUCH AN ATTENTION-HOG...
...NO ONE'S GONNA NOTICE ME CHANGING OVER HERE.
YES! SNAP ALL THE PICS YOU WANT! AND TAKE PLENTY OF NOTES.
BECAUSE THIS IS YOUR FRONT PAGE STORY, RIGHT HERE!
OKAY. JUST GOTTA KEEP HIM BUSY TILL YOU'RE AT FULL POWER...
MR. JAMESON? ARE YOU--?
I'M FINE, MS. BRANT! STOP MOTHERING ME!
SO THAT'S YOUR GAME? WELL YOU'RE NOT GETTING ONE OUNCE OF INK!
'CAUSE AS FAR AS I'M CONCERNED, YOU'RE A CLOWN WHO BELONGS IN THE FUNNY PAGES.
AND AT THE DAILY BUGLE WE DON'T HAVE FUNNY PAGES!

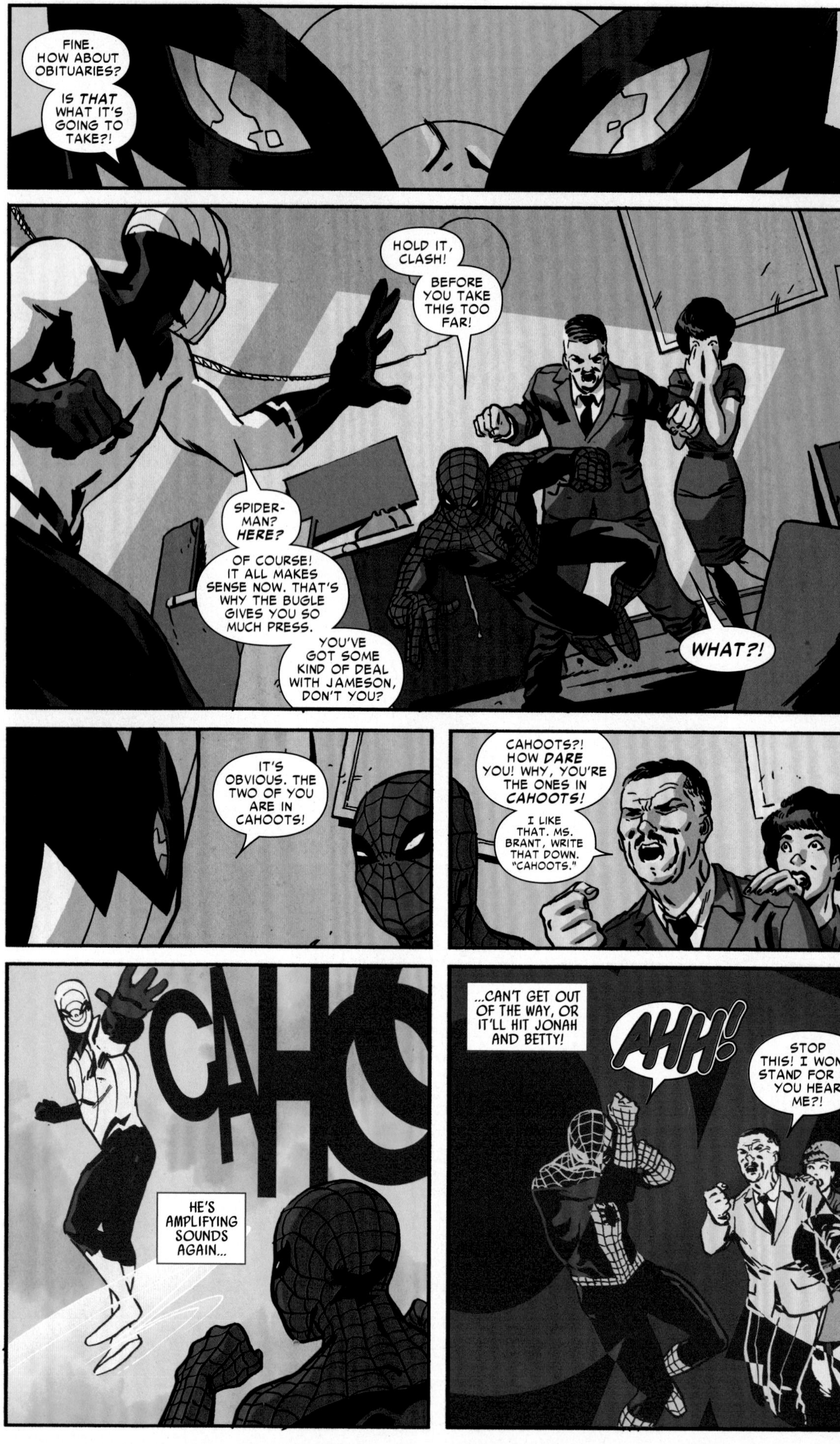
FINE. HOW ABOUT OBITUARIES?
IS *THAT* WHAT IT'S GOING TO TAKE?!
HOLD IT, CLASH!
BEFORE YOU TAKE THIS TOO FAR!
SPIDER-MAN? *HERE?*
OF COURSE! IT ALL MAKES SENSE NOW. THAT'S WHY THE BUGLE GIVES YOU SO MUCH PRESS.
YOU'VE GOT SOME KIND OF DEAL WITH JAMESON, DON'T YOU?
WHAT?!
IT'S OBVIOUS. THE TWO OF YOU ARE IN CAHOOTS!
CAHOOTS?! HOW *DARE* YOU! WHY, YOU'RE THE ONES IN *CAHOOTS!*
I LIKE THAT. MS. BRANT, WRITE THAT DOWN. "CAHOOTS."
CAHO
HE'S AMPLIFYING SOUNDS AGAIN...
...CAN'T GET OUT OF THE WAY, OR IT'LL HIT JONAH AND BETTY!
AHH!
STOP THIS! I WON'T STAND FOR IT! YOU HEAR ME?!

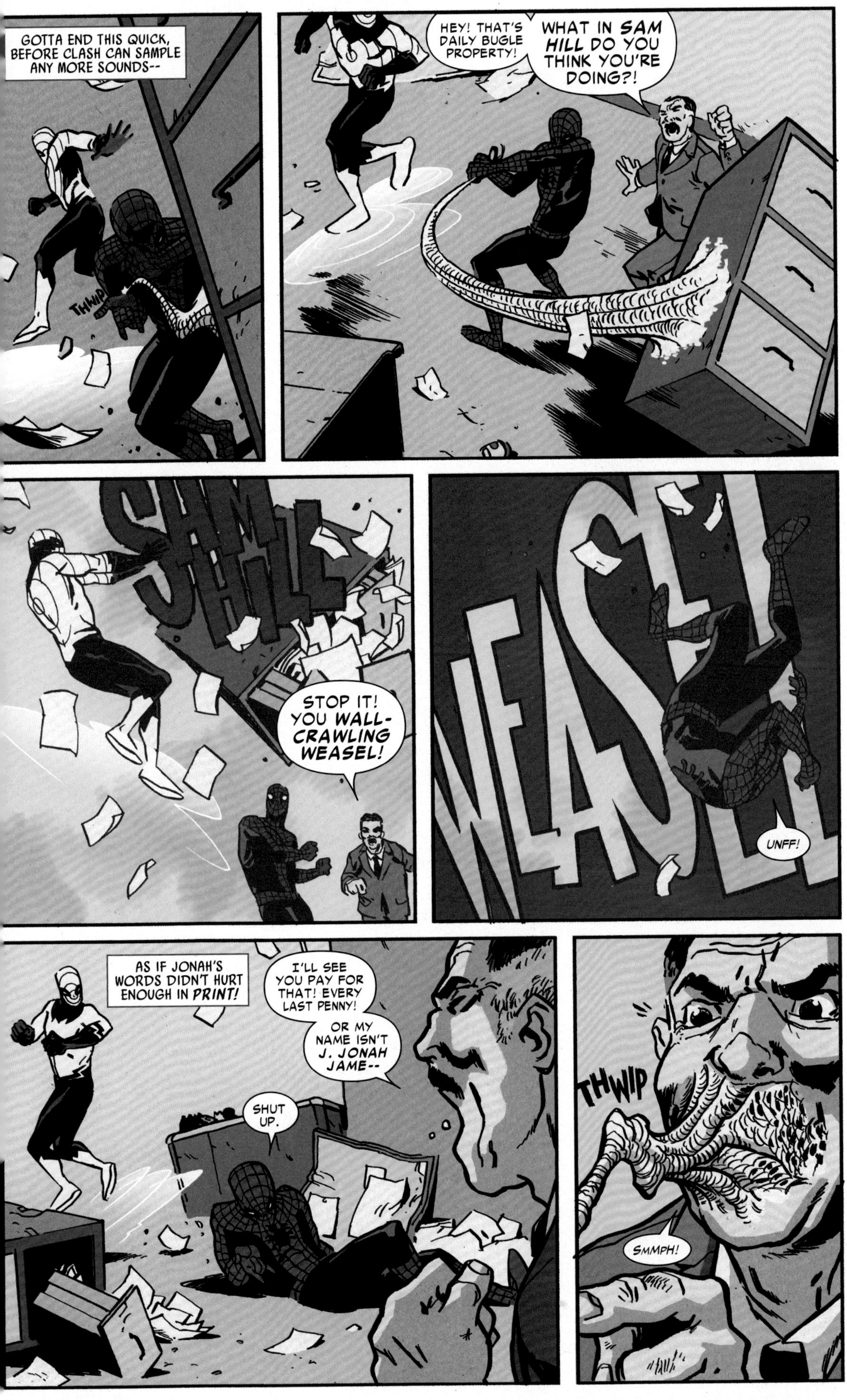

GOTTA END THIS QUICK, BEFORE CLASH CAN SAMPLE ANY MORE SOUNDS--
THWIP
HEY! THAT'S DAILY BUGLE PROPERTY!
WHAT IN SAM HILL DO YOU THINK YOU'RE DOING?!
SAM HILL
STOP IT! YOU WALL-CRAWLING WEASEL!
WEASEL
UNFF!
AS IF JONAH'S WORDS DIDN'T HURT ENOUGH IN PRINT!
I'LL SEE YOU PAY FOR THAT! EVERY LAST PENNY!
OR MY NAME ISN'T J. JONAH JAME--
SHUT UP.
THWIP
SMMPH!

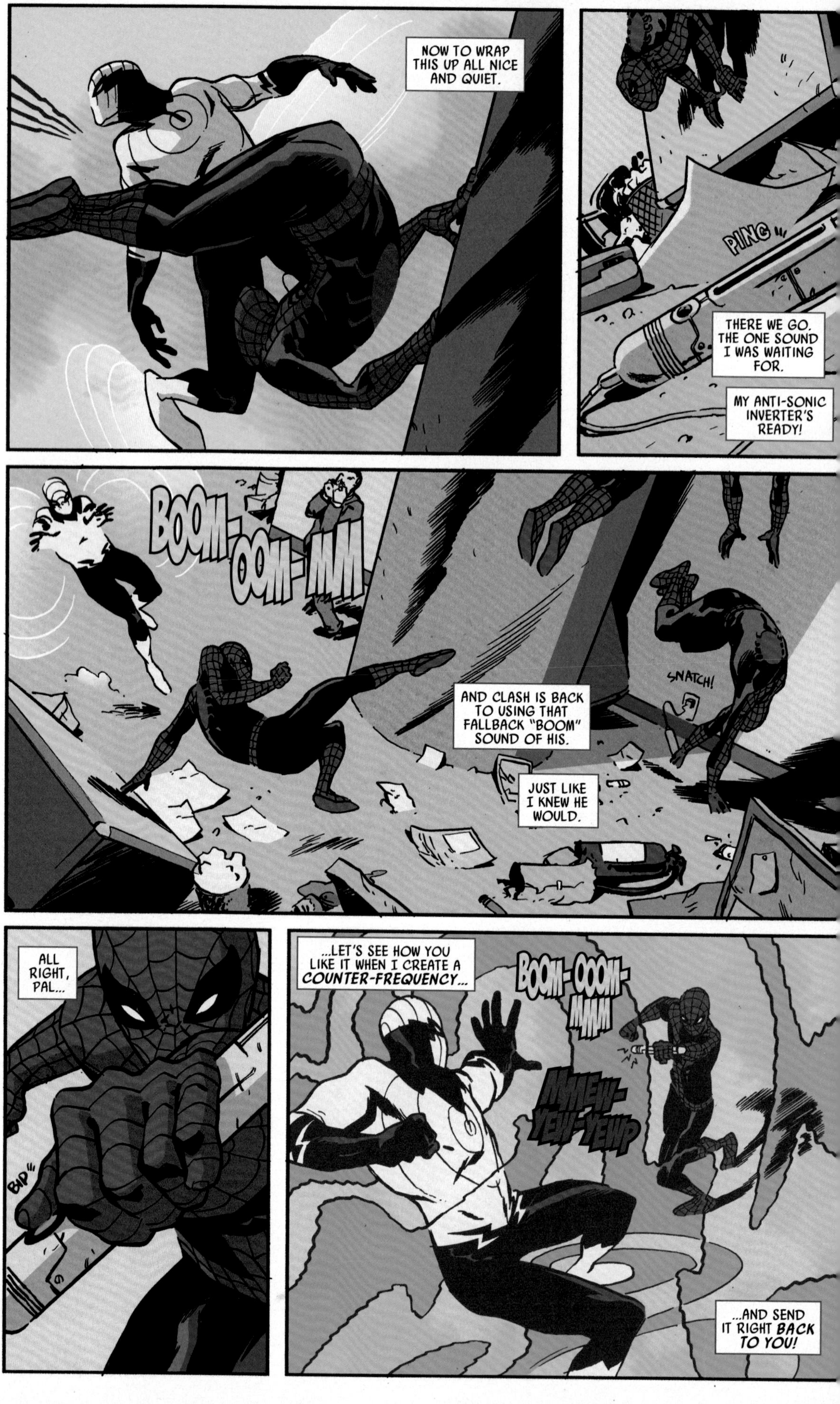
NOW TO WRAP THIS UP ALL NICE AND QUIET.
PING
THERE WE GO. THE ONE SOUND I WAS WAITING FOR.
MY ANTI-SONIC INVERTER'S READY!
BOOM-OOM-MM
SNATCH!
AND CLASH IS BACK TO USING THAT FALLBACK "BOOM" SOUND OF HIS.
JUST LIKE I KNEW HE WOULD.
ALL RIGHT, PAL...
BIP
...LET'S SEE HOW YOU LIKE IT WHEN I CREATE A COUNTER-FREQUENCY...
BOOM-OOM-MMM
MMEW-YEW-YEWP
...AND SEND IT RIGHT BACK TO YOU!

GYAHH!

YEWWW- YEW-YEW!

C-CLEVER! THOUGH NOT CLEVER ENOUGH!

BET IF I INCREASE THE AMPLITUDE AND FREQUENCY...

...THE SOUND BUFFERS IN MY SUIT WILL HOLD UP...

...BETTER THAN YOUR LITTLE TOY!

EEEEE EEEEE

ZRAP

YAHH!

NNHH!

EEEEEEEE EEEEE

NICE TRY, SPIDEY, BUT YOU LOSE!

HE--HE JUST OUT-SCIENCED ME. BUT THAT'S NEVER HAPPENED TO ME BEFORE! EVER!

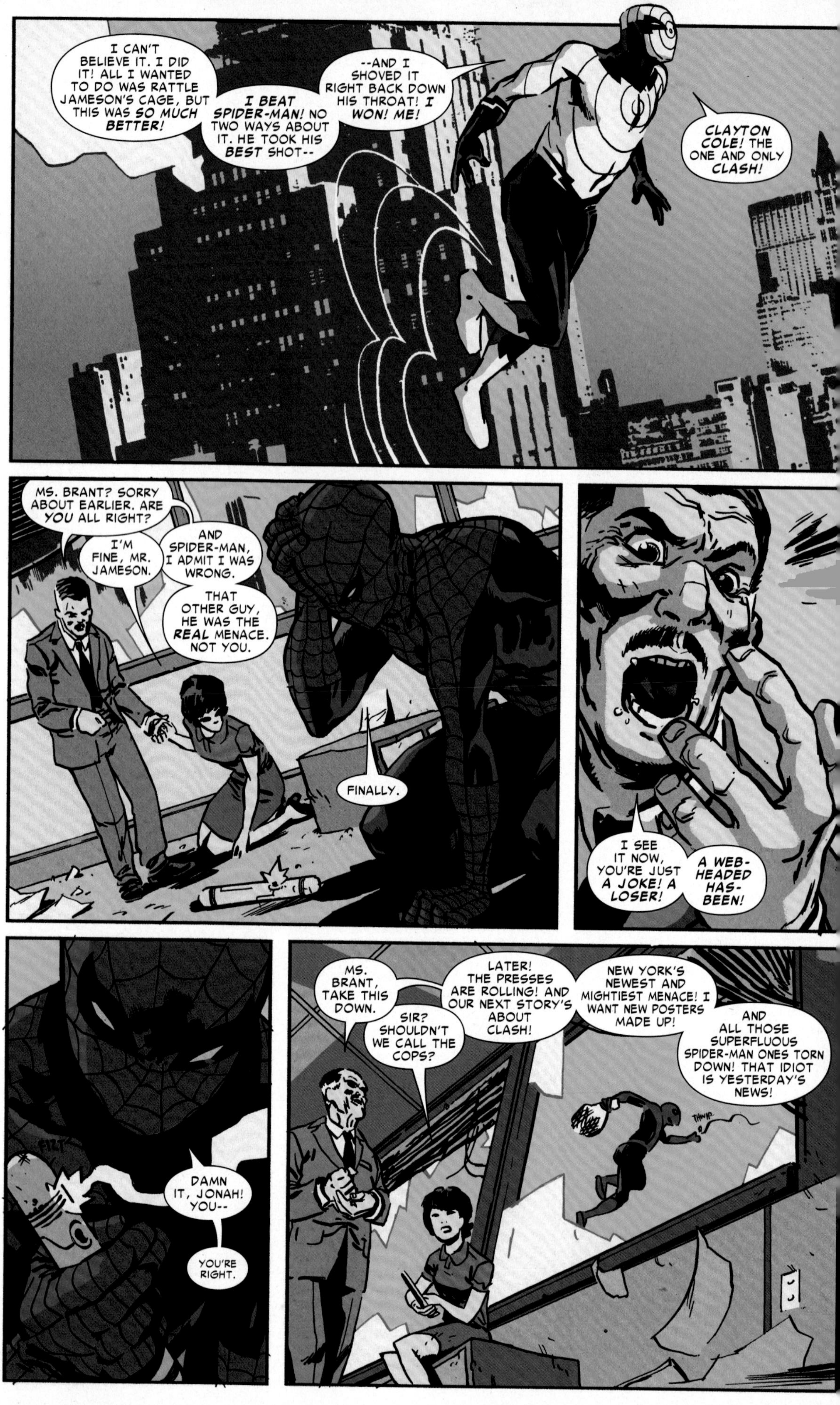
I CAN'T BELIEVE IT. I DID IT! ALL I WANTED TO DO WAS RATTLE JAMESON'S CAGE, BUT THIS WAS SO MUCH BETTER!
I BEAT SPIDER-MAN! NO TWO WAYS ABOUT IT. HE TOOK HIS BEST SHOT--
--AND I SHOVED IT RIGHT BACK DOWN HIS THROAT! I WON! ME!
CLAYTON COLE! THE ONE AND ONLY CLASH!
MS. BRANT? SORRY ABOUT EARLIER. ARE YOU ALL RIGHT?
I'M FINE, MR. JAMESON.
AND SPIDER-MAN, I ADMIT I WAS WRONG.
THAT OTHER GUY, HE WAS THE REAL MENACE. NOT YOU.
FINALLY.
I SEE IT NOW, YOU'RE JUST A JOKE! A LOSER!
A WEB-HEADED HAS-BEEN!
DAMN IT, JONAH! YOU--
YOU'RE RIGHT.
MS. BRANT, TAKE THIS DOWN.
SIR? SHOULDN'T WE CALL THE COPS?
LATER! THE PRESSES ARE ROLLING! AND OUR NEXT STORY'S ABOUT CLASH!
NEW YORK'S NEWEST AND MIGHTIEST MENACE! I WANT NEW POSTERS MADE UP!
AND ALL THOSE SUPERFLUOUS SPIDER-MAN ONES TORN DOWN! THAT IDIOT IS YESTERDAY'S NEWS!

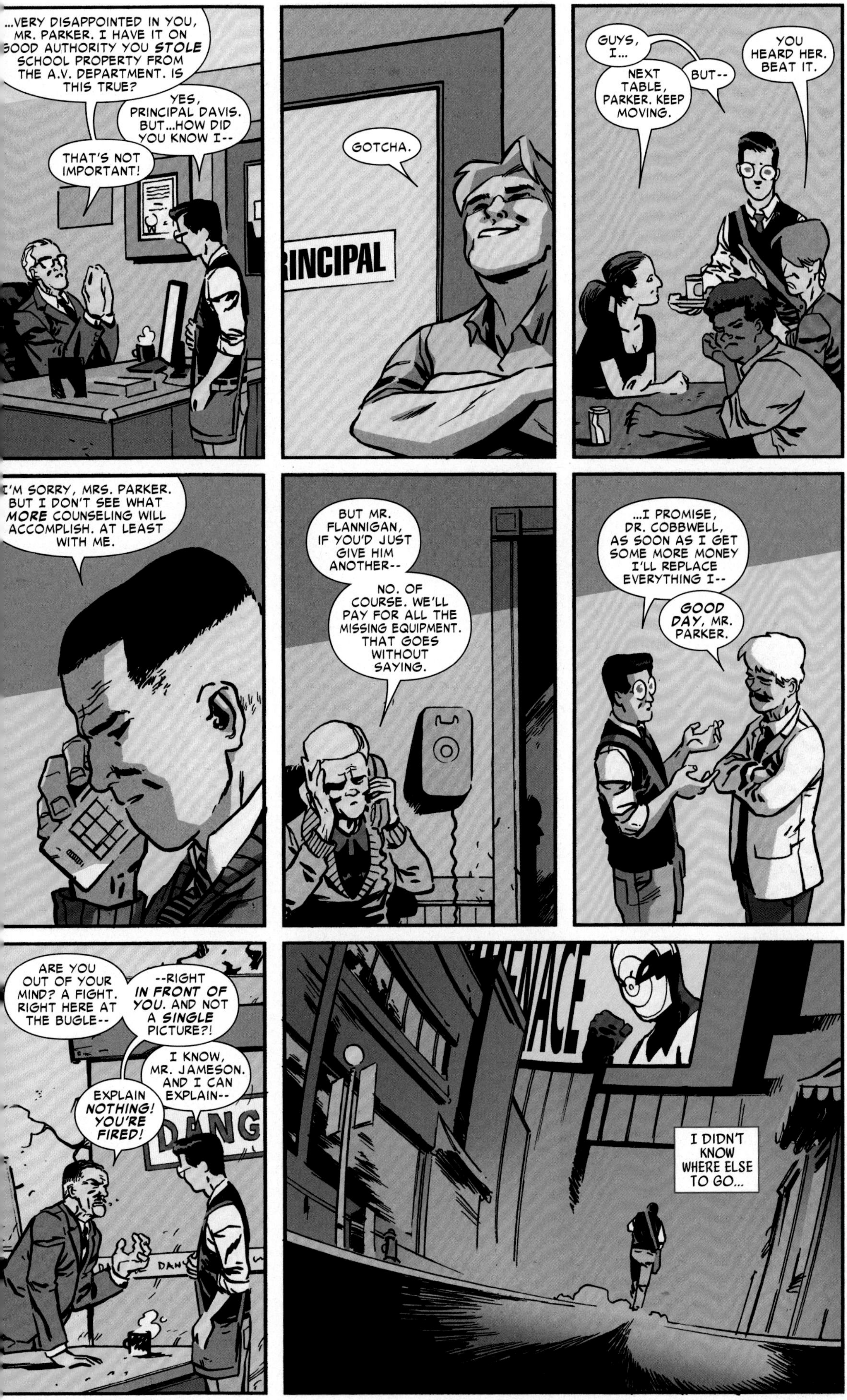

...VERY DISAPPOINTED IN YOU, MR. PARKER. I HAVE IT ON GOOD AUTHORITY YOU STOLE SCHOOL PROPERTY FROM THE A.V. DEPARTMENT. IS THIS TRUE?
YES, PRINCIPAL DAVIS. BUT...HOW DID YOU KNOW I--
THAT'S NOT IMPORTANT!
GOTCHA.
PRINCIPAL
GUYS, I...
NEXT TABLE, PARKER. KEEP MOVING.
BUT--
YOU HEARD HER. BEAT IT.
I'M SORRY, MRS. PARKER. BUT I DON'T SEE WHAT MORE COUNSELING WILL ACCOMPLISH. AT LEAST WITH ME.
BUT MR. FLANNIGAN, IF YOU'D JUST GIVE HIM ANOTHER--
NO. OF COURSE. WE'LL PAY FOR ALL THE MISSING EQUIPMENT. THAT GOES WITHOUT SAYING.
...I PROMISE, DR. COBBWELL, AS SOON AS I GET SOME MORE MONEY I'LL REPLACE EVERYTHING I--
GOOD DAY, MR. PARKER.
ARE YOU OUT OF YOUR MIND? A FIGHT. RIGHT HERE AT THE BUGLE--
--RIGHT IN FRONT OF YOU. AND NOT A SINGLE PICTURE?!
I KNOW, MR. JAMESON. AND I CAN EXPLAIN--
EXPLAIN NOTHING! YOU'RE FIRED!
I DIDN'T KNOW WHERE ELSE TO GO...

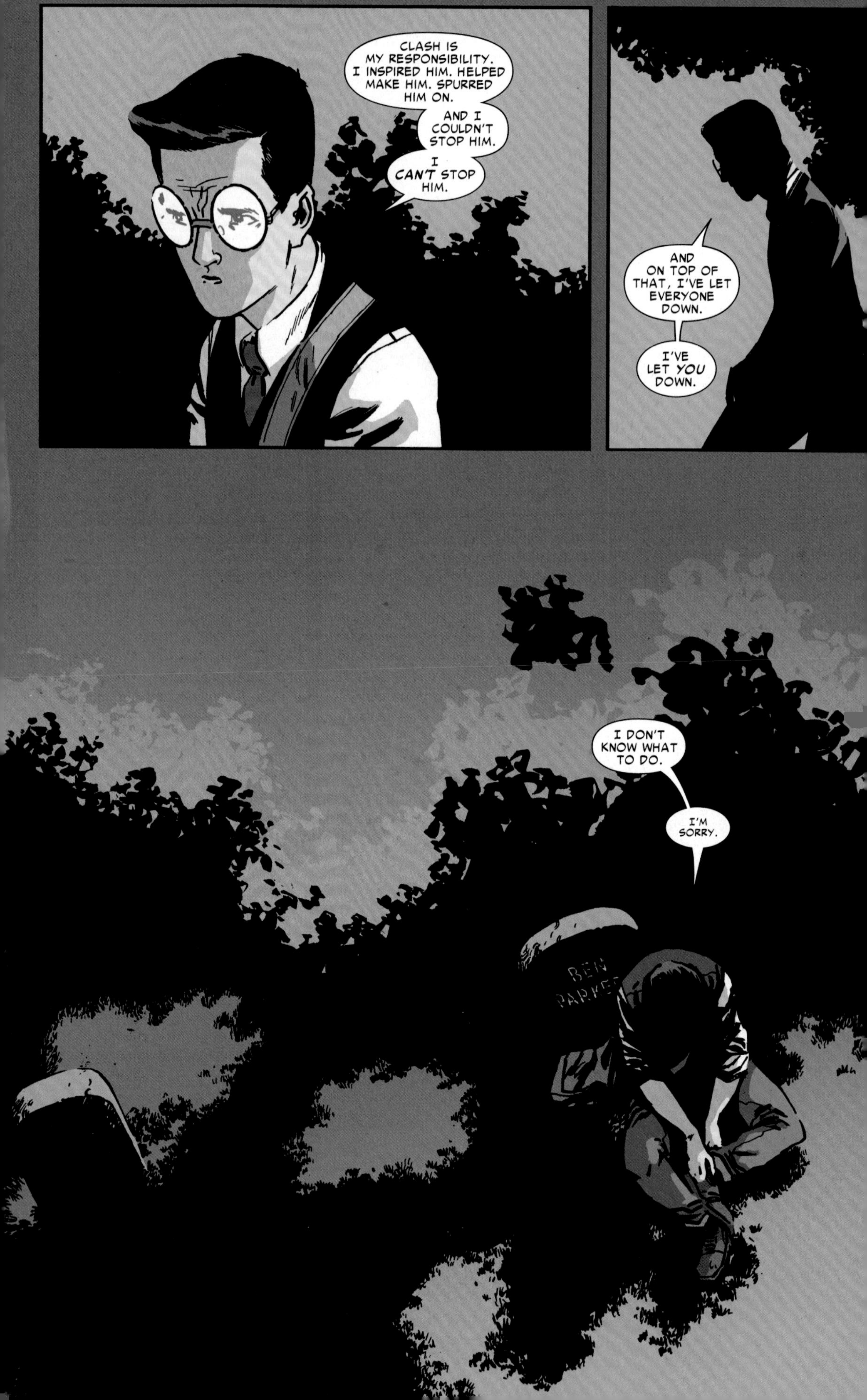
CLASH IS MY RESPONSIBILITY. I INSPIRED HIM. HELPED MAKE HIM. SPURRED HIM ON.
AND I COULDN'T STOP HIM.
I CAN'T STOP HIM.
AND ON TOP OF THAT, I'VE LET EVERYONE DOWN.
I'VE LET YOU DOWN.
I DON'T KNOW WHAT TO DO.
I'M SORRY.
BEN PARKER

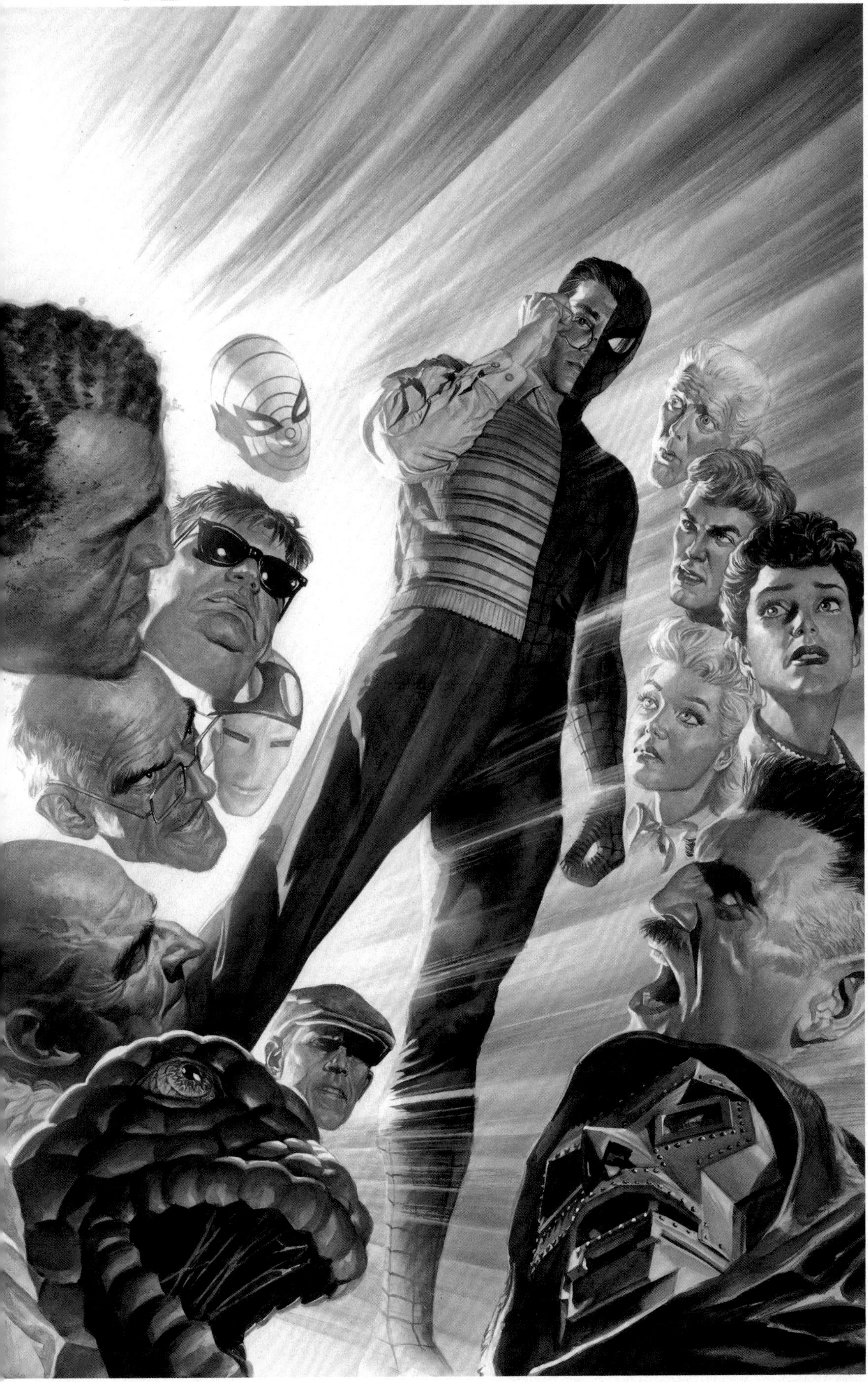

1.5

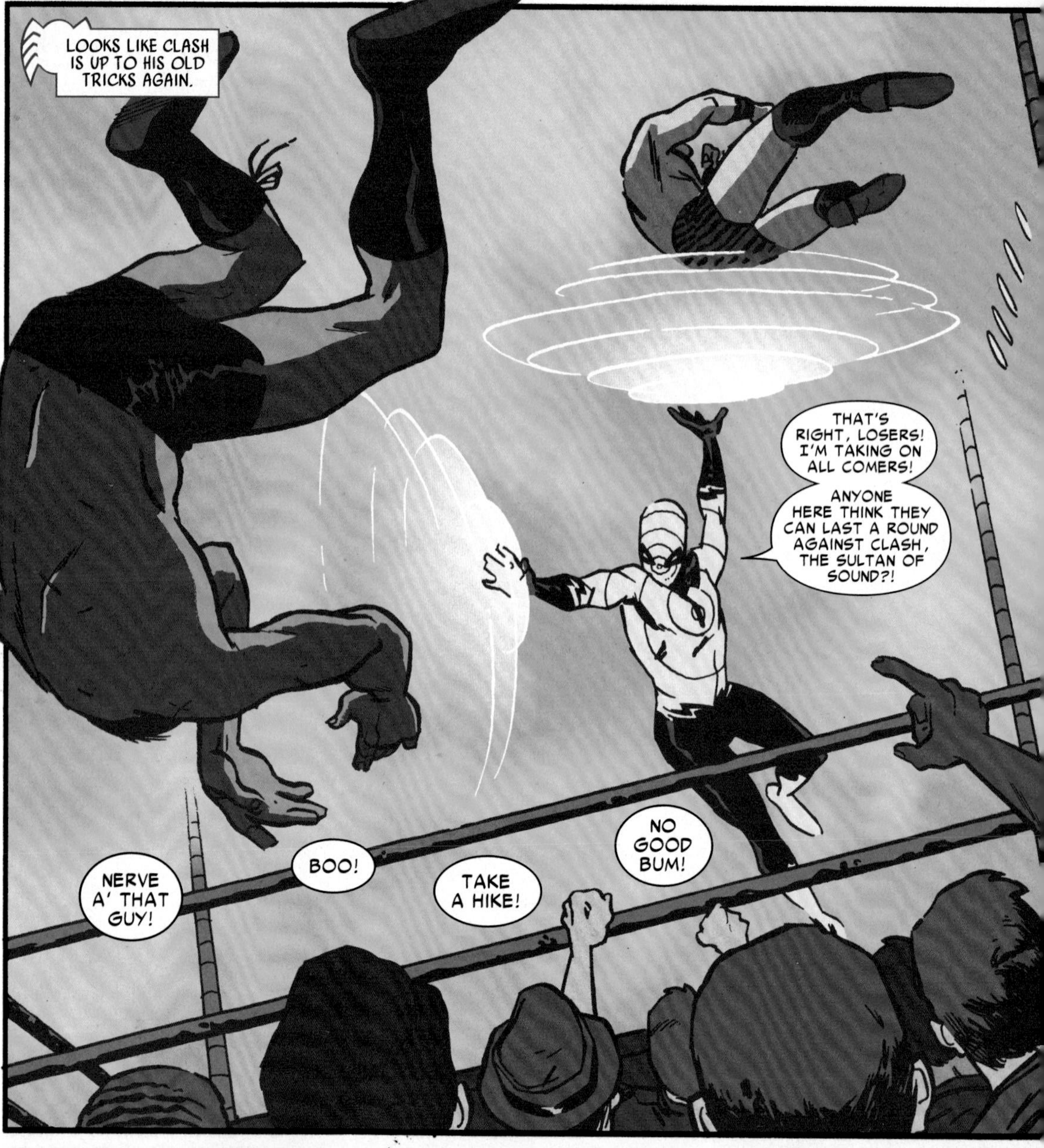
LOOKS LIKE CLASH IS UP TO HIS OLD TRICKS AGAIN.
THAT'S RIGHT, LOSERS! I'M TAKING ON ALL COMERS!
ANYONE HERE THINK THEY CAN LAST A ROUND AGAINST CLASH, THE SULTAN OF SOUND?!
NERVE A' THAT GUY!
BOO!
TAKE A HIKE!
NO GOOD BUM!

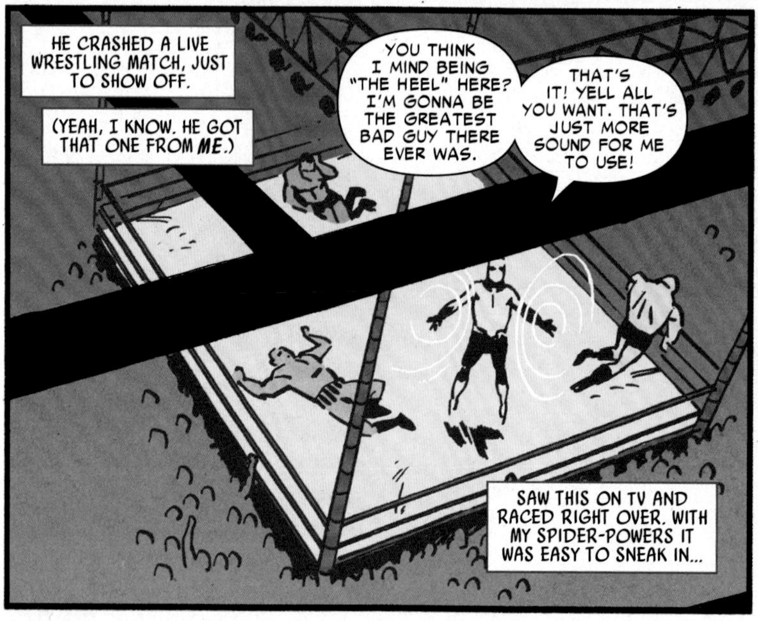
HE CRASHED A LIVE WRESTLING MATCH, JUST TO SHOW OFF.
(YEAH, I KNOW. HE GOT THAT ONE FROM ME.)
YOU THINK I MIND BEING "THE HEEL" HERE? I'M GONNA BE THE GREATEST BAD GUY THERE EVER WAS.
THAT'S IT! YELL ALL YOU WANT. THAT'S JUST MORE SOUND FOR ME TO USE!
SAW THIS ON TV AND RACED RIGHT OVER. WITH MY SPIDER-POWERS IT WAS EASY TO SNEAK IN...

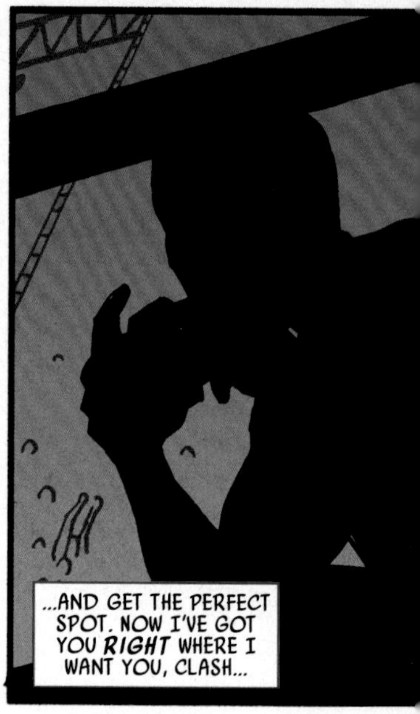
...AND GET THE PERFECT SPOT. NOW I'VE GOT YOU RIGHT WHERE I WANT YOU, CLASH...

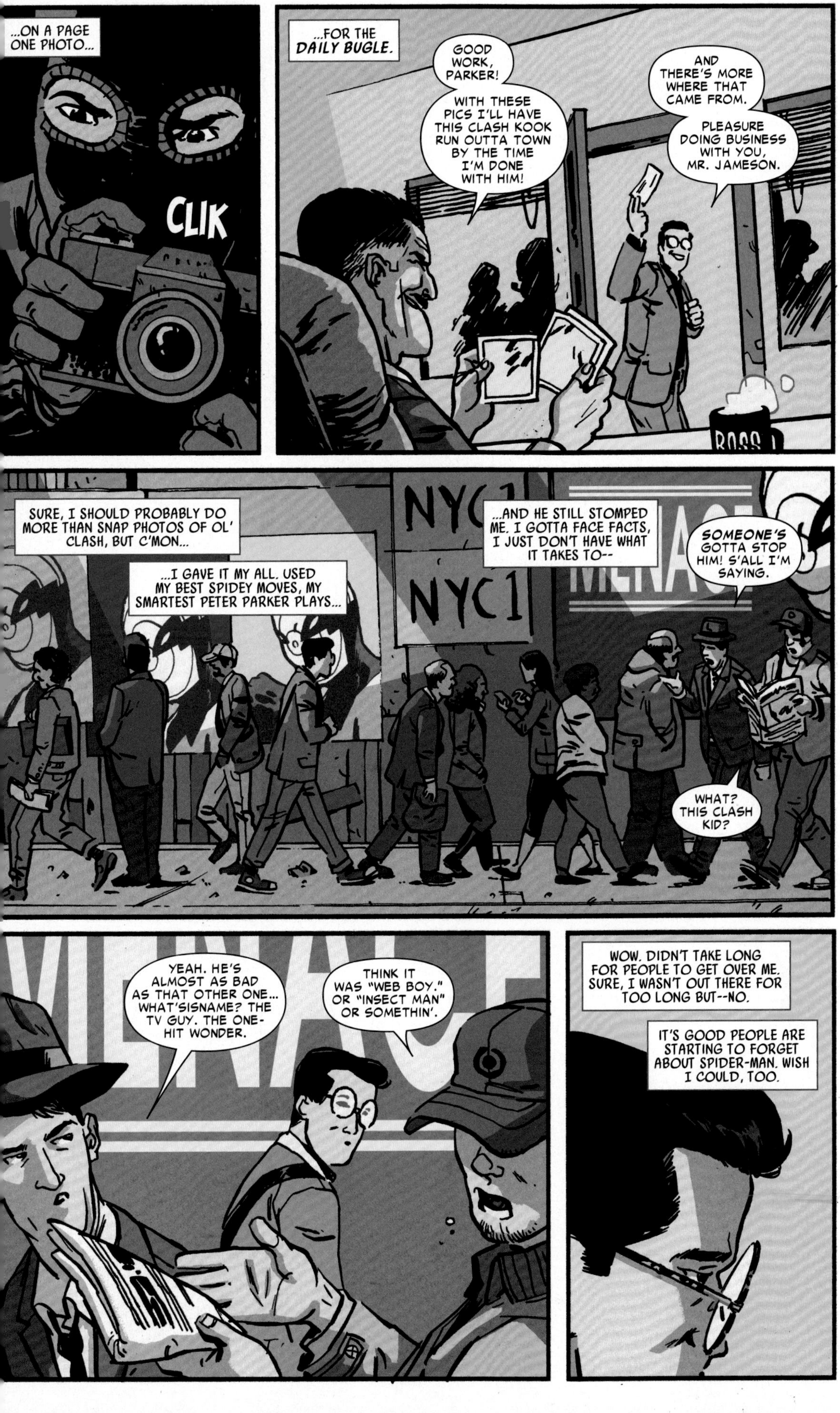
...ON A PAGE ONE PHOTO...
CLIK
...FOR THE DAILY BUGLE.
GOOD WORK, PARKER!
WITH THESE PICS I'LL HAVE THIS CLASH KOOK RUN OUTTA TOWN BY THE TIME I'M DONE WITH HIM!
AND THERE'S MORE WHERE THAT CAME FROM.
PLEASURE DOING BUSINESS WITH YOU, MR. JAMESON.
SURE, I SHOULD PROBABLY DO MORE THAN SNAP PHOTOS OF OL' CLASH, BUT C'MON...
...I GAVE IT MY ALL. USED MY BEST SPIDEY MOVES, MY SMARTEST PETER PARKER PLAYS...
NYC1
NYC1
...AND HE STILL STOMPED ME. I GOTTA FACE FACTS, I JUST DON'T HAVE WHAT IT TAKES TO--
SOMEONE'S GOTTA STOP HIM! S'ALL I'M SAYING.
WHAT? THIS CLASH KID?
YEAH. HE'S ALMOST AS BAD AS THAT OTHER ONE... WHAT'SISNAME? THE TV GUY. THE ONE-HIT WONDER.
THINK IT WAS "WEB BOY." OR "INSECT MAN" OR SOMETHIN'.
WOW. DIDN'T TAKE LONG FOR PEOPLE TO GET OVER ME. SURE, I WASN'T OUT THERE FOR TOO LONG BUT--NO.
IT'S GOOD PEOPLE ARE STARTING TO FORGET ABOUT SPIDER-MAN. WISH I COULD, TOO.

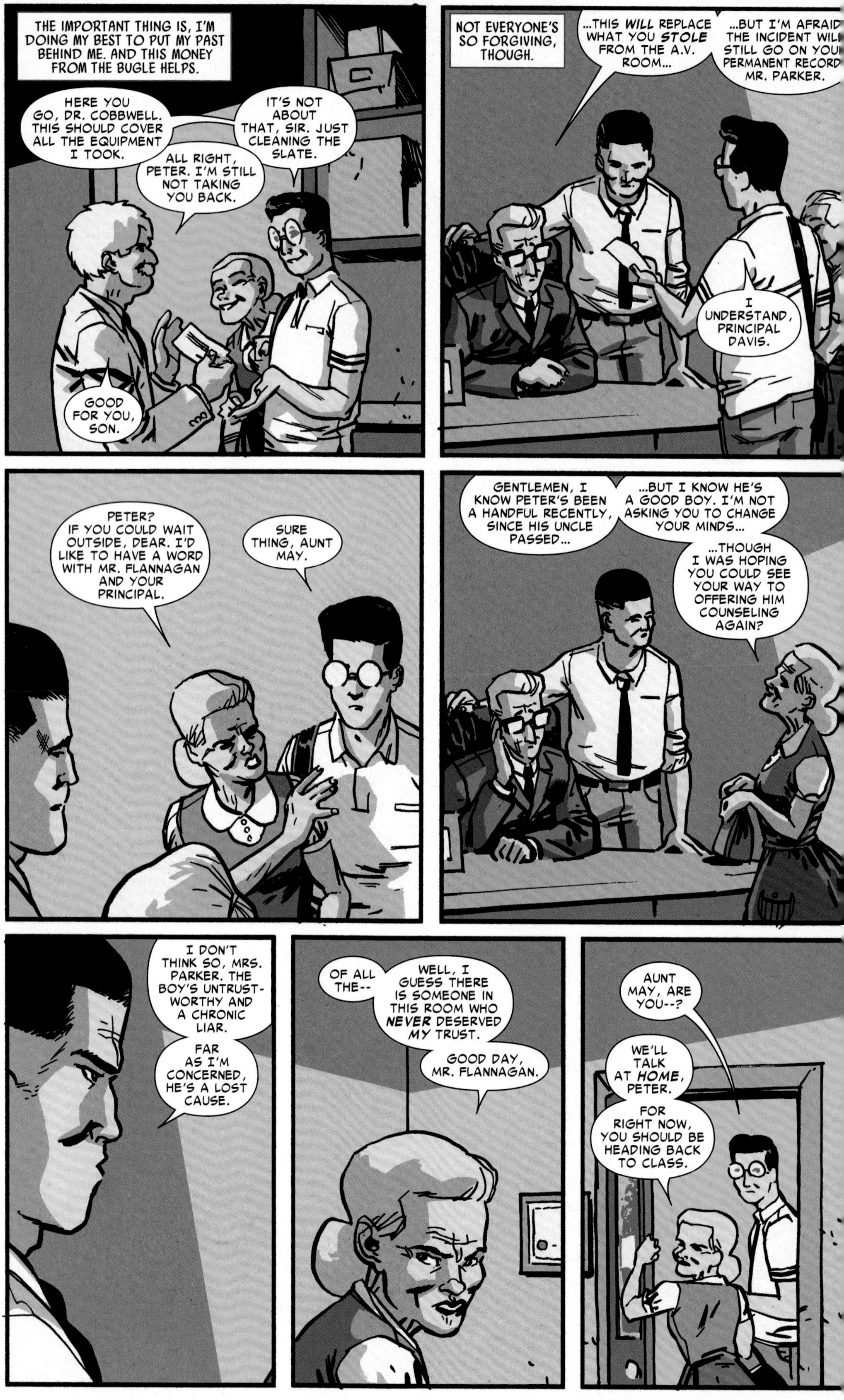
THE IMPORTANT THING IS, I'M DOING MY BEST TO PUT MY PAST BEHIND ME. AND THIS MONEY FROM THE BUGLE HELPS.
HERE YOU GO, DR. COBBWELL. THIS SHOULD COVER ALL THE EQUIPMENT I TOOK.
ALL RIGHT, PETER. I'M STILL NOT TAKING YOU BACK.
IT'S NOT ABOUT THAT, SIR. JUST CLEANING THE SLATE.
GOOD FOR YOU, SON.
NOT EVERYONE'S SO FORGIVING, THOUGH.
...THIS WILL REPLACE WHAT YOU STOLE FROM THE A.V. ROOM...
...BUT I'M AFRAID THE INCIDENT WILL STILL GO ON YOUR PERMANENT RECORD, MR. PARKER.
I UNDERSTAND, PRINCIPAL DAVIS.
PETER? IF YOU COULD WAIT OUTSIDE, DEAR. I'D LIKE TO HAVE A WORD WITH MR. FLANNAGAN AND YOUR PRINCIPAL.
SURE THING, AUNT MAY.
GENTLEMEN, I KNOW PETER'S BEEN A HANDFUL RECENTLY, SINCE HIS UNCLE PASSED...
...BUT I KNOW HE'S A GOOD BOY. I'M NOT ASKING YOU TO CHANGE YOUR MINDS...
...THOUGH I WAS HOPING YOU COULD SEE YOUR WAY TO OFFERING HIM COUNSELING AGAIN?
I DON'T THINK SO, MRS. PARKER. THE BOY'S UNTRUST-WORTHY AND A CHRONIC LIAR.
FAR AS I'M CONCERNED, HE'S A LOST CAUSE.
OF ALL THE--
WELL, I GUESS THERE IS SOMEONE IN THIS ROOM WHO NEVER DESERVED MY TRUST.
GOOD DAY, MR. FLANNAGAN.
AUNT MAY, ARE YOU--?
WE'LL TALK AT HOME, PETER.
FOR RIGHT NOW, YOU SHOULD BE HEADING BACK TO CLASS.

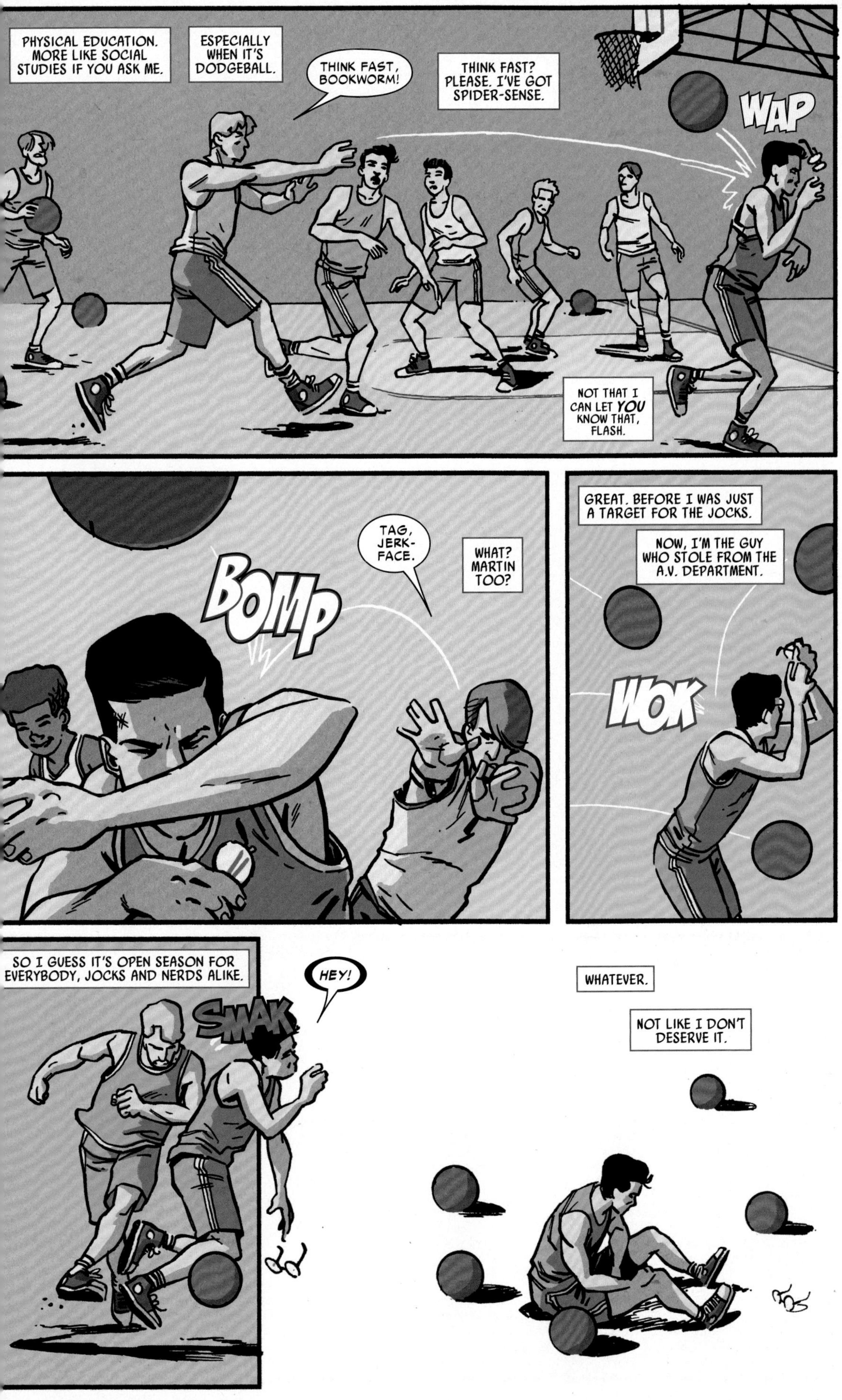
PHYSICAL EDUCATION. MORE LIKE SOCIAL STUDIES IF YOU ASK ME.
ESPECIALLY WHEN IT'S DODGEBALL.
THINK FAST, BOOKWORM!
THINK FAST? PLEASE. I'VE GOT SPIDER-SENSE.
WAP
NOT THAT I CAN LET YOU KNOW THAT, FLASH.
BOMP
TAG, JERK-FACE.
WHAT? MARTIN TOO?
GREAT. BEFORE I WAS JUST A TARGET FOR THE JOCKS.
NOW, I'M THE GUY WHO STOLE FROM THE A.V. DEPARTMENT.
WOK
SO I GUESS IT'S OPEN SEASON FOR EVERYBODY, JOCKS AND NERDS ALIKE.
SMAK
HEY!
WHATEVER.
NOT LIKE I DON'T DESERVE IT.

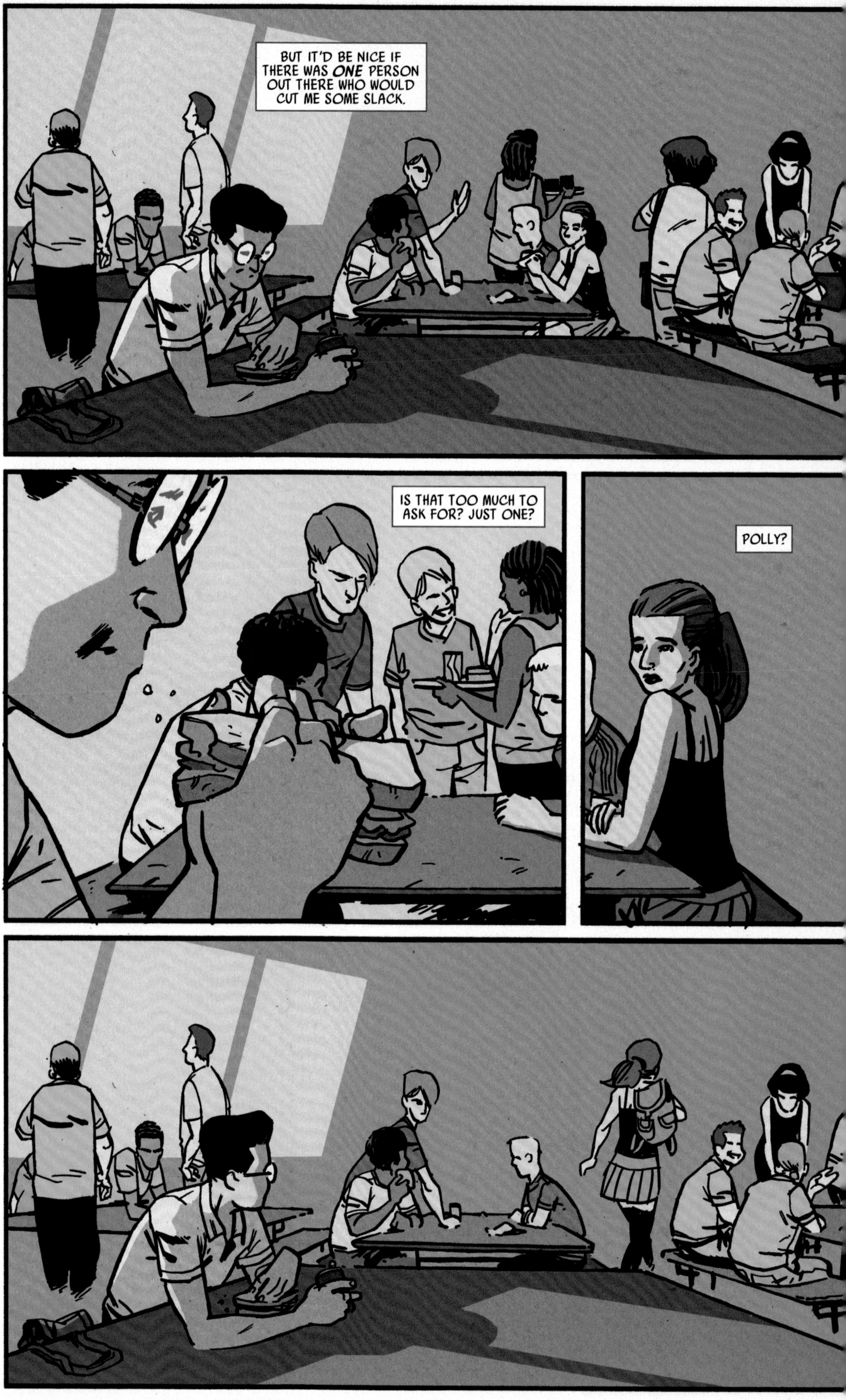
BUT IT'D BE NICE IF THERE WAS ONE PERSON OUT THERE WHO WOULD CUT ME SOME SLACK.
IS THAT TOO MUCH TO ASK FOR? JUST ONE?
POLLY?

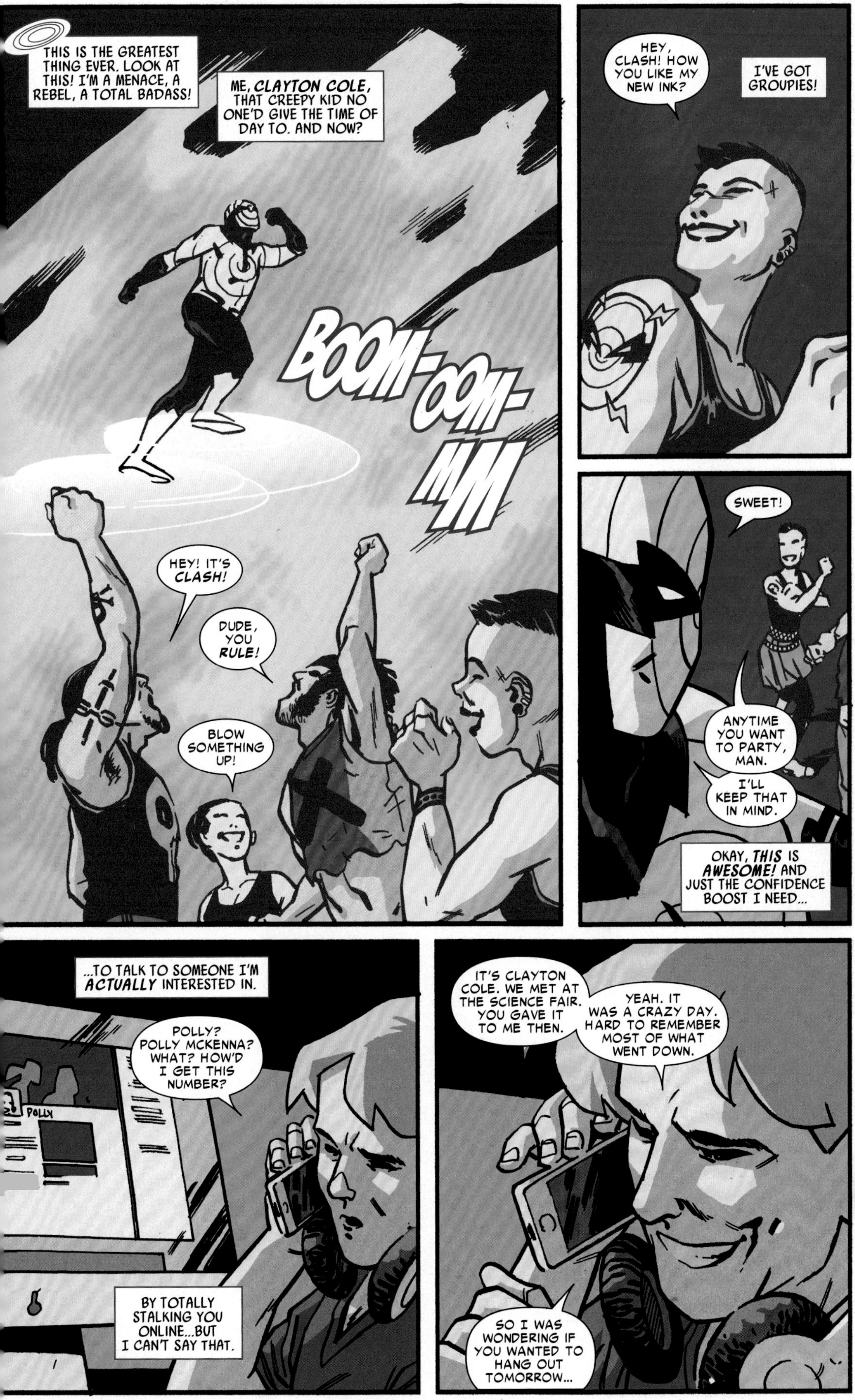
THIS IS THE GREATEST THING EVER. LOOK AT THIS! I'M A MENACE, A REBEL, A TOTAL BADASS!
ME, CLAYTON COLE, THAT CREEPY KID NO ONE'D GIVE THE TIME OF DAY TO. AND NOW?
BOOM-OOM-MM
HEY! IT'S CLASH!
DUDE, YOU RULE!
BLOW SOMETHING UP!
HEY, CLASH! HOW YOU LIKE MY NEW INK?
I'VE GOT GROUPIES!
SWEET!
ANYTIME YOU WANT TO PARTY, MAN.
I'LL KEEP THAT IN MIND.
OKAY, THIS IS AWESOME! AND JUST THE CONFIDENCE BOOST I NEED...
...TO TALK TO SOMEONE I'M ACTUALLY INTERESTED IN.
POLLY? POLLY MCKENNA? WHAT? HOW'D I GET THIS NUMBER?
POLLY
BY TOTALLY STALKING YOU ONLINE...BUT I CAN'T SAY THAT.
IT'S CLAYTON COLE. WE MET AT THE SCIENCE FAIR. YOU GAVE IT TO ME THEN.
YEAH. IT WAS A CRAZY DAY. HARD TO REMEMBER MOST OF WHAT WENT DOWN.
SO I WAS WONDERING IF YOU WANTED TO HANG OUT TOMORROW...

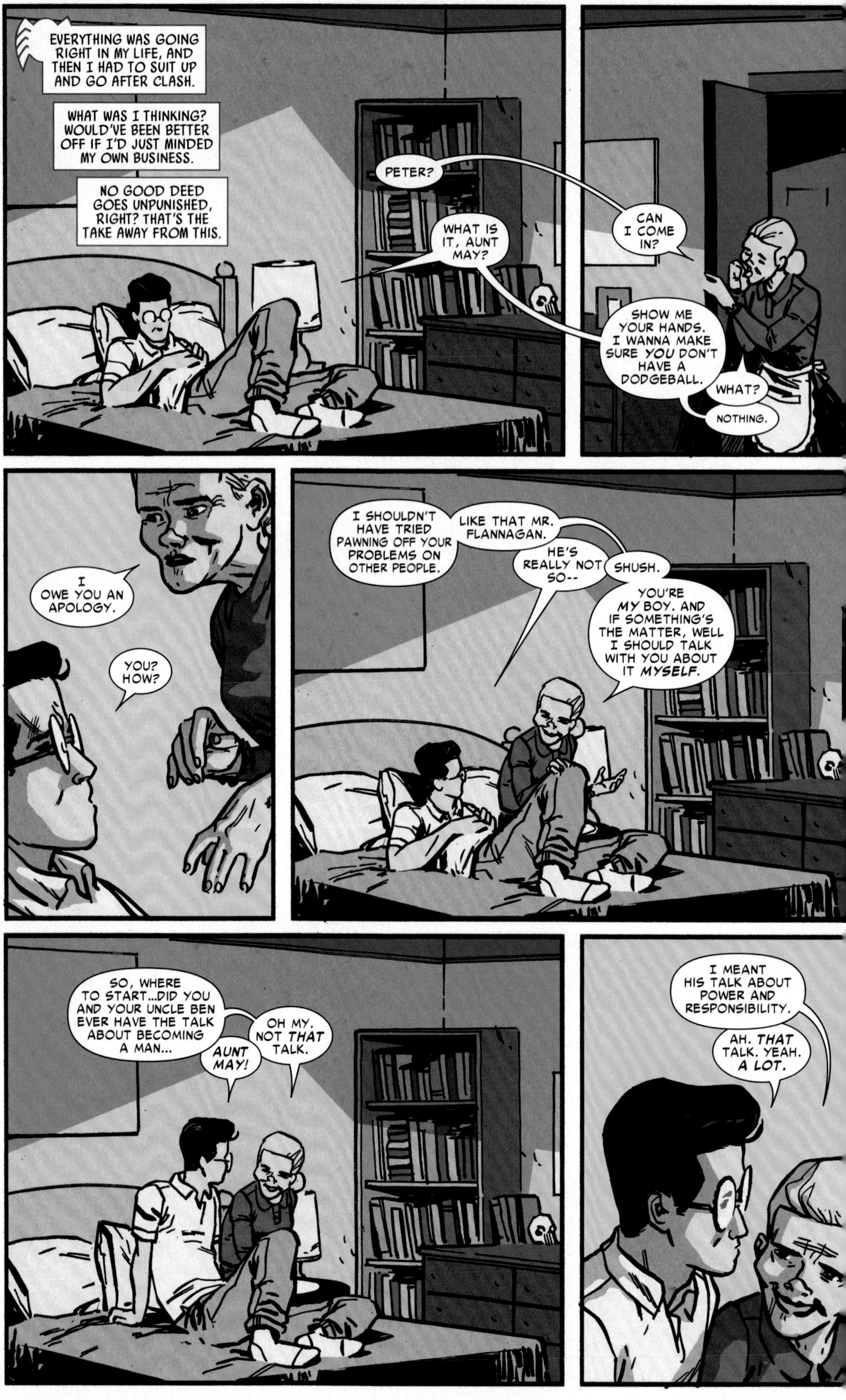
EVERYTHING WAS GOING RIGHT IN MY LIFE, AND THEN I HAD TO SUIT UP AND GO AFTER CLASH.
WHAT WAS I THINKING? WOULD'VE BEEN BETTER OFF IF I'D JUST MINDED MY OWN BUSINESS.
NO GOOD DEED GOES UNPUNISHED, RIGHT? THAT'S THE TAKE AWAY FROM THIS.
PETER?
CAN I COME IN?
WHAT IS IT, AUNT MAY?
SHOW ME YOUR HANDS. I WANNA MAKE SURE YOU DON'T HAVE A DODGEBALL.
WHAT?
NOTHING.
I OWE YOU AN APOLOGY.
YOU? HOW?
I SHOULDN'T HAVE TRIED PAWNING OFF YOUR PROBLEMS ON OTHER PEOPLE.
LIKE THAT MR. FLANNAGAN.
HE'S REALLY NOT SO--
SHUSH.
YOU'RE MY BOY. AND IF SOMETHING'S THE MATTER, WELL I SHOULD TALK WITH YOU ABOUT IT MYSELF.
SO, WHERE TO START...DID YOU AND YOUR UNCLE BEN EVER HAVE THE TALK ABOUT BECOMING A MAN...
AUNT MAY!
OH MY. NOT THAT TALK.
I MEANT HIS TALK ABOUT POWER AND RESPONSIBILITY.
AH. THAT TALK. YEAH. A LOT.

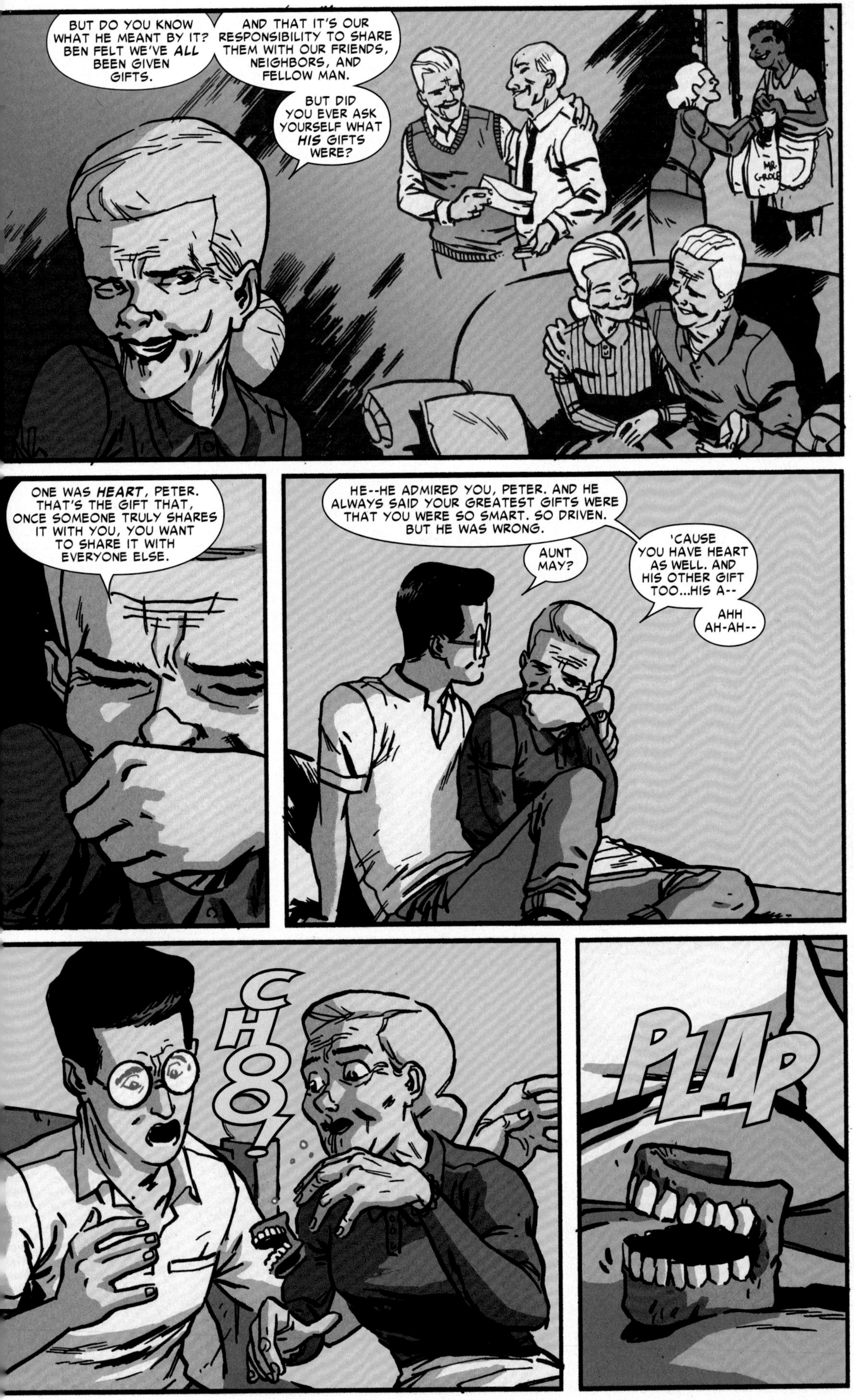
BUT DO YOU KNOW WHAT HE MEANT BY IT? BEN FELT WE'VE ALL BEEN GIVEN GIFTS.
AND THAT IT'S OUR RESPONSIBILITY TO SHARE THEM WITH OUR FRIENDS, NEIGHBORS, AND FELLOW MAN.
BUT DID YOU EVER ASK YOURSELF WHAT HIS GIFTS WERE?
ONE WAS HEART, PETER. THAT'S THE GIFT THAT, ONCE SOMEONE TRULY SHARES IT WITH YOU, YOU WANT TO SHARE IT WITH EVERYONE ELSE.
HE--HE ADMIRED YOU, PETER. AND HE ALWAYS SAID YOUR GREATEST GIFTS WERE THAT YOU WERE SO SMART. SO DRIVEN. BUT HE WAS WRONG.
AUNT MAY?
'CAUSE YOU HAVE HEART AS WELL. AND HIS OTHER GIFT TOO...HIS A--
AHH AH-AH--
CHOO!
PLAP

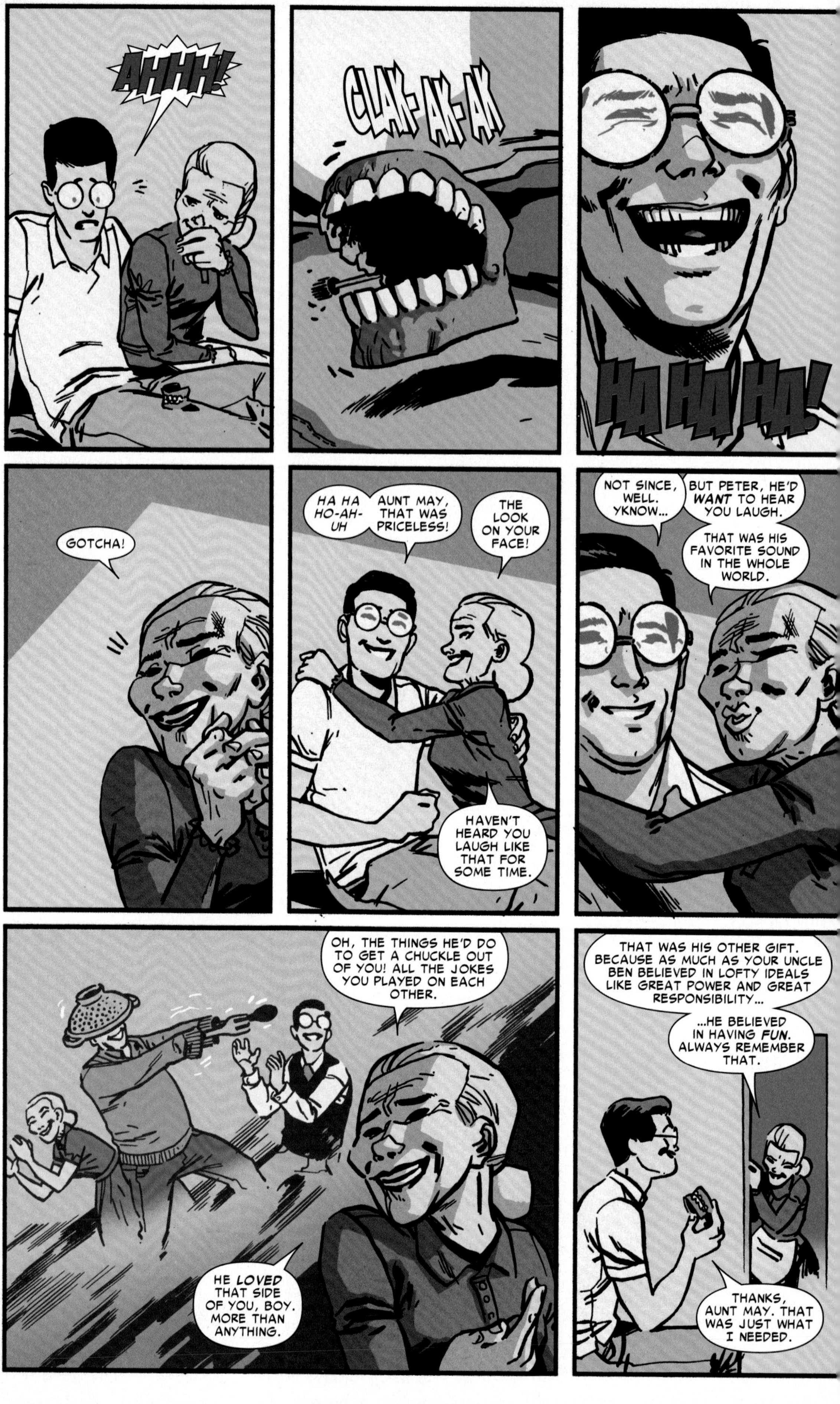
AHHH!
CLAK-AK-AK
HA HA HA!
GOTCHA!
HA HA HO-AH-UH
AUNT MAY, THAT WAS PRICELESS!
THE LOOK ON YOUR FACE!
HAVEN'T HEARD YOU LAUGH LIKE THAT FOR SOME TIME.
NOT SINCE, WELL. YKNOW...
BUT PETER, HE'D *WANT* TO HEAR YOU LAUGH.
THAT WAS HIS FAVORITE SOUND IN THE WHOLE WORLD.
OH, THE THINGS HE'D DO TO GET A CHUCKLE OUT OF YOU! ALL THE JOKES YOU PLAYED ON EACH OTHER.
HE *LOVED* THAT SIDE OF YOU, BOY. MORE THAN ANYTHING.
THAT WAS HIS OTHER GIFT. BECAUSE AS MUCH AS YOUR UNCLE BEN BELIEVED IN LOFTY IDEALS LIKE GREAT POWER AND GREAT RESPONSIBILITY...
...HE BELIEVED IN HAVING *FUN*. ALWAYS REMEMBER THAT.
THANKS, AUNT MAY. THAT WAS JUST WHAT I NEEDED.

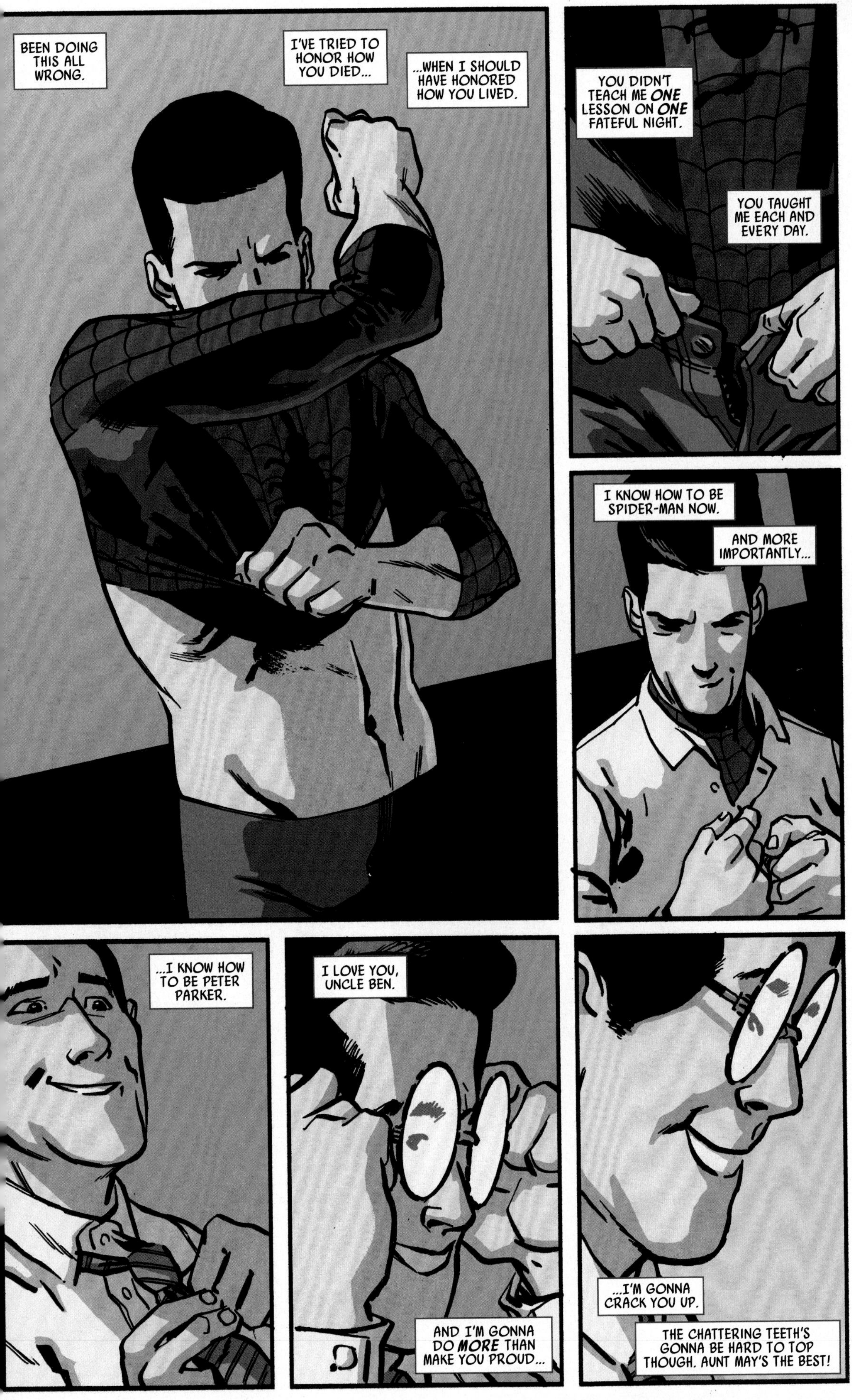
BEEN DOING THIS ALL WRONG.
I'VE TRIED TO HONOR HOW YOU DIED...
...WHEN I SHOULD HAVE HONORED HOW YOU LIVED.
YOU DIDN'T TEACH ME ONE LESSON ON ONE FATEFUL NIGHT.
YOU TAUGHT ME EACH AND EVERY DAY.
I KNOW HOW TO BE SPIDER-MAN NOW.
AND MORE IMPORTANTLY...
...I KNOW HOW TO BE PETER PARKER.
I LOVE YOU, UNCLE BEN.
AND I'M GONNA DO MORE THAN MAKE YOU PROUD...
...I'M GONNA CRACK YOU UP.
THE CHATTERING TEETH'S GONNA BE HARD TO TOP THOUGH. AUNT MAY'S THE BEST!

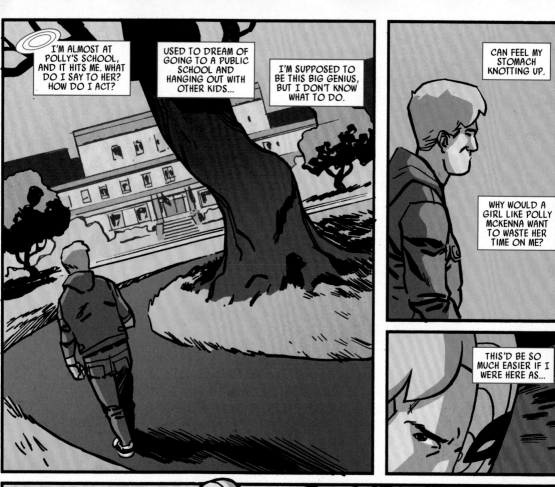

I'M ALMOST AT POLLY'S SCHOOL, AND IT HITS ME. WHAT DO I SAY TO HER? HOW DO I ACT?

USED TO DREAM OF GOING TO A PUBLIC SCHOOL AND HANGING OUT WITH OTHER KIDS...

I'M SUPPOSED TO BE THIS BIG GENIUS, BUT I DON'T KNOW WHAT TO DO.

CAN FEEL MY STOMACH KNOTTING UP.

WHY WOULD A GIRL LIKE POLLY MCKENNA WANT TO WASTE HER TIME ON ME?

THIS'D BE SO MUCH EASIER IF I WERE HERE AS...

MIDTOWN HIGH! IT'S YOUR LUCKY DAY! YOU'RE GETTING A SPECIAL GUEST APPEARANCE...

...FROM CLASH!

RUN FOR IT! IT'S THAT FREAK FROM THE BUGLE!

SOMEONE HIT THE ALARM!

CALL THE COPS!

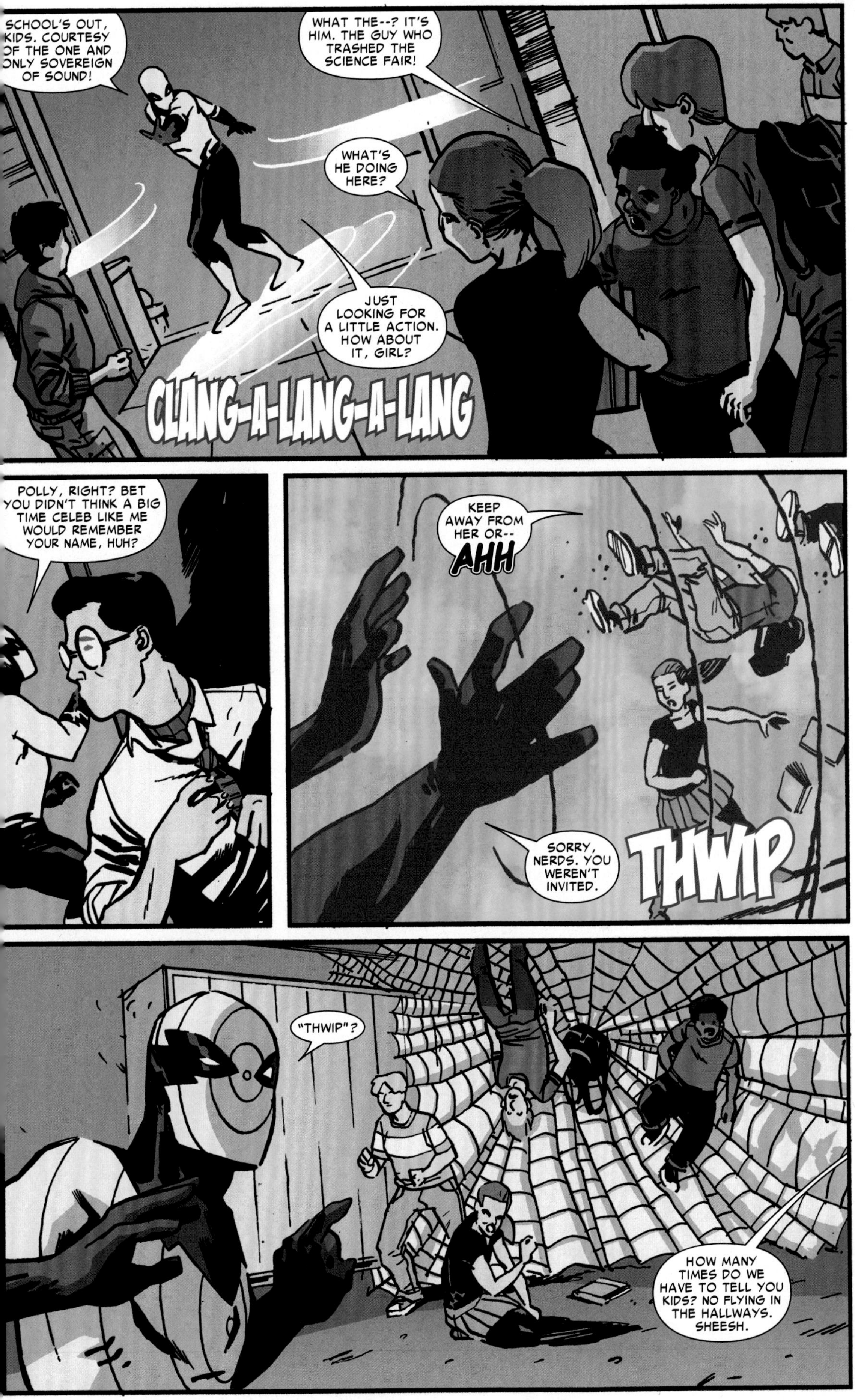
SCHOOL'S OUT, KIDS. COURTESY OF THE ONE AND ONLY SOVEREIGN OF SOUND!
WHAT THE--? IT'S HIM. THE GUY WHO TRASHED THE SCIENCE FAIR!
WHAT'S HE DOING HERE?
JUST LOOKING FOR A LITTLE ACTION. HOW ABOUT IT, GIRL?
CLANG-A-LANG-A-LANG
POLLY, RIGHT? BET YOU DIDN'T THINK A BIG TIME CELEB LIKE ME WOULD REMEMBER YOUR NAME, HUH?
KEEP AWAY FROM HER OR-- AHH
SORRY, NERDS. YOU WEREN'T INVITED.
THWIP
"THWIP"?
HOW MANY TIMES DO WE HAVE TO TELL YOU KIDS? NO FLYING IN THE HALLWAYS. SHEESH.

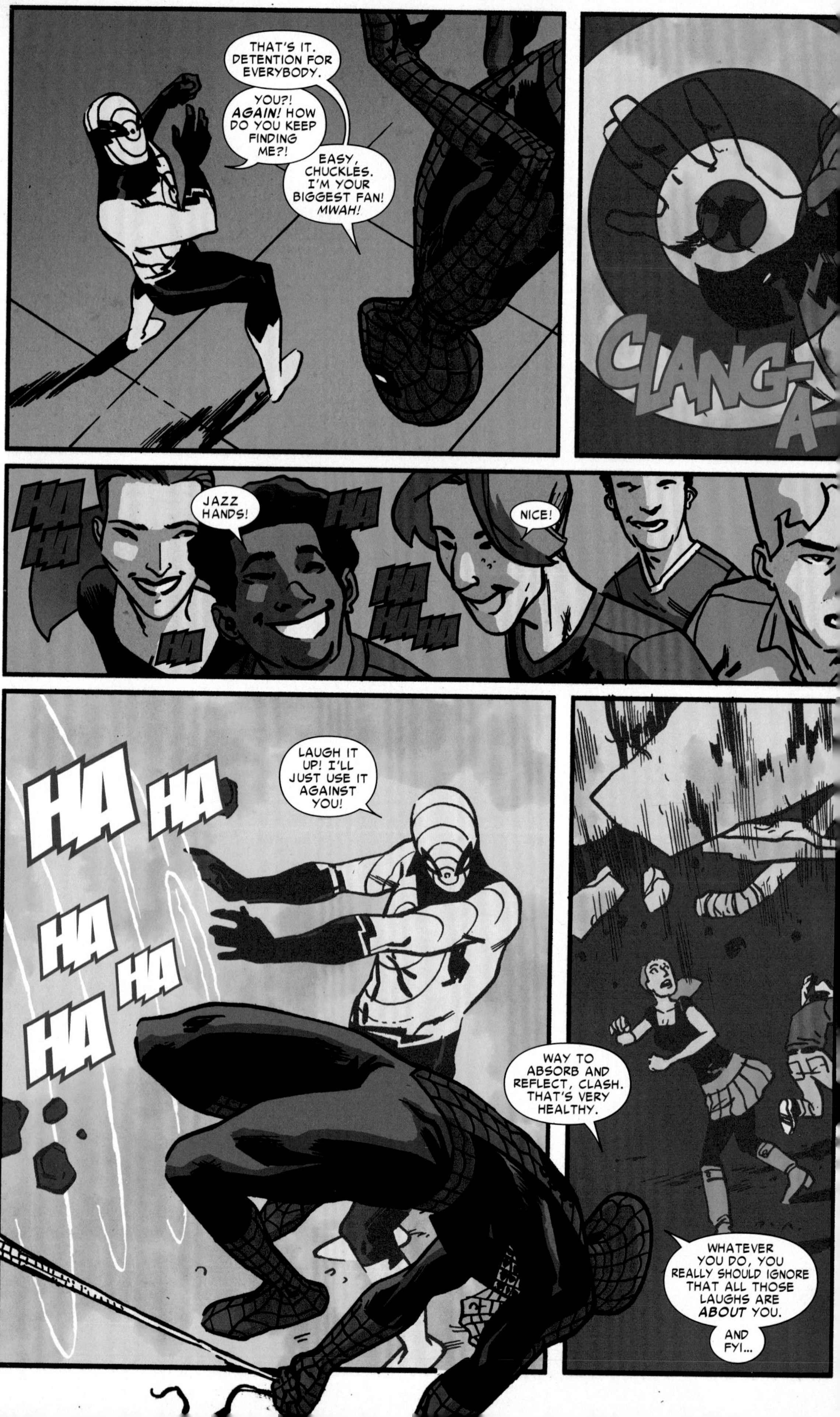
THAT'S IT. DETENTION FOR EVERYBODY.
YOU?! AGAIN! HOW DO YOU KEEP FINDING ME?!
EASY, CHUCKLES. I'M YOUR BIGGEST FAN! MWAH!
CLANG-A-
HA HA
JAZZ HANDS!
HA
HA
HA HA HA
NICE!
HA HA
LAUGH IT UP! I'LL JUST USE IT AGAINST YOU!
HA HA HA
WAY TO ABSORB AND REFLECT, CLASH. THAT'S VERY HEALTHY.
WHATEVER YOU DO, YOU REALLY SHOULD IGNORE THAT ALL THOSE LAUGHS ARE ABOUT YOU.
AND FYI...

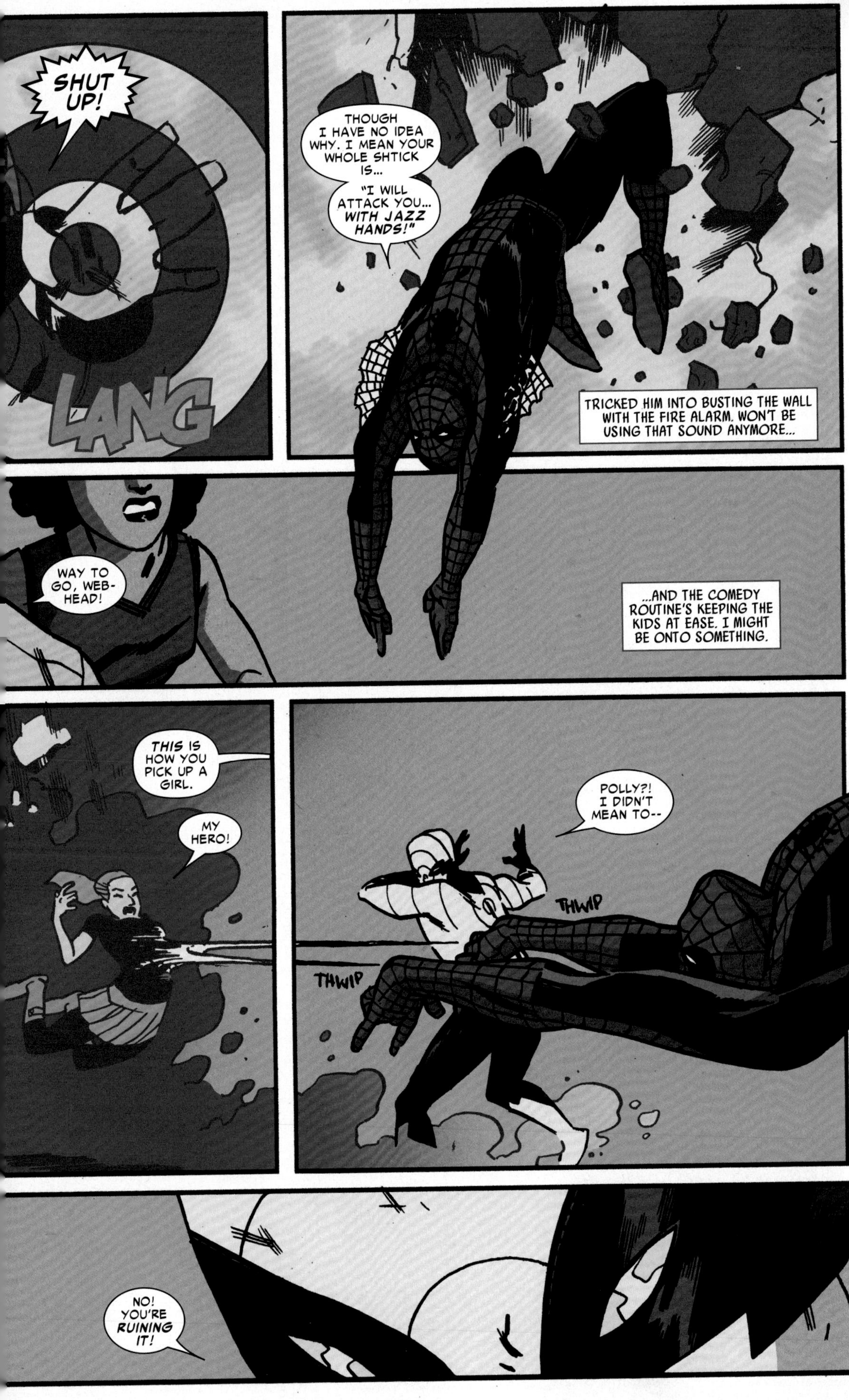
SHUT UP!
LANG
THOUGH I HAVE NO IDEA WHY. I MEAN YOUR WHOLE SHTICK IS...
"I WILL ATTACK YOU... WITH JAZZ HANDS!"
TRICKED HIM INTO BUSTING THE WALL WITH THE FIRE ALARM. WON'T BE USING THAT SOUND ANYMORE...
WAY TO GO, WEB-HEAD!
...AND THE COMEDY ROUTINE'S KEEPING THE KIDS AT EASE. I MIGHT BE ONTO SOMETHING.
THIS IS HOW YOU PICK UP A GIRL.
MY HERO!
POLLY?! I DIDN'T MEAN TO--
THWIP
THWIP
NO! YOU'RE RUINING IT!

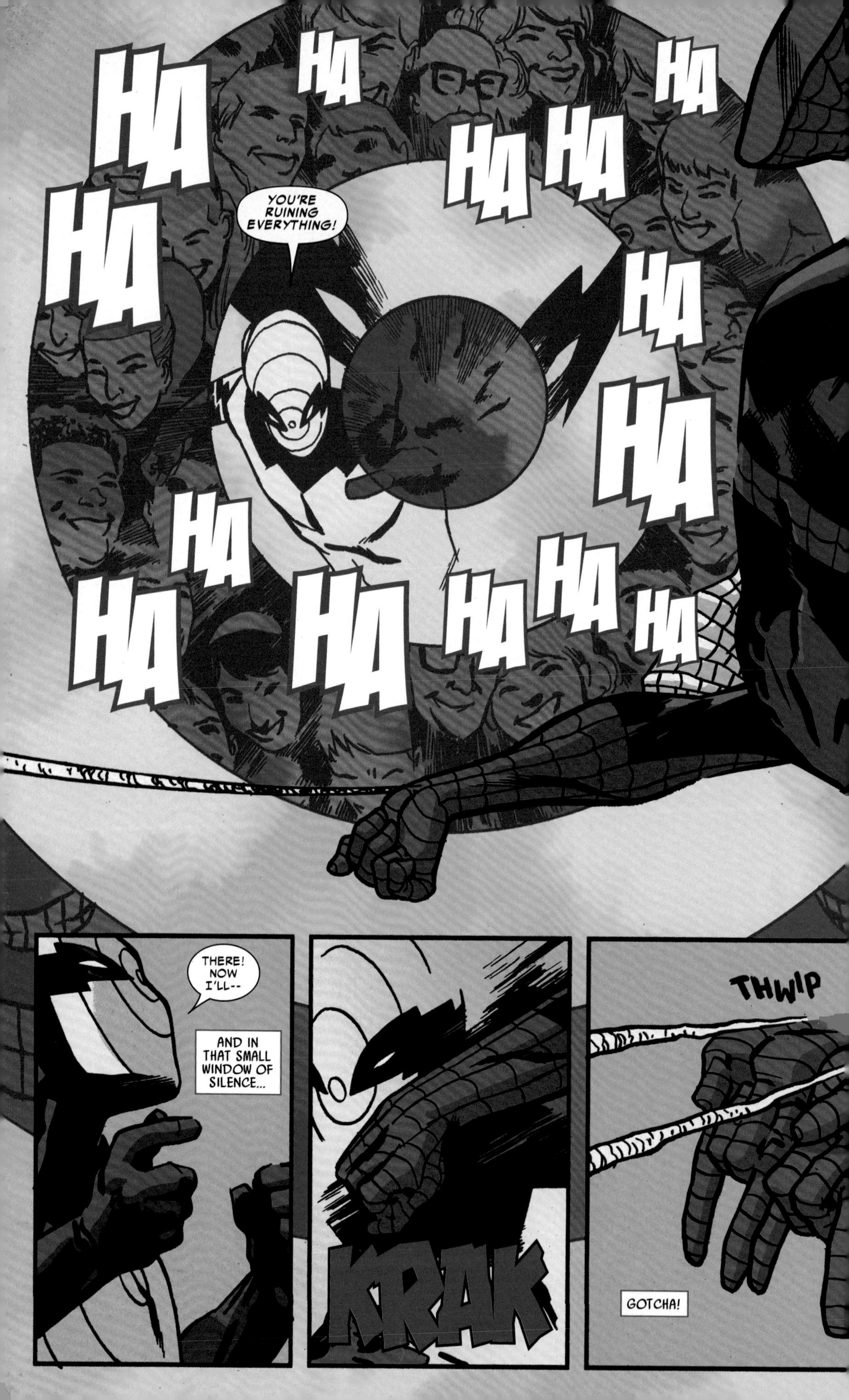
HA
HA
HA
HA
HA
YOU'RE RUINING EVERYTHING!
HA
HA
HA
HA
HA
HA
HA
HA
HA
THERE! NOW I'LL--
AND IN THAT SMALL WINDOW OF SILENCE...
KRAK
THWIP
GOTCHA!

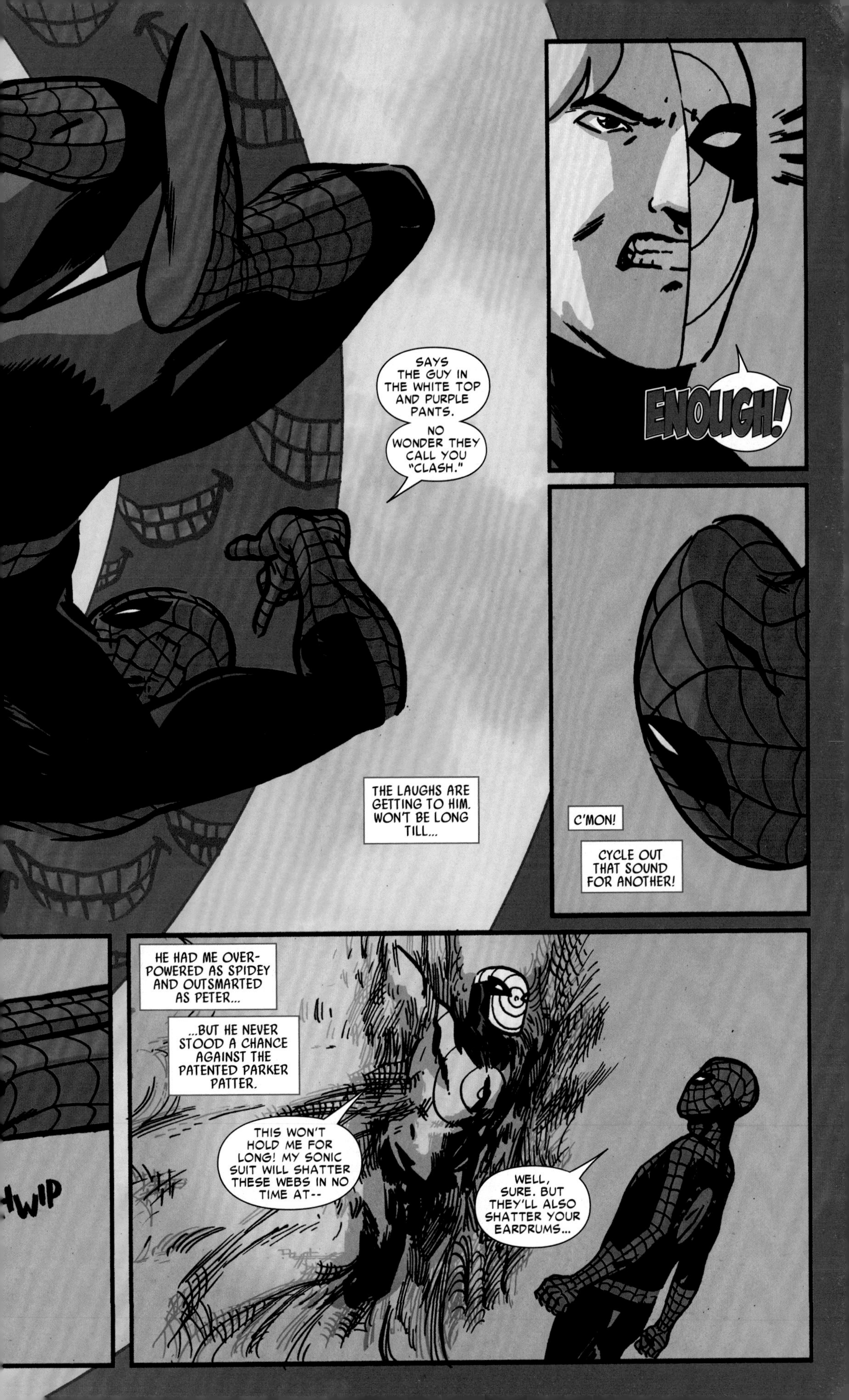
SAYS THE GUY IN THE WHITE TOP AND PURPLE PANTS.
NO WONDER THEY CALL YOU "CLASH."
ENOUGH!
THE LAUGHS ARE GETTING TO HIM. WON'T BE LONG TILL...
C'MON!
CYCLE OUT THAT SOUND FOR ANOTHER!
TWIP
HE HAD ME OVER-POWERED AS SPIDEY AND OUTSMARTED AS PETER...
...BUT HE NEVER STOOD A CHANCE AGAINST THE PATENTED PARKER PATTER.
THIS WON'T HOLD ME FOR LONG! MY SONIC SUIT WILL SHATTER THESE WEBS IN NO TIME AT--
WELL, SURE. BUT THEY'LL ALSO SHATTER YOUR EARDRUMS...

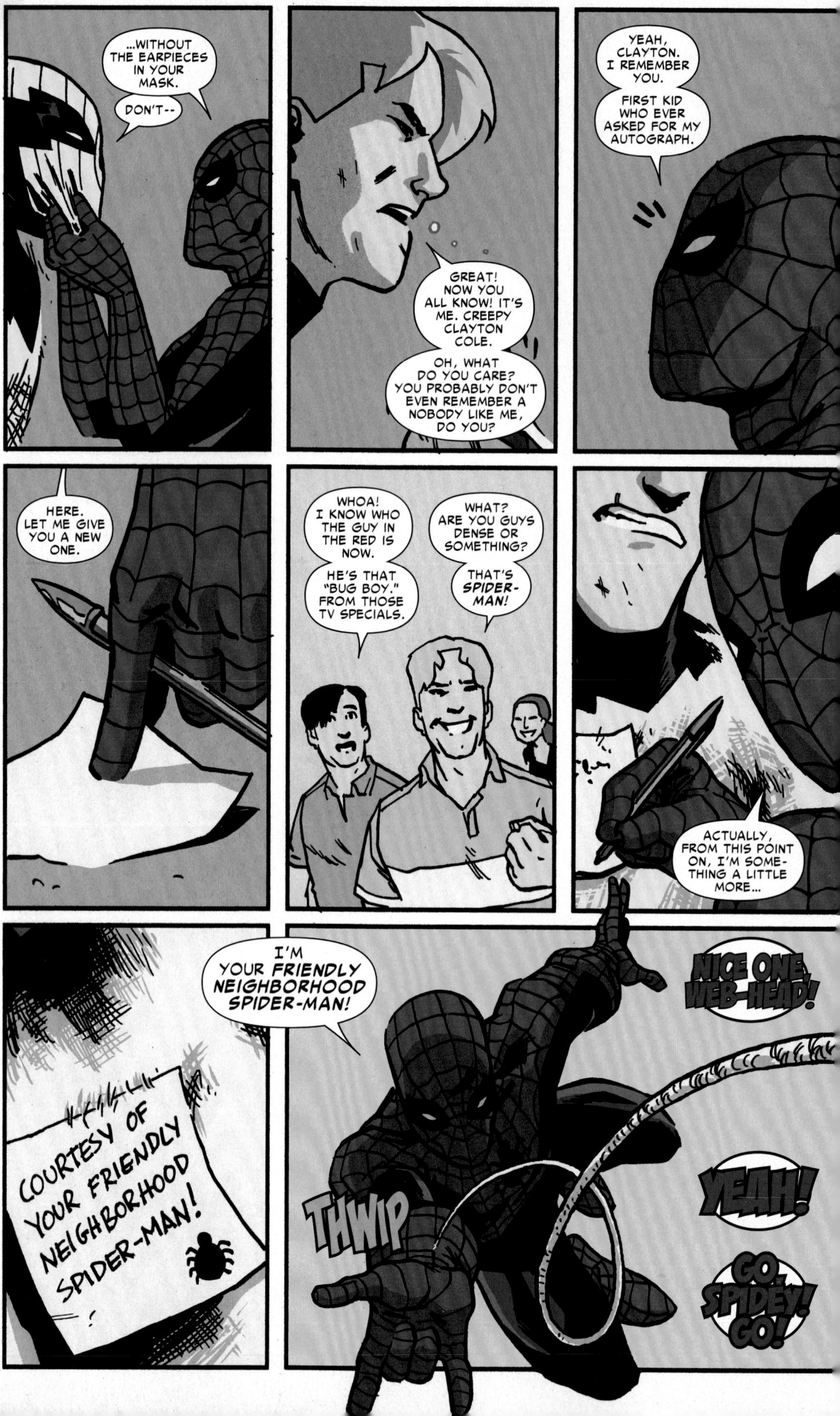
...WITHOUT THE EARPIECES IN YOUR MASK.
DON'T--
GREAT! NOW YOU ALL KNOW! IT'S ME. CREEPY CLAYTON COLE.
OH, WHAT DO YOU CARE? YOU PROBABLY DON'T EVEN REMEMBER A NOBODY LIKE ME, DO YOU?
YEAH, CLAYTON. I REMEMBER YOU.
FIRST KID WHO EVER ASKED FOR MY AUTOGRAPH.
HERE. LET ME GIVE YOU A NEW ONE.
WHOA! I KNOW WHO THE GUY IN THE RED IS NOW.
HE'S THAT "BUG BOY." FROM THOSE TV SPECIALS.
WHAT? ARE YOU GUYS DENSE OR SOMETHING?
THAT'S SPIDER-MAN!
ACTUALLY, FROM THIS POINT ON, I'M SOME-THING A LITTLE MORE...
COURTESY OF YOUR FRIENDLY NEIGHBORHOOD SPIDER-MAN!
I'M YOUR FRIENDLY NEIGHBORHOOD SPIDER-MAN!
NICE ONE, WEB-HEAD!
THWIP
YEAH!
GO, SPIDEY! GO!

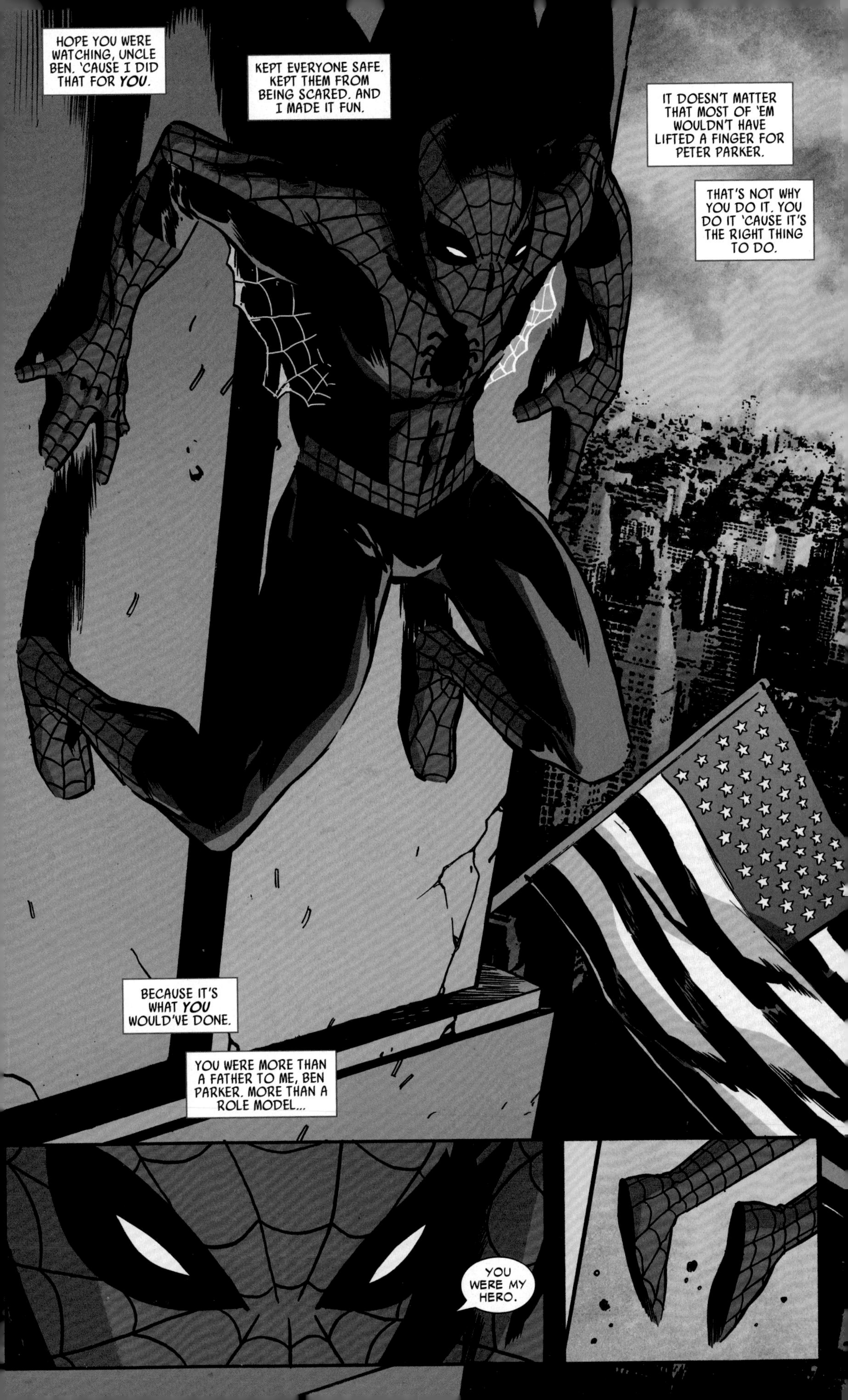
HOPE YOU WERE WATCHING, UNCLE BEN. 'CAUSE I DID THAT FOR *YOU*.
KEPT EVERYONE SAFE. KEPT THEM FROM BEING SCARED. AND I MADE IT FUN.
IT DOESN'T MATTER THAT MOST OF 'EM WOULDN'T HAVE LIFTED A FINGER FOR PETER PARKER.
THAT'S NOT WHY YOU DO IT. YOU DO IT 'CAUSE IT'S THE RIGHT THING TO DO.
BECAUSE IT'S WHAT *YOU* WOULD'VE DONE.
YOU WERE MORE THAN A FATHER TO ME, BEN PARKER. MORE THAN A ROLE MODEL...
YOU WERE MY HERO.

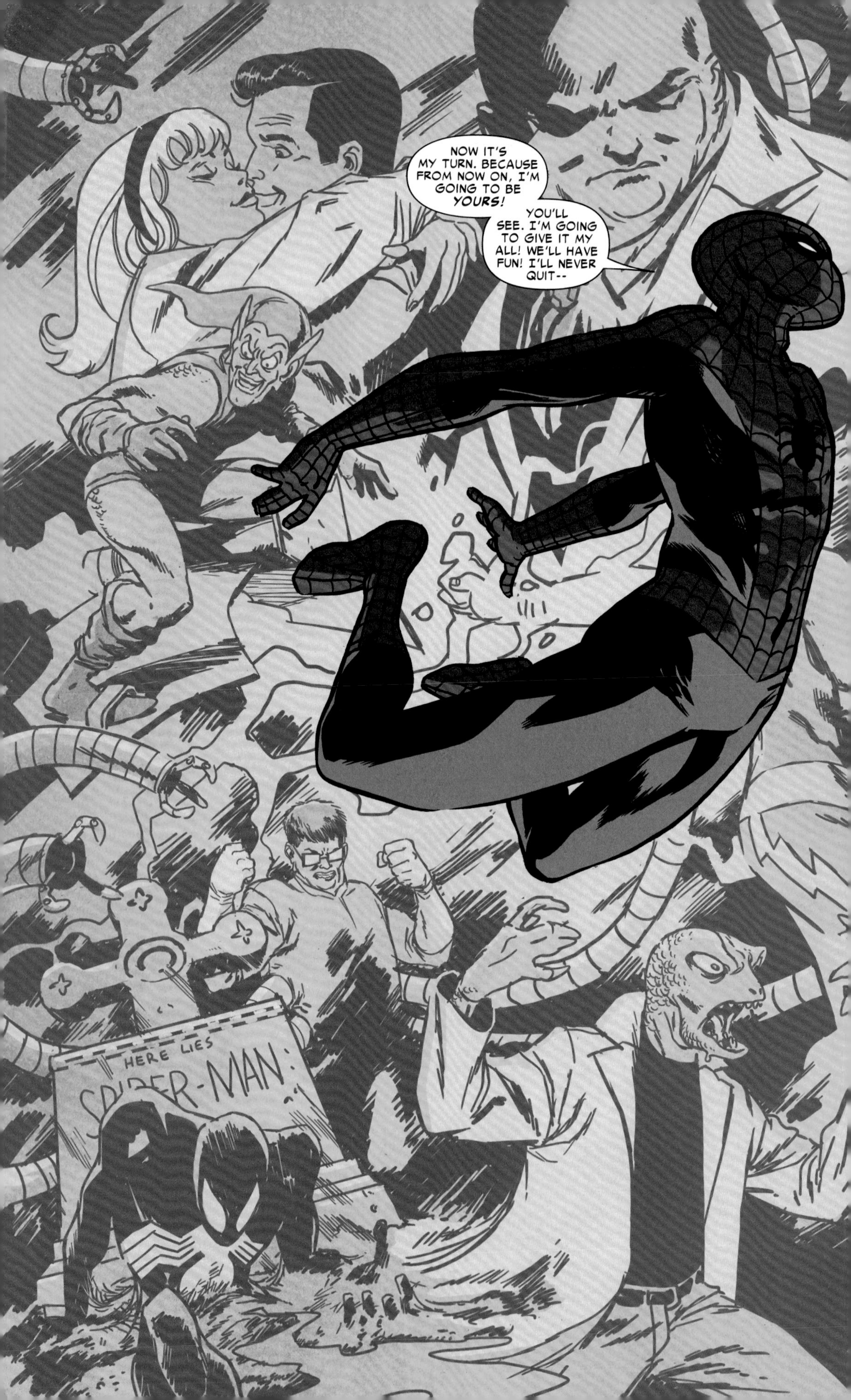
NOW IT'S MY TURN. BECAUSE FROM NOW ON, I'M GOING TO BE *YOURS!*
YOU'LL SEE. I'M GOING TO GIVE IT MY ALL! WE'LL HAVE FUN! I'LL NEVER QUIT--
HERE LIES SPIDER-MAN

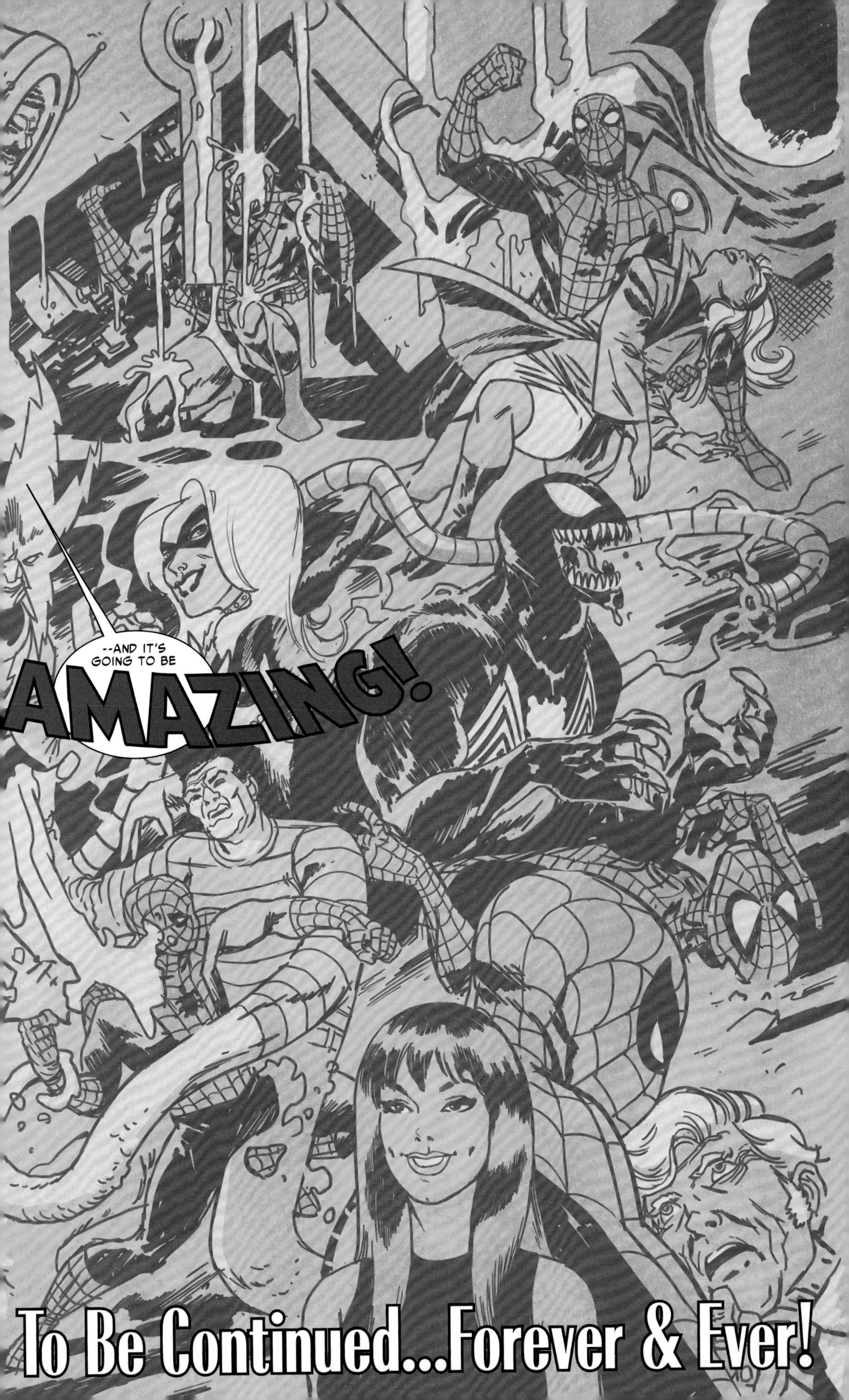
--AND IT'S GOING TO BE
AMAZING!
To Be Continued...Forever & Ever!

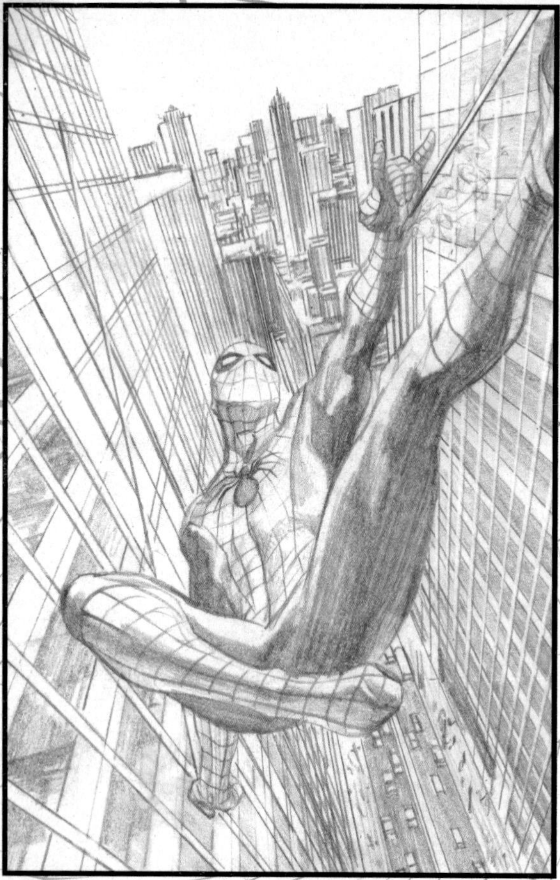
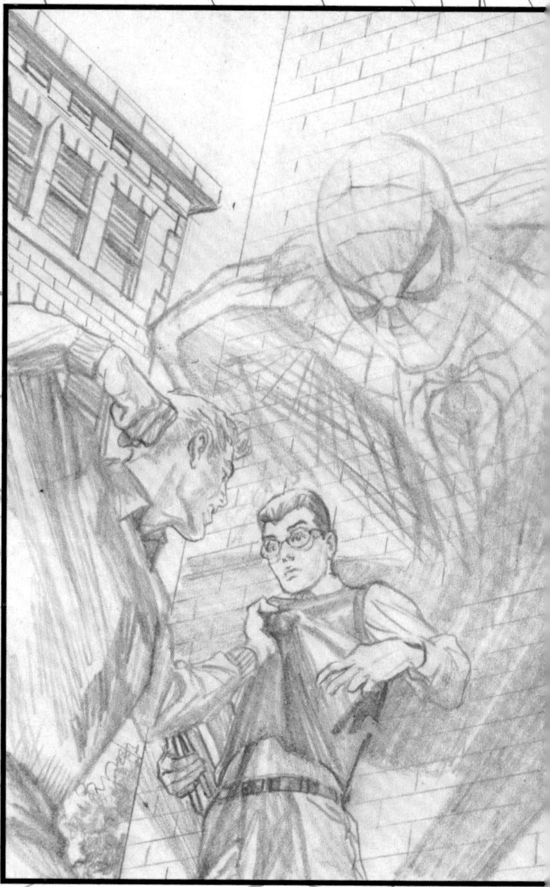
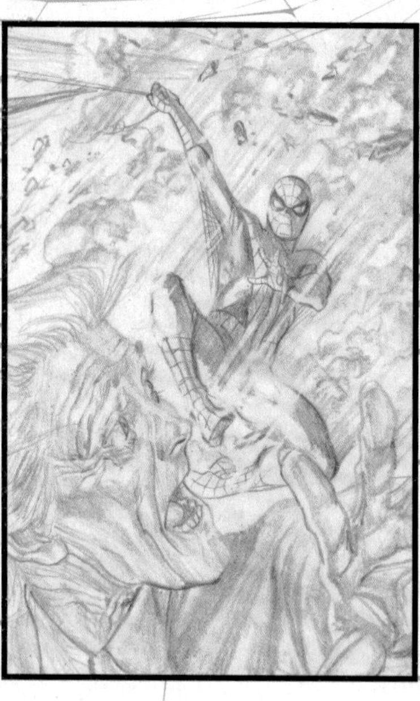
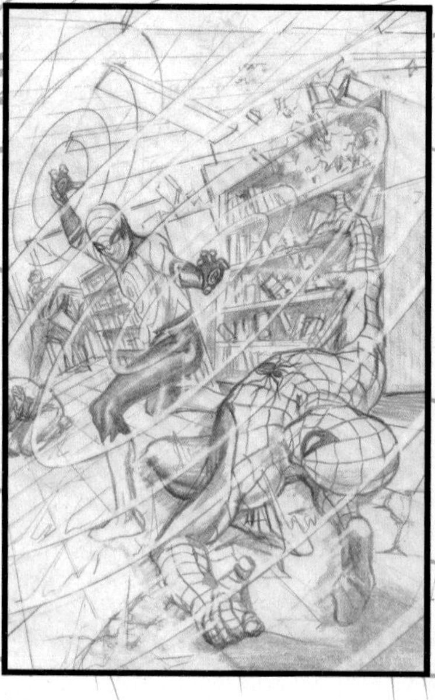
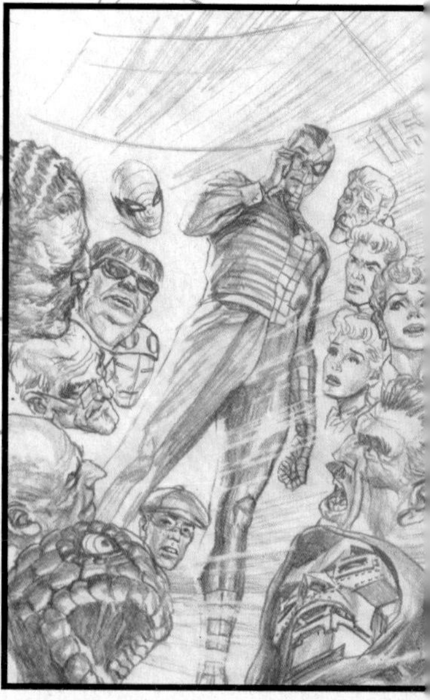

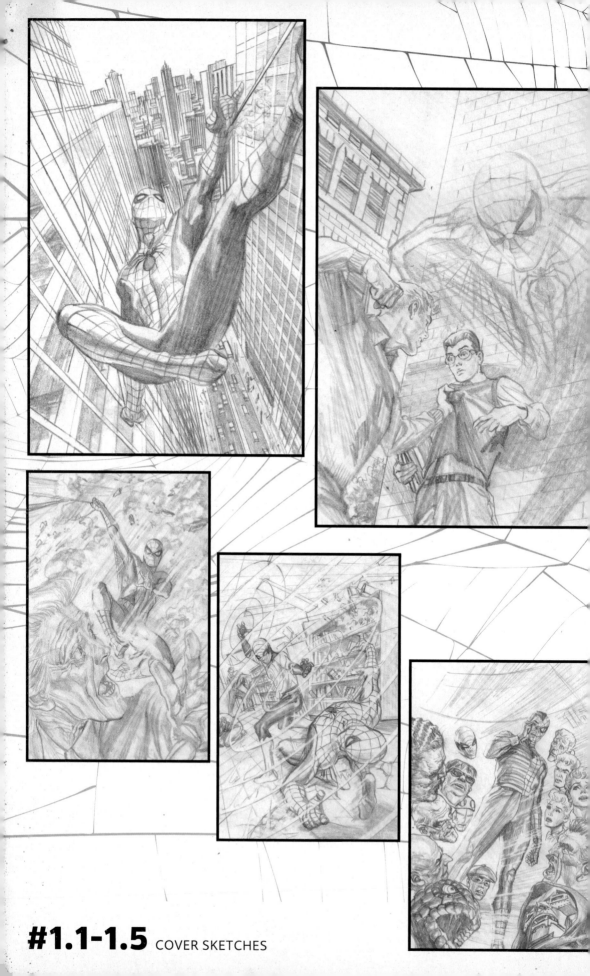

#1.1-1.5 COVER SKETCHES